Cultural Struggle & Development in Southern Africa

Cultural Struggle & Development in Southern Africa

Edited by Preben Kaarsholm

Associate Professor in International Development Studies,
Roskilde University Centre
Formerly Research Fellow, Centre for Research in the Humanities,
University of Copenhagen

Baobab Books
HARARE
James Currey
LONDON
Heinemann
PORTSMOUTH (N.H.)

Baobab Books
A division of Academic Books Pvt. Ltd.
P.O. Box 567
Harare, Zimbabwe

James Currey Ltd
54b Thornhill Square
Islington
London N1 1BE

Heinemann Educational Books, Inc.
361 Hanover Street
Portsmouth, NH 03801–3959

© James Currey Ltd 1991
First published 1991

British Library Cataloguing in Publication Data
Cultural struggle & development in Southern Africa
1. Southern Africa. Cultural processes.
I. Kaarsholm, Preben
306. 0968

ISBN 0-85255-212-2 (Cloth)
ISBN 0-85255-211-4 (Paper)

ISBN 0-435-08062-8 (Heinemann)

91 92 93 94 95 9 8 7 6 5 4 3 2 1

Typeset by Bente Jensen at the
Centre for Research in the Humanities
at the University of Copenhagen
Printed by Villiers Publishers, London N6

Contents

Part Three: The Culture and Politics of Popular Participation

Notes on Contributors

John M. MacKenzie is a historian at the University of Lancaster in England. He has published two widely used books on imperialist popular culture - *Propaganda and Empire: The Manipulation of British Popular Opinion, 1890-1960* (1985) and the anthology *Imperialism and Popular Culture* (1986). In 1988 he published *The Empire of Nature: Hunting, Conservation and British Imperialism.*

Preben Kaarsholm was trained in comparative literature and works for International Development Studies at Roskilde University Centre. His ideas about romantic anti-capitalism were presented in a book on Thomas Mann and German right-wing thinking in 1976. He is interested in colonial history and modern Third World development and has published articles on imperialist ideology in Britain, the Boer War, and cultural developments in Zimbabwe.

Stephen Williams is an art historian and until recently director of the Mzilikazi Art and Craft Centre in Bulawayo's oldest 'high-density suburb'. He now works for the National Museum of Botswana in Gaborone. He has been active in PF-ZAPU, worked for a while at Simukai collective cooperative, and taken a special interest in the development of new courses of art instruction in Zimbabwe.

Kimani Gecau teaches English-language literature at the University of Zimbabwe in Harare. He is a Kenyan by birth and used to work for the Department of Literature at the University of Nairobi together with Ngugi wa Thiong'o and Micere Mugo. Like these two colleagues, he had to leave Kenya after the failed coup attempt against the Daniel arap Moi government in August 1982.

David Caute is a historian and was for some time a Research Fellow at All Souls' College, Oxford. For more than twenty years, however, he has made a living writing books and in journalism. He has written a book of reportage and a novel about Zimbabwe's road to independence - *Under the Skin: The Death of White Rhodesia* and *The K-Factor* (both from 1983). In 1986, he published *The Espionage of the Saints: Two Essays on Silence and the State* which contains 'Marechera and the Colonel'.

Ken Manungo is chief oral historian with the National Archives of Zimbabwe in Harare and has been in charge of the Shona section of the Archives' Oral History Programme. He has collected a large number of life histories and has concentrated especially on experiences during the liberation struggle. He is working on a Ph. D. thesis on the wartime interaction between peasants and guerillas in the Chiweshe area.

Norma Kriger is South African by birth and teaches political science at The Johns Hopkins University in Baltimore. Her doctoral dissertation on 'Struggles for Independence: Rural Conflicts in Zimbabwe's War of Liberation' from 1985 was based on field work undertaken in Mutoko District in north-eastern Zimbabwe.

Terence Ranger is Rhodes Professor of Race Relations in the University of Oxford and a Fellow of St. Antony's College, Oxford. He taught in Rhodesia between 1957 and 1963, when he was deported because of his membership of the National Democratic Party and active support for the African nationalist movement. He is the author of a large number of writings on the history of anti-colonial resistance in Southern Africa, among them *Revolt in Southern Rhodesia, 1896-97, The African Voice in Southern Rhodesia* and *Peasant Consciousness and Guerilla War in Zimbabwe.* A forthcoming book is entitled *Voices from the Rocks: The Modern History of the Matopos.*

Welshman Ncube is Chairman of the Department of Public Law in the University of Zimbabwe. With Alice Armstrong, he has edited a book on *Women and Law in Southern Africa,* and he has published a number of articles on human rights and development.

Shephard Nzombe is Chairman of the Department of Private Law, University of Zimbabwe. He has specialized in questions of labour law and trade union rights, but has also written on constitutional development and is a member of the editorial board of the *Journal of Social Change and Development.*

Kate Crehan took her doctorate in anthropology at the University of Manchester. She has worked as a research fellow with the African Studies Centre, University of Cambridge and now has a post with the New School for Social Research in New York. She has spent extended periods doing field work in Zambia's North-Western Province.

Notes on Contributors

Luke Mhlaba was born at Kezi in Matabeleland. Between 1978 and 1980 he worked for the information department of PF-ZAPU in Lusaka, and after Zimbabwe's independence he became a journalist with the *Chronicle* in Bulawayo. He studied for his law degree in Harare and at Pau in France, and since 1988 he has been employed by the Faculty of Law at the University of Zimbabwe.

Bodil Folke Frederiksen graduated in English literature, but is now an Associate Professor in International Development Studies, Roskilde University Centre. Her ongoing research is on urban subcultures in Kenya, and her special interest is the use of literary texts as source material for an understanding of everyday-life experience, and the ways in which texts circulate and are used within the local community.

Jeff Guy was born at Pietermaritzburg and teaches history at the University of Trondheim in Norway. For eleven years he worked for the National University of Lesotho and played a major role in setting up the university's Oral History Project. His publications include *The Destruction of the Zulu Kingdom* and *The Heretic: A Study of the Life of John William Colenso*.

Motlatsi Thabane is completing a doctorate in history at the National University of Lesotho. His research is on the effects of migrant labour on the contemporary history of Lesotho, and his interviews have contributed significantly to the development of oral history in the region.

Acknowledgements

The essays contained in the present collection are rewritten versions of papers presented to a workshop on 'Culture and Development in Southern Africa' held at the Centre for Research in the Humanities at the University of Copenhagen in April 1988. The workshop as well as the publication were made possible by financial support from DANIDA and the Danish Council for Research on Developing Countries. Thanks to this support copies are being distributed in Africa. Special thanks are due to Bente Jensen of the Centre for Research in the Humanities for typing manuscripts on to disk and formatting them.

Introduction

Preben Kaarsholm

It can be argued that 'classical' understandings of societal development contain two notions of culture - one in which culture represents the traditional, that which is pre-existing and contrary to development, and another in which culture stands for a set of institutions and genres that emerges as a consequence and reflection of development. This applies both to the development and modernization theories which came into existence in the context of post-Second World War decolonization, and to Marxist theories of the progression of modes of production and of capitalism in particular. In both cases, development is seen as based on economic growth, as a sequence of transformations which takes off at an identifiable point in time, and as an irreversible process that explodes an earlier state of cultural inertia, irrationality and simple reproduction to replace it with a modern complexity of profit- and participation-oriented institutions, dynamic, calculating personalities as well as duality of mass and 'high' cultures which have become liberated from traditional religious functions and from direct links with the cyclical regeneration of local communities.

In important respects, the development of the colonial and postcolonial societies in Southern Africa in the twentieth century does not conform with this paradigm. In the Union and later Republic of South Africa, for example, an extremely dynamic history of capitalist production and accumulation has unfolded in a much more ambiguous relationship with cultural preconditions and effects. While, on the one hand, economic modernization has been accompanied by the establishment of participatory and democratic political institutions and a differentiated system of culture for the ruling white minority, it has at the same time based itself on conditions of enforced cultural traditionalism and non-development for the African majority.

Apartheid represents a particularly glaring variety of colonial semi-modernization, in which, by means of purposeful social engineering, society is turned into a federation of mutually dependent developed and non-developed sectors - a grotesque miniature of an imperialist global order, in which poor areas are restricted to providing the resources and labour power for the development of the rich. While the control and benefits of industrialization, accumulation and urbanization have been reserved for a white fraction of the population, the African majority in South Africa has been marginalized as a fundamentally rural and powerless surplus population with only vulnerable roots in carefully manipulated reserves or homelands structured around allegedly traditional cultures and forms of government. Thus, in South Africa, development has so far taken place without the effects of any universal cultural modernization - on the contrary, it has in many respects presupposed the conservation of vast areas of traditionalism.

To take another example: Zimbabwe shares with South Africa a history of colonization, of partial modernization and of racial division, but was formally decolonized, in 1980, in a manner South Africa has never experienced, and had majority rule established in the wake of a gruesome and protracted anti-colonial struggle. After independence, however, development in Zimbabwe has continued to be restricted by many colonial features. In economic terms, control, ownership and distribution of wealth are still extremely unevenly balanced, the geography and social worlds of both town and countryside are as fundamentally, if less formally, segregated as in the heyday of imperialism, and as far as the modernization of politics and culture is concerned, there are huge gaps between the needs and languages of the different groups of the population.

While, for a time, these gaps were hidden away under the dominating confrontation between white settler rule and African nationalism, the nationalist consensus of the immediate post-1980 period is now rapidly being replaced by genuine disagreements about which direction the development of institutions should take and about the role of democracy. Debates concerning the introduction of a one-party constitution after the lapse of the transitional Lancaster House agreement in 1990 have shown a division between, on the one hand, the idea that nationalist control is paramount to democracy and that independent development would benefit most from a system of institutions in harmony with traditional African notions of social control, and, on the other hand, the view that a more radical process of transformation of political and cultural life in the form of expanding rather than restricting pluralist representation and of actively promoting the articulation of differences is needed as a precondition for further growth and a more equitable distribution of influence and wealth.

So what has emerged in the process of development in Zimbabwe is not so much a dismantling of tradition and the emergence of an alternative new and abruptly modern culture. It is rather a contradiction between a redefined body of tradition on the one hand, having its roots in the anti-colonial programmes for a cultural renaissance of the nationalist movements during the struggle for independence, and on the other hand, an ambition to move beyond this redefinition towards a radically different type of cultural struggle - a new forum and agenda for debates between the conflicting interests and diverging understandings of development of different classes, sexes, generations, language groups, or other categories in which people might choose to place the priorities in their definition of themselves.

The texts included in this publication are all aimed at describing the complexities of the relationship between cultural struggle and development in a number of Southern African situations. All of them, in different ways, present problematizations of any simple dualism of modernization and cultural tradition and of envisaging a modern culture as a superstructure arising mechanically out of economic growth and accumulation. They tend to agree that an understanding of the dialectics of modern development must bring into play a much deeper historical perspective than is usually the case when development theorists set up projects. History, rather than tradition in a static or anthropological sense, sets the conditions for the development of modernity.

The essays cover an extensive geographical field. Zimbabwe is treated most substantially because the majority of the contributors are Zimbabweans or Zimbabwe scholars. South Africa, its satellite reservoirs of labour, and cultures which are both violently divided and violently mixed, are covered by Jeff Guy and Motlatsi Thabane. Kate Crehan deals with conflicts of understanding between developers, politicians and peasants in Zambia. Two essays, by Kimani Gecau and Bodil Folke Frederiksen respectively, take their point of departure outside the region, in Kenya, but in doing so they bring Southern Africa into enlightening perspective. Gecau provides a parallel between the history of anti- and post-colonial culture in Kenya and that in Zimbabwe; Frederiksen juxtaposes the urban youth cultures of Nairobi and those of the townships of Johannesburg. The opening article, by John MacKenzie, gives an overview of aspects of the cultural history of the whole Southern African region.

3

In all of the essays, central themes within the discussion of cultural struggles and development are *traditions* and *democracy*. The plural of traditions is important. What is being discussed is a variety of often conflicting frameworks and discourses - African political, cultural and ethnic traditions, colonial and anti-colonial traditions, traditions of government, the traditions of nationalism and of modern political and cultural institutions. They are all full of contradictions within themselves and do not represent unambiguous positions *vis-à-vis* development. And they are all traditions which have been, if not invented, then at least thoroughly manipulated by the developments of modern history, as many of the articles show (cf. Hobsbawm and Ranger 1983; Vail 1989).

Colonial traditions figure prominently at the beginning of the collection. John MacKenzie describes the colonization of nature in Southern Africa as a prelude to the colonization of peoples and societies and discusses the way this is reflected in literature dealing with travel, hunting or conservation from late-nineteenth century imperialism to the present day. He traces the development of attitudes towards wild animals and ideas of natural beauty from expropriation by white colonizers to the policies concerning nature parks and animal reserves in post-independence Southern African societies. It is a tale of continuity as well as of change - the ongoing war against poachers in many African states seems to carry on a colonial tradition of caring more for wild animals and resources of spectacle than for the needs of local human beings, having to make a living out of nature. MacKenzie's article is an example of the inspiring boom which seems to be taking place at present within environment and conservation history (cf. Anderson and Grove 1988; MacKenzie 1988; Beinart 1989; Ranger (forthcoming)).

Conceptions of nature and of what is 'natural' or authentic are also central to my essay on war literature in Rhodesia and Zimbabwe. The essay deals with a double relationship of change and continuity - first, between a British tradition of imperialist writing and the war novels of colonial Rhodesia, and second, between the latter and post-independence Zimbabwean literature about the liberation war. Often the war novels strive to look beyond the disasters of war to a more healthy and 'natural' society which is not burdened by the complex problems of democracy and modernization - a romantic anti-capitalism which can be found in examples of colonial as well as of anti-colonial literature. Stephen Williams, in his article on pictorial art and sculpture in Rhodesia and Zimbabwe, points to the escapism of the colonial tradition of painting, its obsession with landscapes and natural scenary which have been emptied of anything human or social - a theme which has been investigated recently also by J. M. Coetzee in South Africa (Coetzee 1988:36-62). As an alternative, Williams sketches the principles of a post-colonial art policy in which the artist serves the development of human and social capacities for communication and is allowed scope for free experimentation.

Colonial cultural traditions also appear in subsequent articles. Dambudzo Marechera's Oxford accent and horse-riding outfit which are described in an anecdote by David Caute, may have been intended as a joke, but also represented a real problem for this 'modernist of underdevelopment' (cf. Berman 1982: 232). Continuity and the possibilities of change are also the central concerns of Welshman Ncube and Shephard Nzombe in their mapping out of constitutional development from colonization to independence. Is multi-party democracy part of a western tradition and colonial heritage from which an African nation must liberate itself in order to attain independence and autonomy? Or is there a universal framework within which constitutional and political rights can be discussed, and where the criteria for a definition of democracy can be sought? (cf. Shivji 1988; Beckmann *et al.* (forthcoming); Moyo 1990). And is there a need to move beyond the antagonism between colonialism and anti-colonialism as a basic framework of understanding in order to formulate an adequate political agenda for Southern African societies today?

A group of essays in the collection concern itself particularly with traditions of anti-colonial culture and politics. Kimani Gecau describes the evolution of a counter-culture of songs and theatre in Kenya in relation to the struggle for independence. He sees a specific tradition developing from the Mau Mau revolt onwards - a tradition which is eventually betrayed by 'neo-colonial' politicians, but which can still be appealed to by groups seeking a more radical transformation. Ken Manungo presents a harmonious picture of collaboration between peasants and guerillas during Zimbabwe's war of liberation. The anti-colonial struggle was a genuine people's war, and as a tradition it has continued to inspire popular efforts after independence.

Norma Kriger expresses a gloomier view. In the region she studied, which borders that of Manungo's field work, anti-colonial co-operation between peasants and guerillas was far from idyllic, and people would exploit the war situation to strengthen their positions in the context of overlapping everyday conflicts of interest -

5

between sexes, generations, or clans. Rather than a heroic age, the war years were a nightmare for a lot of ordinary people caught in the cross-fire, and the tradition which survives most powerfully is one of hate, fear and violence. At the same time, instead of working towards social transformation, guerillas would often ally themselves opportunistically with traditional leaders and conservative forces in African rural communities. Thus certain aspects of the war did not provide much incentive for a democratization of social relations in the countryside after 1980 (cf. Phimister 1988).

In contrast, Terence Ranger writes about healing and reconciliation. He describes the work of religious institutions which have themselves been caught up in contradictions between colonialism and anti-colonialism - spirit mediums, independent and missionary Christian churches. The use by guerillas of spirit mediums to mobilize local support during the war is well-known from Ranger's earlier work as well as from that of David Lan (Ranger 1985; Lan 1985), but according to Ranger at least some of the Christian churches fulfilled a similar mediating function. In parallel, he sees religious institutions after the war working more or less in unison to relieve the traumas of the war and of post-independence economic differentiation.

Ranger's essay points to the extreme adaptability of cultural forms, and several other contributions describe how cultural traditions over time become appropriated by different groupings and are manipulated to serve very contradictory purposes. Kaarsholm illustrates how different conceptions of African cultural tradition have been promoted in Rhodesia and Zimbabwe by colonialist and nationalist politicians. Bodil Folke Frederiksen writes about self-identification in the urban slums of Nairobi, about Islamic and 'Nubian' cultures that are chosen consciously by people in the attempt, not just to survive, but to articulate coherence and ambition and come to terms with a situation of radical poverty and uprootedness. In this world, images also crop up of South Africa - of Sophiatown as an ideal of autonomy and social organization.

Jeff Guy's and Motlatsi Thabane's essay on Basotho gangs in Johannesburg describes how an even 'wilder' range of cultures can be mixed to offer identification and space, and how the function of ethnicity can be one of both subversiveness and subordination. In the lives of the migrant workers interviewed, the understanding of class is extricably bound up with that of ethnicity. At the same time, the ethnicity in question is far removed from any traditional culture of the 'homeland'. Culture has been transformed to make it possible for people to keep up a role in a historical development which would otherwise have deprived them more completely of control over their own lives (cf. Rudolph and Rudolph 1967).

In important respects, it is the relations between culture and power in a community which decide opportunities for grassroots participation in development. Kate Crehan describes in detail some of the problems that development projects may encounter when they attempt to build up participation and self-reliance in the countryside. If local networks for providing social security and exerting influence are disregarded, the effort to promote self-reliance may bring about a weakening of the poorest groups rather than the intended opposite. The development dialogue takes place not only in a context of conflicting interests, but also within a universe of 'struggles over meaning' between different notions of what development implies between different groups of the local population, politicians and the representatives of development agencies. Democratization, in the sense of providing scope and opportunity for these different voices to be articulated and contested, seems a precondition for economic improvement.

In his essay, Kimani Gecau underlines the role of popular culture in formulating Utopias, building self-respect and mobilizing people for change in a national perspective. Luke Mhlaba takes this argument further by pointing to the need to strengthen local cultural resources and not be blinded by a national level of discourse which to majority groups within the population is just an abstraction. The colonial heritage is one of 'cultural alienation', and the 'cultural renaissance' which Mhlaba sees as a precondition for development necessarily involves decentralization:

> If we consider a cultural renaissance, i.e. a rejection of political and social *mimétisme* and its replacement by institutions and values grounded in the African experience, which are more conducive to a development based on self-reliance, we must logically reject the present Jacobin structure of the African state, characterized as it is by heavy centralization.

The alternative, according to Mhlaba, is a looser, federation-like form of nation state, a giving up of one-party systems which are more in harmony with a European history of centralization than with African traditions, and pluralistic language, education and media policies which will allow otherwise marginalized groups the possibility of making themselves heard.

7

The essays are not in agreement, and present problems rather than solutions. Luke Mhlaba's anti-Jacobinism, for example, differs considerably from the Marxist approach of Welshman Ncube and Shephard Nzombe which would favour a more centralist perspective and regard Mhlaba's concern for local languages and cultural institutions as promoting divisions and weakening broader popular aspirations based on class interest. Similarly, the present publication contains differing views on cultural nationalism, on ethnicity and on the dynamics of liberation struggles. There is a point, however, in bringing out a collection which represents a forum for discussion rather than a unified programme for change, and it is to be hoped that the essays can help to stimulate further debates.

The collection also presents an argument in favour of a broader and more interdisciplinary understanding of development studies in which investigations of cultural struggle and contributions from history and the humanities enter into meaningful dialogue with political and economic analysis. Finally, by bringing together contributions from scholars based in Southern Africa with those of researchers working in Europe and the United States, the collection gives an example of a dialogue between two environments which need to be able to communicate in an unchauvinistic, tolerant and open manner in order for both of them to be able to develop their insights.

References

Anderson, David and Grove, Richard (eds.) (1988) *Conservation in Africa*, Cambridge.

Beckmann, Björn, Brandell, Inga and Rudebeck, Lars (eds.) (forthcoming) *When Does Democracy Make Sense? Political Economy and Political Rights in the Third World with Some European Comparisons*, Uppsala.

Beinart, William (ed.) (1989) *The Politics of Conservation in Southern Africa, Special Issue of the Journal of Southern African Studies*, vol. 15, no. 2, January.

Berman, Marshall (1982) *All That Is Solid Melts into Air. The Experience of Modernity*, London.

Coetzee, J. M. (1988) *White Writing: On the Culture of Letters in South Africa*, New Haven.

Hobsbawm, Eric and Ranger, Terence (eds.) (1983) *The Invention of Tradition*, Cambridge.

Lan, David (1985) *Guns and Rain: Guerillas and Spirit Mediums in Zimbabwe*, Harare.

MacKenzie, John M. (1988)*The Empire of Nature. Hunting, Conservation and British Imperialism*, Manchester.

Moyo, Jonathan (1990) 'The One-Party State' in: *Parade*, July.

Phimister, Ian (1988) 'The Combined and Contradictory Inheritance of the Struggle against Colonialism' in: Colin Stoneman (ed.) *Zimbabwe's Prospects: Issues of Race, Class and Capital in Southern Africa*, London.

Ranger, Terence (1985) *Peasant Consciousness and Guerilla War in Zimbabwe*, Harare.

Ranger, Terence (forthcoming) *Voices from the Rocks. The Modern History of the Matopos*, Harare.

Rudolph, Lloyd and Rudolph, Susanne Hoeber (1967) *The Modernity of Tradition: Political Development in India*, Chicago.

Shivji, Issa G. (1988) *Fight my Beloved Continent: New Democracy in Africa*, Harare.

Vail, Leroy (ed.) (1989) *The Creation of Tribalism in Southern Africa*, London.

Part One

Colonial Ideology and Post-Independence Culture

Part One

Capital Markets and
Performance Measures

The Natural World and the Popular Consciousness in Southern Africa: The European Appropriation of Nature

John M. MacKenzie

Introduction

Wild animals were a central fact of existence for most African peoples in Southern Africa. They presented both a threat and an opportunity, a danger to stock, crops and human life, but a source of meat, receptacles, tools, ornament, jewellery, raiment and trade goods. They were important in the physical and moral training of the young and were a source of environmental and biological knowledge; they played a significant role in magic, divination and ritual and were the subject of myth and fable; they offered a welcome addition to diet in normal times and they constituted an emergency resource in time of crisis; the distribution of the products of the chase was a crucial aspect of social relations and Africans were introduced to the international economy through ivory and horns, hides and skins. Hunting inspired much ingenuity in the manufacture of weapons, traps, snares and gins and the construction of trip wires, deadfalls and pitfalls. It prompted deeds of valour, celebrated in poetry and song, and could act as a significant route to meritocratic advance.

These may sound like the grossly inflated claims of the obsessive specialist emerging from two to three years of eating and drinking hunting, as it were, but they are claims which seem to be amply vindicated by a wide range of sources. The full significance of wild animals to African culture and socio-economic structures has been obscured to modern scholars for a number of reasons. The widespread, prolific and immensely varied game resources of

Africa had been virtually exterminated south of the Limpopo by the end of the Boer War; a similar destruction had taken place in Zimbabwe and to a lesser extent in Zambia by the inter-war years. The lingering influence of notions of economic evolution led most to accept that while hunting was obviously of great importance to hunting and gathering peoples (though even with them its proportionate contribution to diet was invariably less than fifty per cent) it could only have marginal significance for herders and cultivators. Moreover, by the inter-war years policies of separating human settlement from animal habitat were far advanced, and game legislation had set about restricting social access to hunting, transforming it into a ritual of the élite and Africans into poachers. Scientific ideas and administrative action, particularly associated with tsetse control, hastened this process, as did labour migration and urbanization.

Thus by the 1930s Schapera and Goodwin could suggest that hunting 'is nowhere a regular occupation', that 'it is carried out fairly sporadically' and that its products could not be described in any way as 'a staple food', though they made a partial, if qualified, exception of Botswana where 'game may be an important source of food' (Goodwin and Schapera 1937: 141). In the same decade Audrey Richards, in her survey of the diet of the Bemba of Zambia, found that while the Bemba looked back to a golden age of hunting and regarded animals as a crucial aspect of magic and ritual, they could not match words with present performance (Richards 1939). She viewed with scepticism the idea that hunting had ever been as practically significant as her respondents seemed to indicate.

Historians have tended to view hunting merely as a survival mechanism, an inferior form of economic activity adopted only in times of crisis. Thus Leonard Thompson, writing of the disruption of the Sotho by the Nguni migrations of the 1820s, described 'demoralized survivors' wandering around 'contriving to live on game or veld plants,' which, together with the emergence of canni- balism, served to illustrate 'the collapse of the social and moral order' (Wilson and Thompson 1969: 395). William Beinart has sug- gested that in Pondoland hunting became particularly important in times of stress, providing 'a major source of meat in the 1820s and 1830s' (Beinart 1980: 128). Peter Delius, writing of the economy of the Pedi, has noted that the cattle losses experienced in the 1820s 'presumably increased the importance of hunting, and by 1839 they lived "chiefly by the chase, on millet, and on beans" ' (Delius 1980: 301). More contentiously, the historian of the Shona of Zimbabwe has asserted that hunting was taken up only in time of famine (Beach 1977: 39-40).

No doubt hunting did become more important when other forms of subsistence failed, but this should not obscure the fact that it could be a significant source of meat and domestic commodities, as well as trade goods, even in normal times. Delius, reflecting a new sensitivity to the full range of African economic opportunities, recognizes an ambiguity in the expected balance of Pedi activities:

> The gradual re-accumulation of cattle reduced this dependence on the hunt, but in accounts of the region in the 1860s, hunting is given equal prominence with agriculture and cattle-keeping as constituting the economic bases of local societies (Delius 1980: 301-2).

Delius sees this continuing importance of hunting as being related to the use of guns and the development of trade, but he acknow-ledges that it is difficult to draw clear distinctions between hunting for trading purposes and its role in everyday subsistence. This is an important caveat, for historians have long been concerned with animal products as trade goods without evincing much interest in the process by which animal becomes product or the precise rela-tionship between the 'external' trading sector - utilizing only one part of the animal - and the other products of the chase used 'internally'.

Hunting was a raid upon nature, which, though labour-intensive, could be immediately productive in a manner which contrasted with the slower processes of herding or cultivation. Different priori-ties - meat, domestic items or trade goods - would have prevailed at different times, partly depending on the scale and social organiza-tion of the particular hunt. It was perhaps this very combination of opportunity which ensured the continuing prestige and popularity of hunting, together with the opportunities it afforded for redistri-bution or appropriation according to the status of the participants. Among historians who have begun to spot its importance, Philip Bonner has argued, most suggestively, that the Swazi and Zulu aris-tocracies were able to control the size and reproduction of individ-ual homesteads through, among other things, 'the organization of "hunts" which provided for a more substantial proportion of subsis-tence than is normally acknowledged' (Bonner 1980: 85).

Myths of origin involving great hunters, explanations of migra-tion in terms of the search for superior hunting grounds, and hunting tales of one sort or another have become familiar in the oral record throughout Southern and Central (as well as East) Africa. A study of the Bisa of the Luangwa Valley of Zambia in the 1960s helps to explain the cultural prominence of hunting among otherwise agricultural peoples. Stuart Marks found that Bisa hunters had high prestige often matched by political authority. Specialist hunting guilds deployed a wide range of practical techniques as well as magic, and hunting shrines were carefully maintained. Success rates were high and yields good, though the time devoted to hunting, in comparison with other economic activities, was relatively low (Marks 1976). Thus, relative to effort, hunting was highly productive. The Bisa are a special case in so far as their hunting opportunities have survived into modern times, but this survival may well represent conditions that obtained for many more African peoples throughout Southern Africa in the past.

Nineteenth-century travellers' accounts certainly abound in descriptions of African hunting in almost every part of the subcontinent. It would be tedious to enumerate these in detail, so all I offer here is a brief survey larded by some particularly juicy quotations. In the rest of the article I shall attempt to revalue the significance of African hunting, chart its appropriation by a dominant white culture, and assess its role in resistance and adaptation.

African Hunting

The missionary John Brownless described the Xhosa as 'passionately fond' of the chase 'as an active and animating amusement' (Wilson and Thompson 1969: 110, 235; Steedman 1835: vol.1, 21-5). They organized large-scale communal hunts for all the large game in the expanses of unpopulated country between chieftaincies (which were thus effectively game preserves). Most of their meat came from game, for as one commentator has put it, they were prodigal of game, but sparing of their cattle (Wilson and Thompson 1969: 254). The northern Nguni displayed a similar predilection for hunting, although the balance between cultivation and the chase naturally varied according to the quality of the land and the quantity of game available. The search for good hunting grounds may have been one cause of the movements of the northern Nguni in the late eighteenth century and their methods were transferred to other parts of south Central Africa during the *mfecane*. There are a number of detailed descriptions of Zulu hunting which indicate the large numbers of people involved and the elaboration of the fences and pits used in game drives (Baldwin 1894: 42, 74; Beinart 1980: 124-6; Ritter 1955: 205-15).

The extent of similar 'works' was described by many of the visitors to the territory of the southern Sotho in the first half of the nineteenth century. Cornwallis Harris, for example, described 'a long line of pitfalls used for entrapping game':

> Upwards of sixty of these were dug close together in a treble line; a high thorn fence extending in the form of a crescent a mile on either side, in such a manner that gnoos, quaggas and other animals may easily be driven into them. They are carefully concealed by grass, and their circumscribed dimensions render escape almost impossible. Heaps of whitened bones bore ample testimony to the destruction they had occasioned (Harris 1852: 49, 94).

At Kolobeng, David Livingstone saw a very large pit or *hopo* in frequent use. Around his mission sixty or seventy head of large game were killed each week providing a good deal of protein to what would otherwise have been 'an exclusively vegetable diet' (Livingstone 1857: 26). As is well known, each of the Sotho-Tswana peoples had clearly defined western hunting grounds, inhabited by client hunters, from whom tribute was levied.

Such tribute fed the wide range of crafts associated with animal products. The Sotho practised highly skilled ivory carving as well as superb leatherwork. Tanning and sewing were a masculine employment, and the high regard in which it was held is evidenced by the fact that men of superior status participated in stitching karosses. The results were of excellent quality, soft and beautifully sewn. Almost everywhere the poor wore antelope skins and the rich garments made up of jackal and cat furs. Sandals were made of buffalo or giraffe hide, as were shields, while women wore a kaross and kilt generally of impala skin. In 1890, when H. Anderson Bryden hunted in Botswana and carefully observed the trade in animal products the finest karosses were fetching over £6 each. The kaross industry of the Tswana remained very important even then. 'No other people can so deftly shape and sew them' (Bryden 1893: 60-2).

The importance of hunting was very apparent at the court of Mzilikazi, king of the Ndebele, when Cornwallis Harris visited him in the 1830s. Animal products were everywhere, and Mzilikazi's heralds praised the king in terms of his hunting exploits, making both visual and aural animal imitations.

Advancing slowly towards the waggons, he opened the exhibition by roaring and charging, in frantic imitation of the king of beasts - then placing his arm before his mouth, and swinging it rapidly in pantomime representation of the elephant, he threw his trunk above his head and shrilly trumpeted. He next ran on tiptoe imitating the ostrich; and lastly, humbling himself in the dust, wept like an infant. At each interval of the scene he recounted the matchless prowess and mighty conquests of his illustrious monarch, and made the hills re-echo with his praise (Harris 1852: 96).

Perhaps this extolling of hunting prowess was based in economic reality. Harris saw the products of the chase as more important to the subsistence of ordinary people than the products of herding. The king's cattle were herded throughout the country 'and furnish employment to a considerable portion of his lieges, who are precariously maintained by his bounty, but depend chiefly for support upon their success in hunting' (Harris 1852: 114-5, 138-40).

When the Ndebele crossed the Limpopo to their new territory in Zimbabwe they took their hunting practices with them. The missionary T. M. Thomas observed Ndebele hunts involving several thousand warriors whose labour time was thus consumed in a period of seasonal underemployment (Child 1968: 68-72; Cobbing 1976: 174-5; Thomas 1893: 116-7). Some of the Shona peoples gave tribute in animal products to the Ndebele. They set traps and snares and training in their use was an important part of the education of the young (Bullock 1950: 40-41). They also had large-scale hunts using *mambure* or nets. Karl Mauch described one he saw in the Chibi district and Thomas Baines drew one he witnessed in the Lomagundi district (Bernhard 1971: 220; Burke 1969: 159-61). These hunts involved a great deal of labour, albeit briefly deployed, and were more likely to be undertaken by people in good heart, not when driven to it by famine.

In the upper Zambezi Valley Lozi hunts were particularly extensive, and were clearly an important part of the economy and culture of Barotseland. David Livingstone described the avid hunting of the Lozi and their Kololo aristocracy (Coillard 1897: 600; Livingstone 1857: 204-5, 217; Tabler 1963: 43). Enormous numbers of the 'prodigious herds' of waterbuck like lechwe were killed every year;

there were large-scale hippo hunts as well as the great annual elephant hunt. Later in the century, partly under European influence, Lewanika seems to have increased the scale and frequency of the hunts as well as elaborating the ritual associated with them. The hunt became a central part of state ceremonial. In 1889 he gave a Martini-Henry rifle to his son Letia, and the prince's first kills were met with congratulations from around the kingdom. The hunt had become a rite of passage to the chieftaincy. Lewanika reserved a particular area for his exclusive use and had a hunting lodge built within it. In 1895 three great hunting expeditions took place. The king commanded one of the hunts from an ant-hill, where he waited while the animals were driven towards him by hundreds of men. He insisted on making the first kill, piercing the animal with a weapon in his own hand. 'Alas,' wrote the missionary François Coillard, 'the pretensions of royalty multiply in an alarming manner; ceremonies are becoming more and more complicated...' (Coillard 1897: 591). Lewanika was inventing tradition in the middle of Africa. The last of these great Barotse hunts took place in 1913.

Each Lozi hunter erected an altar 'where he dedicates the first-fruits of his hunting and some of the vertebrae or horns of the animals.' Lewanika's great village, before he ascended the Lozi throne, was full of 'heaps of heads and horns of every kind of animal' while on its edge was a shrub loaded with vertebrae. Every hunter's tomb was decorated with skulls, horns or tusks, depending on the animals he most favoured in the hunt. Sewing was a masculine prerogative and 'it was the hunter's privilege to dress and stitch the skins of the animals he chased and to embroider a garment for his bride' (Coillard 1897: 598; Mackintosh 1907: 342, 346).

European Hunting

Lewanika's activities represented the last great flourishing of African hunting (particularly of the 'state' variety) at a time when nature was finally being appropriated by Europeans throughout Southern Africa. There were a succession of phases to this progressive annexation of the faunal abundance of the sub-continent. The first was marked by the sheer firepower of the well-armed hunter-trader operating beyond the frontier, from the Cape in the eighteenth century and progressing deeper into Africa in the course of the nineteenth before virtually disappearing in the years before the First World War. Hunter-trading became part of the Southern

African myth in the nineteenth century, as many works of juvenile literature - like W.H.G. Kingston's *Hendricks the Hunter*, R.M. Ballantyne's *The Settler and the Savage* and G.A. Henty's *The Young Colonists* - indicate. Hunter-trading interacted with the work of the publicists, the natural history explorers like Thunberg, Sparrman, Le Vaillant, Barrow, Lichtenstein, Burchell and Smith, and the celebrated international hunters, Cornwallis Harris, Roualeyn Gordon Cumming, W. C. Baldwin and others, who publizised their exploits to a Europe increasingly enthralled by the hunting cult. They greatly contributed to the myth which was to influence exploration, conquest and settlement later in the century as the works of Selous and the correspondence of members of Rhodes's pioneer column amply testify. During this period African hunting was undoubtedly stepped up to meet the voracious demands of hunter-traders (most of whom traded more than they hunted, invariably at highly advantageous terms of trade). Where European hunters travelled, African camp followers enjoyed a meat bonanza. So profligate were the white hunters that they usually left a train of wounded animals in their wake which could be picked off by African hunters.

All settlers are, initially, asset-strippers. In the second phase game constituted a vital expansionist resource, a ready source of meat, a means of paying labour, as well as offering trade items to supplement other forms of economic activity. Lands for settlement were often judged according to the relative abundance of game. Moreover, hunting added impetus to frontier expansion since it was of course an exceptionally land extensive activity. But game was a wasting asset. It offered only a temporary subsidy to frontier settler or trekker. As settlement was consolidated the game was shot out, or, disturbed, moved on. Nor was this necessarily a disadvantage to the farmers. As herds were built up, the balance between the pastoral and the hunting sectors of the frontiersman's economy changed. It was no longer in his interests to have animal competitors for the grazing. Migratory herds, particularly of springbok, might still appear and could be shot at will to protect the pasturage, offering large quantities of meat and skins in the process. In the Boer republics many farmers alternated between farming in the growing season and more distant hunting expeditions in the winter. Some moved their stock to winter grazing where game might still be found, on the low veld, for example, a practice which continued up to the First World War.

As I have described elsewhere, game acted as a subsidy to a variety of other activities (MacKenzie 1987). Missionaries often fed their followers or paid for church building on the strength of their prowess with the gun. Livingstone built his church at Kolobeng by this method and it was particularly common in Central Africa. Prospectors, explorers and a variety of imperial concerns helped to finance their operations through ivory, skins and the distribution of meat. As the accounts of almost all travellers testify, meat was a vital means of propitiating Africans through whose lands they passed. Later, game meat acted as a subsidy to major engineering works, like railway lines, when these passed through game-rich regions. James Stevenson-Hamilton described the importance of the meat subsidy to the building of South African railway lines, 'including that of the Selati railway itself [which passed through the Sabi game reserve] ... the game as a matter of course always provided free meat, and thus cheapened working expenses' (Stevenson-Hamilton 1937: 126).

At these processes accelerated in the later nineteenth century, it was not just Africans who found it increasingly difficult to gain access to the faunal resource. Access to game progressively became a marker of class status among whites. The disappearance of hunting opportunities may well have furthered the impoverishment of poor whites in the Transvaal and thus developed social differentiation among the Boers (Trapido 1980: 356, 359). This was confirmed by game legislation. Proprietorial rights to game were established in relation to private lands. A licensing system was introduced which increasingly turned hunting into an élite recreation and exemptions for bona fide travellers were eventually removed, although those for officials and the police survived rather longer (game was also of course exploited for practical purposes in time of war). As the utilitarian aspects of hunting declined, its status as the perquisite of the élite became increasingly important. As with most sports a 'code' now came into operation; 'clean kills' became the order of the day and all methods adjudged cruel, like the use of spears, poison, traps, snares or pits were banned. Thus Europeans created a set of legal and moral criteria which specifically excluded Africans. Africans were also excluded by the operation of gun laws and the decline of iron-working and crafts associated with hunting.

By this time whites had become acutely aware of the decline of game stocks. Two species, the blaaubok and the quagga, had become extinct while others no longer survived in vast tracts of Southern Africa where formerly they had been abundant. Herds of increasingly rare antelope were beginning to be 'preserved' on private estates.

John M. MacKenzie

The development of notions of preservation and conservation marked the final stages of the appropriation of nature. The concept of land segregation has usually been studied in terms of its human and radical dimensions. But it should be remembered that racial segregation was preceded by efforts to separate animal habitat from human settlement. The need for a game reserve was first perceived by the government of the South African Republic and the reservation of land for animals was begun there and in Natal in the 1890s. The British later became enthusiastic exponents of the idea in colonies throughout the continent. The idea of the reserve was based on a number of premises. The co-existence of humans and animals was incompatible. African hunting was inadmissible - in Darwinian terms it was regressive and in any case the methods adopted by Africans were unacceptable. The only hope for the survival of game - and for the 'civilization' of Africans - lay in the provision of separate territory where it would be protected. Elite white hunting could continue to take place in remote regions or in controlled hunting areas.

The dangers of allowing animals to co-exist with humans seemed to be confirmed by the capacity of game to transmit rinderpest (from which game had suffered drastically in the mid-90s) and East Coast fever, and, above all, to harbour tsetse. So far as African access to game was concerned the new policies were neatly summed up by the warden of the Sabi game reserve (later the Kruger National Park), James Stevenson-Hamilton. In the early years of the twentieth century

the native inhabitants of the low veld looked upon game as their natural food, in fact as their chief support, and every track within miles of a habitation was dotted at short intervals with every variety of snare and other device for entrapping birds and beasts known to kaffir ingenuity. Besides this every kraal contained a horde of nondescript dogs, usually of the lurcher type, used solely for hunting, and a considerable number of the men were in possession of firearms of one kind or another. It may therefore be realized that the initial task was no sinecure (Stevenson-Hamilton 1940: 25).

The task was of course to transform these hunters into 'poachers' in order to frustrate their hunting activities.

The clearance of Africans out of the new reserves, combined with extensive shooting of game in the areas inhabited by Africans, were the twin motors of the new policy, given international sanction by the Convention for the Preservation of Wild Animals, Birds and Fish in Africa, signed in London in 1900, and the Agreement for the Protection of the Fauna and Flora of Africa of 1933.[1] The conservationist lobby, represented by the Society for the Preservation of the Fauna of the Empire in London and various societies in Southern Africa which later fused into the Wildlife Protection Society of South Africa, set about insisting that game meat was not an appropriate foodstuff for Africans, despite the assiduous use of it for precisely that purpose by hunters, explorers, missionaries, prospectors, railway builders, miners and farmers. One member of the London society asserted categorically that 'Meat is not part of the routine diet of the African native.' Securing meat by hunting 'is the stamp of primitiveness' from which Europeans should lead him by teaching him 'the meat-securing methods which are practised by the more cultured races'. This would involve a 'discouragement of native slaughter' and 'teaching of the keeping and breeding of domestic animals such as cattle, pigs, sheep, fowls and ducks' (Journal of the Society for the Preservation of the Fauna of the Empire, XII, 1930: 56). In effect, game meat was to be subjected to sumptuary laws; it could be eaten only by those who treated hunting as sport; African labour time was not to be devoted to its pursuit. Hunting was not just a distraction from settled agriculture but a consumer of male labour time which should be directed into labour migration.

National Parks

The development of national parks introduced a new phase to the white appropriation of nature. The 'preservation' phase, associated with the early attempts at game legislation and the establishment of reserves, was part of the transformation of hunting into a sport of the élite. Species would survive and game be protected in order to supply recreation to those qualified to pursue it. Reserves were established by gubernatorial or ministerial decree; they could be deproclaimed as easily as they were first declared. Most observers thought they would be temporary - at the very least it was thought that their prime function was to stock adjacent hunting areas. Very

---

[1] A full survey of the conservation movement, the activities of the Society for the Preservation of the Fauna of the Empire and of the international agreements of the period can be found in MacKenzie 1988a.

little was spent on their management and they were invariably designed to inhibit rather than promote human access. Their rangers, where they were were appointed at all, were usually ex-hunters and had an entirely nineteenth-century approach to animals. 'Vermin' were to be shot at will and exterminated as far as possible. In this category came lions, crocodiles and, above all, hunting dogs. Reserves were thus a policy of the hunting era.

The national parks, which first emerged in the inter-war years and became virtually a flood after the Second World War, were very different. They were given legislative sanction and measures were introduced to ensure that it would be difficult to subvert them. Since it was intended that they should be, as far as possible, self-financing, accessibility was crucial. They were to be a vast outdoor zoo, an African rural idyll, designed to show a combination of urbanized whites and international tourists what the 'real' Africa was like. They were dependent upon the internal combustion engine and could scarcely have developed without it. Criteria of animal value now took a dramatic shift representing this change of function. Whereas the practical hunter judges animals according to edibility, the sportsman judges them according to sporting characteristics, the excellence of the chase they provide and their 'pluck' in resisting death. The notion of 'vermin' is invariably a sportsman's category, vermin being the predators who deny him 'sport' (sometimes, however, 'vermin' can become a protected species - like the fox in England or the tiger in India - if they become amenable to sport). The national parks introduced a wholly new criterion - 'viewability'. Animals underwent somersaults in reputation. The lion, formerly vermin, was the most notable case of this. Viewers of the 'real' Africa wanted lions and lots of them. Rangers, almost overnight, gave up shooting them and started protecting them.

The creation of national parks did, however, confirm a number of trends already apparent in the establishment of reserves. First, the conservation lobby insisted that they had to be large. This was essential, so it was thought, to permit animal migration and to ensure adequate insulation from regions of human settlement. Second, if conservation objectives were to be achieved and 'poaching' eliminated, then all people and their habitations not required for the running of the park needed to be moved out. Third, national parks greatly increased the respectability of game preservation. In the post-Second World War period in particular, conservation seemed to be a visionary movement emblematic of a brighter post-war prospect. The protection of game had moved through a spectrum from being the policy of the imperial right to a favoured strategy of an internationalist left, in which guise it was enthusiastically taken over by African politicians north of the Limpopo.

Resistance and Adaptation

In the endless stream of television programmes about African wildlife shown in Britain the villains are always African 'poachers'. I have yet to hear the massive assault upon game by Europeans in the nineteenth and twentieth centuries mentioned at all. Conservation has become the source of a new Whiggism, all developments in the past being judged according to whether they further or retard this prime good of the later twentieth century. The heaping of blame upon Africans was begun in the nineteenth century - it was a convenient justification for the legal and preservationist policies of the period as blaming the rural poor was for the game laws in Britain - but some at least apportioned a good deal of the responsibility to technology. Livingstone described the game resources of Southern Africa as 'melting like snows in the sun' as Africans acquired guns. Sir John Kirk was quite clear about distinguishing between the traditional and the modern: 'It is wonderful how little effect natives with spears, traps and arrows have on game in a country, and how suddenly it disappears before the gun and the rifle' (Cd 3189, lxxix: 25). Others, like Selous, were much cruder, arguing for the total elimination of all African hunting. In any case the major depredations on African wildlife, notably the rhino, were - and remain - stimulated by the international economy.

In most parts of Southern Africa hunting has progressively ceased to be a common activity of Africans or a significant contributor to their diet. Not only have the animals become segregated, but Africans have become densely packed in reserves and homelands where the sheer pressure of human occupation ensures that wildlife cannot survive. In some places, where game survived, 'poaching' became a significant area of resistance to colonial rule just as it has long been an important source of social disaffection and rural protest in Britain. But in many parts of Southern Africa this particular route to resistance has simply disappeared. It may well be that African culture has been as much deprived by these developments as African diet or socio-economic relations.

Yet hunting repeatedly makes elusive, but highly suggestive, appearances in the record of resistance and reminiscence, adaptation and traditional survival. John Chilembwe, it will be remembered, was an able big-game hunter who attempted to finance his mission, as many Europeans had done, by shooting elephants and from the sale of the resulting ivory. He also sold meat and tried to keep his followers fed on the products of his gun. In this he was joined by several of his associates, most notably John Gray Kufa. They were largely attempting to emulate contemporary European practice. The Nyasaland authorities, however, became increasingly reluctant to issue gun and game licences to him. He had a gun confiscated in 1908 and was refused a licence in 1913. These obstacles to what he viewed, on the basis of good precedent, as a legitimate means of keeping his mission going contributed to the grievances that drove him to rebellion (Shepperson and Price 1958: 56, 139, 147, 175, 232-3, 243, 458, 462).

Audrey Richards found that Bemba labour migrants on the Copperbelt regarded their home territory as a land of hunting and wove a romantic thread of reminiscence around recollections of the chase. They attempted to recreate hunting traditions although their opportunities to translate these into practice were limited. They were restricted by game laws and the disappearance of game, for which, as Richards laconically reports, whites blamed blacks and blacks blamed whites (Richards 1939: 283, 343, 350, 366). The Gwembe Tonga of Zambia, for whom hunting had been a major part of their economy and their culture, attempted to maintain hunting rituals and pour libations in honour of hunting ancestors when hunting had ceased to be of any practical significance to them (Scudder 1962: 189-201).

Africans of the new petty bourgeoisie and of missionary Ethiopianism attempted to adopt European practices, both for recreational and for financial purposes. Sol Plaatje, in his Mafeking days, prized his reputation as a crack shot. Hunting small game was, apparently, one of his 'few forms of relaxation' (Willan 1984: illustration opposite 148). In 1931 Herbert Dhlomo, in an article on 'Bantu and Leisure' clearly saw hunting as an 'advanced' recreation. Holidaying, motoring and hunting, he argued, were 'out of the question at this stage of their development' (Couzens 1982: 330). Nature had been so effectively appropriated by whites that Africans should see one of their longest standing activities, one of the richest aspects of their cultural life, as a recreational form that they might ultimately grow into. This is as richly ironic as the effort to impart Baden-Powell's scouting techniques to African 'pathfinders'.

Yet white authorities could be ambivalent about African hunting when it suited them. In 1916 Solomon ka Dinuzulu, in keeping with Zulu tradition, called a ritual hunt to end the period of mourning for his father. The authorities were outraged, seeing it as a blatant attempt to increase royal influence. In 1934, however, the ritual hunt, following Solomon's own death in 1933, took place with the authorities' support, the enthusiastic interest of anthropologists and under the lenses of the film cameras (Marks 1986: 31, 42-43).[2] It had become part of the the picturesque characteristics of royal authority, now atavistically encouraged by a government that found traditional élites useful. I do not know how successful this hunt was, but it surely cannot have matched in 'bags' the great hunts of the nineteenth century. The killing may well have been ritualized too, yet another symbol of the appropriation of nature. It is surely significant - and again richly ironic - that in 1925 Solomon ka Dinuzulu went to the lengths of financing a hunting expedition to East Africa so that he could secure two fine tusks to present to the Prince of Wales on his visit to Natal (Marks 1986: 20).

Scholars have generally ignored hunting or relegated it to only a marginal position in studies of African societies in transition. It has paled into apparent insignificance beside agricultural decline, labour migration, urbanization and rural impoverishment. Yet a good deal of evidence suggests that it had a far greater economic, and certainly cultural, importance than has generally been recognized. It has undoubtedly had great cultural significance in the establishment and maintenance of white power in Africa. As well as fulfilling many practical functions, it has remained a symbol of dominance to this day. A South African arms dealer, commenting recently on gun sales and the spread of classes in marksmanship, remarked 'After all we are a hunting nation.' As a host of works, including juvenile literature, have pointed out, Boer sharpshooting in the Boer War (and both before and since) was based on practice

---

[2] It has been said that the ritual hunts among the Zulu re-emphasized male energy and dominance at a time when the women were illustrating their helplessness and submission through the *isililo* or wailing (Gaitskell 1986: 343). This may be true of the Zulu, but sexual roles relating to hunting may be a good deal more complex among many peoples. It was normally a source of sexual separation and an exhibition of macho characteristics for whites, and some African peoples do see hunting as a distinctively male activity, but it is clear from some accounts that hunting was so labour-intensive - in brief bursts - that women and children could be roped in for the game drive, for skinning and butchering, if not for the actual killing.

on game. G. A. Henty in *The Young Colonists* thought that colonial irregulars were more effective than imperial troops for the same reason (MacKenzie 1988b).

The literature of empire, fictional and documentary, abounds in hunting. Every colonial campaign inspired works on the combination of sport and war. Hunting was part of generalized colonial violence and human and animal 'bags' were easily elided. Even children's literature reflects the profound ambiguities of the hunter's relationship with nature. R.M. Ballantyne wrote in his novel *Black Ivory* that hunting brought out the best in Africans. For him it was a symbol of tranquillity and abundance (contrasting with the slave trade), a means of communal co-operation, a definer of leadership and a source of praise and epic poetry (Ballantyne 1873: 166-73, 250-1). But in *Six Months at the Cape* he depicted the dispossession of Africans as being essentially about nature, animals and hunting. He saw that dispossession as being justified by the fact that Africans had failed adequately to exploit their hunting grounds (Ballantyne 1877: 246-7). He gave this fictional form in *The Settler and the Savage*, and any number of works by his contemporaries and successors depicted the imperial ruler and colonial settler as essentially a hunter. This was given powerful form in Rudyard Kipling's *Jungle Book*, where the wolves are clearly valued above all other animals, for they hunt in packs, have a family life and are ordered and commanded through strong leadership. In Kipling's jungle, animals that hunt are most to be admired, while those that scavenge are hated and despised, and the prey hardly figure at all. It is no accident that Baden-Powell called his junior scouts the 'wolf cubs'.

The restriction of access to hunting as a perquisite of the élite for recreation, military and moral training has been a characteristic of human societies for many centuries. Both Xenophon and Plato pleaded powerfully for such a strategy and it has lain behind countless game laws. Imperialism gave it an international and racial twist which continues to have resonances for white minority rule. The dominance of the hunting ethic was in effect confirmed by twentieth-century conservation in Africa, which emphasized an exclusively élite access to animals and which demonstrated that the ruling race had the power to rearrange nature as well as land and people, to separate game from humans and turn the former into a spectacle available to those with the cars, the time and the money to appreciate it. The only place of the African hunter within such a scheme was an extra-legal one, as the much-despised poacher. Here was an aspect of imperial propaganda, based on international agreements, which secured ready acceptance at the periphery.

John M. MacKenzie

References

Baldwin, W. C. (1894) *African Hunting and Adventure from Natal to the Zambezi*, London.

Ballantyne, R. M. (1873) *Black Ivory*, London.

Ballantyne, R. M. (1877) *Six Months at the Cape*, London.

Beach, D. N. (1977) 'The Shona economy' in: R. Palmer and N. Parsons, *The Roots of Rural Poverty*, London.

Beinart, William (1980) 'Production and the material basis of chieftainship' in: Shula Marks and Anthony Atmore (eds.) *Economy and Society in Pre-Industrial South Africa*, London.

Bernhard, F. O. (ed.) (1971) *Karl Mauch*, Cape Town.

Bonner, Philip (1980) 'Classes, the mode of production and the State in pre-colonial Swaziland' in: Shula Marks and Anthony Atmore (eds.) *Economy and Society in Pre-Industrial South Africa*, London.

Bullock, Charles (1950) *The Mashona and the Matebele*, Cape Town.

Burke, E. E. (ed.) (1969) *The Journals of Karl Mauch*, Salisbury.

Bryden, H. A. (1893) *Gun and Camera in Southern Africa*, London.

Cd 3189 (1906) Parliamentary Papers: *Correspondence relating to the Preservation of Wild Animals in Africa*, lxxix: Memorandum by Sir John Kirk, 31 July 1897, London.

Child, Harold (1968) *The Ndebele*, Salisbury.

Cobbing, J. R. D. (1976)*The Ndebele under the Khumalos, 1820-96*, unpublished Ph. D. thesis, University of Lancaster.

Coillard, François (1897) *On the Threshold of Central Africa*, London.

Couzens, Tim (1982) 'Moralizing Leisure Time' in: Shula Marks and Richard Rathbone (eds.), *Industrialisation and Social Change in South Africa*, London.

Delius, Peter (1980) 'Migrant labour and the Pedi, 1840-80' in: Shula Marks and Anthony Atmore (eds.) *Economy and Society in Pre-Industrial South Africa*, London.

Gaitskell, Deborah (1982) '"Wailing for purity": prayer unions, African mothers and adolescent daughters 1912-40', in: Shula Marks and Richard Rathbone (eds.) *Industrialisation and Social Change in South Africa*, London.

Harris, William Cornwallis (1852) *The Wild Sports of Southern Africa*, London.

Journal of the Society for the Preservation of the Fauna of the Empire, XII (1930).

Livingstone, David (1857) *Missionary Travels and Researches in South Africa*, London.

MacKenzie, John M. (1987) 'Chivalry, social Darwinism and ritualised killing; the hunting ethos in Central Africa to 1914' in: D. Anderson and R. Grove (eds.), *Conservation in Africa*, Cambridge.

MacKenzie, John M. (1988a) *The Empire of Nature, Hunting, Conservation and British Imperialism*, Manchester.

MacKenzie, John M. (1988b) 'Hunting and the Natural World in Juvenile Literature' in: Jeffrey Richards (ed.) *Imperialism and Juvenile Literature*, Manchester.

Mackintosh, C. W. (1907) *Coillard of the Zambezi*, London.

Marks, Shula (1986) *The Ambiguities of Dependence in South Africa*, Johannesburg.

Marks, Stuart A. (1976) *Large Mammals and a Brave People*, Seattle.

Richards, Audrey I. (1939) *Land, Labour and Diet in Northern Rhodesia*, London.

Ritter, E. A. (1955) *Shaka Zulu*, London.

Schapera, I. and Goodwin, A.J.H. (1937) 'Work and Wealth' in: I. Schapera (ed.) *The Bantu-speaking Tribes of South Africa*, London.

Scudder, Thayer (1962) *The Ecology of the Gwembe Tonga*, Manchester.

Shepperson, George and Price, Thomas (1958) *Independent African. John Chilembwe and the Origins, Setting and Significance of the African Native Rising of 1915*, Edinburgh.

Steedman, Andrew (1835) *Wanderings and Adventures in the Interior of South Africa*, London.

Stevenson-Hamilton, J. (1940) *Our South African National Parks*, Cape Town.

Stevenson-Hamilton, J. (1937) *South African Eden*, London.

Tabler, E. C. (1963) *Trade and Travel in Early Barotseland*, London.

Thomas, T. M. (1893) *Eleven Years in Central South Africa*, London.

Trapido, Stanley (1980) 'Reflections on land, office and wealth in the South African Republic, 1850-1900' in: Shula Marks and Anthony Atmore (eds.) *Economy and Society in Pre-Industrial South Africa*, London.

Willan, Brian (1984) *Sol Plaatje, South African Nationalist, 1876-1932*, London.

Wilson, Monica and Thompson, Leonard (eds.) (1969) *The Oxford History of South Africa*, vol. 1, Oxford.

From Decadence to Authenticity and Beyond: Fantasies and Mythologies of War in Rhodesia and Zimbabwe, 1965-1985

Preben Kaarsholm

Introduction

The present article examines aspects of the 'struggle for the hearts and minds of people' that was an integral part of the process of de-colonization in Rhodesia from the Unilateral Declaration of Independence in 1965 and the first initiatives of guerrilla warfare on the part of the nationalist movements from March 1966 onwards (Maxey 1975: 55; Martin and Johnson 1980: 9ff.; CIIR 1978) to the in-dependence of Zimbabwe and the ZANU(PF) election victory in 1980.

The struggle has been continued since then in the attempts by Zimbabwean writers, poets and artists, musicians, dramatists and educationalists, media professionals, politicians and co-operative members to consolidate and develop the foundations of a new, autonomous national culture that were established during the war.

One of my central concerns, therefore, is to analyse some of the contradictions involved in the transformation of a cultural hege-mony from a colonial system of legitimation and control to a dif-ferent organization of cultural energies and articulations corre-sponding to and fulfilling the needs of a modern, independent African society, striving to clarify its goals and to mobilize its hu-man and democratic resources for development (cf. Frederiksen and Kaarsholm 1986).

The war was a battle for and against a revolution of society. It was a conflict over land, influence and state power, but also a struggle concerning basic conceptions and terms of expression - a confrontation between different universes of understanding, in which ideas of racial superiority and a whole complex of imperialist and colonial ideology were challenged by growing demands for mental decolonization and notions of African cultural nationalism as well as ideas of radical democracy and socialism.

It was a situation similar to that described by Han Suyin in her beautiful, multi-layered novel of the Malayan emergency, *... and the Rain my Drink* from 1956, through the contrasting of two poems. On the one hand is the Chinese folk song describing the forest as the germinating place of the new world of the partisans - 'I will go to the forest for justice... And become a green-clad man... The wind for my garment and the rain my drink, We build a new heaven and earth.' On the other hand is the universe that is upheld in increasing desperation by the British soldiers and their allies, which finds expression in the quotation of a poem by A. E. Housman - 'These, in the day when heaven was falling, The hour when earth's foundations fled, Followed their mercenary calling And took their wages and are dead. Their shoulders held the sky suspended; They stood, and earth's foundations stay; What God abandoned, these defended, And saved the sum of things for pay' (Suyin 1986: 169, 206).

As the struggle intensified, the war itself became increasingly the dominant theme in the lives of both white and black citizens, of urban as well as rural people. Consequently, the war became also one of the dominant motifs of both white Rhodesian and African revolutionary culture, exemplified on the one side by the spate of belligerent novels published by white authors during UDI, and on the other for example by the suggestive and sometimes arcane nature lyrics of the *chimurenga* and *impi yenkululeku* songs used by the political commissars of the guerrilla armies and by nationalist activists to arouse and mobilize the masses of the Tribal Trust Lands and of the overpopulated townships of Salisbury and Bulawayo.[1]

A good example is 'Mhandu Musango' ('The Enemy in the Bush') by Thomas Mapfumo and the Acid Band: 'Look at the bleached bones in the forest, Lord... Let the murderers kill, Lord... Look at the bones in the forest, Lord... We are dying because we speak the

---

[1] For examples of both white and black culture during the struggle, cf. Frederikse 1982. For *chimurenga* songs, cf. Pongweni 1982. There are a few examples of ZAPU songs in Ndebele and English as well as sometimes very different versions and English translations by Aaron Hodza of the Shona songs translated by Pongweni in the Julie Frederikse papers in the National Archives of Zimbabwe, MS 536/13.

truth, Lord... A miracle is going to happen... We are going to see an omen... Destroy the enemy.'[2]

After 1980, the war has continued to provide a prominent part of the imagery used for the propagation of the new culture and the articulation of the new moral needs of independence, as can be observed in the discourse of official celebrations, in novels and poetry published after independence and in the increasingly wide-spread productions of grassroots theatre.

From 'Classic' Imperialism to African Nationalism

The intention of the present article is to examine and provide inter-pretations of some of the dominating themes in a selection of war novels produced, distributed and read in Rhodesia between 1965 and 1980 and in Zimbabwe between 1980 and 1985. The aim of the interpretation is to point out important topics and patterns and un-derstanding in the two groups of novels and to assess the relation-ship between continuity and change in the war literatures of Rhodesia and Zimbabwe.

Further, I shall attempt to show that outstanding elements of the ideology and mentality of the white Rhodesian war novels are direct continuations of or enter a close dialogue with themes of thought and structures of expression which were prevalent in the literature of the era of 'classic' British imperialism around the turn of the century, in the writings, for example, of authors such as Kipling and John Buchan.

The article therefore addresses two sets of relationships of conti-nuity and change, on the one hand, between the formulations of European imperialism and expansionism at its zenith and the at-tempts of legitimation and self-understanding on the part of the Rhodesian settler colonialists in the last phase of decolonization, and on the other hand, between these instances of Rhodesian ideology and 'mythopoetics' (Chennells 1982: xxiii) and the new literature of independent Zimbabwe.

As will be realized, the ambition of the paper is not unrelated to that expressed in David Maughan-Brown's book *Land, Freedom & Fiction: History and Ideology in Kenya* (London 1985) or in Robert

---

[2] National Archives of Zimbabwe, MS 536/13. Cf. the much longer version in Pongweni 1982: 136, which extends the metaphor of the bones in the forest: 'How can our people rot in the bush? So many anonymous graves in the bush.'

Kavanagh's treatise on *Theatre and Cultural Struggle in South Africa* (London 1985). For one reason or another, however, neither of these two works which both try to utilize Gramscian notions of hegemony have been as helpful as expected. Maughan-Brown seems to get stuck in a repetitive web of Althusserian-Machereyan jargon, and Kavanagh, to my mind, is much too concerned to classify articulations of counter-culture according to his own ideas of correctness of line to arrive at a convincing understanding of the dynamics of cultural struggle and transformation.

Much greater inspiration has been found in the works of Anthony John Chennells on the Rhodesian novel and, more generally, in Hugh Ridley's comparative history of colonialist literatures in English, French and German (Chennells 1982 and Ridley 1983). Dr Chennells has provided indispensable pioneer work in tracing, classifying and introducing the literally hundreds of Rhodesian novels that were published between the conquest of 1890 and independence in 1980, and I have drawn extensively on his expertise and his collection of books. Professor Ridley's survey is remarkable both for the scope of its comparative analysis and for its drawing attention to the variances between metropolitan imperialist and satellite colonial literatures and to the strong elements of cultural pessimism and regression in high imperialist discourse.

A major point in Hugh Ridley's book is that the 'new' imperialism of the late nineteenth century was much more heavily influenced by *fin-de-siècle* ideas of decadence and possible regeneration than is most often assumed, and that 'Imperialist thinkers... tended increasingly to portray imperialism as the corrective to the ills of civilization rather than as the propagator of its benefits' (Ridley 1983: 114f.).

In important respects imperialist ideology represented a programme of 'reactionary modernism' (cf. Kaarsholm 1985b: 54, 1985c: 186 and Herf 1984) and was able to draw on a well-established tradition of 'romantic anti-capitalism' which looked back to the authenticity and health of a craft-based, hierarchical world before the 'fall' into modern commercial civilization.[3]

---

[3] This tradition is also strongly present in such works as J. A. Hobson's book on Ruskin (*John Ruskin Social Reformer*, London 1898) and Robert Blatchford's best-seller *Merrie England* (London 1895). It provided a frame of reference that could be utilized by imperialists and anti-imperialists alike and, as in the case of Blatchford and the *Clarion*, helps to understand some of the apparently self-contradictory crossovers between left and right in late nineteenth and early twentieth century political ideology. Cf. Kaarsholm 1988.

The settler colonies provided a laboratory for experiments with the implementation of imperialist programmes of redressing the evils of modernity, and white colonial culture became infused with notions of an organic closeness to nature and of 'aristocratic democracy' (Ridley 1983: 127; Chennells 1982: 160). Colonial life made it possible to have the best of two worlds, the settlers enjoying a modern egalitarianism among themselves (at least theoretically) and at the same time upholding a vigorously hierarchical 'feudalism' *vis-à-vis* the non-white peoples that had been defeated and alienated from their lands in the process of colonial conquest.

In Southern Africa, the colonial culture soon took on an identity of its own and developed its own criticisms of the imperialism of the metropolis. Or, perhaps more precisely, as Chennells sees in the history of the Rhodesian novel, a contradiction evolved between an 'imperial romance', which saw the colonial endeavour as the acting out in practice of a high imperial purpose, and a 'colonial pastoral' which emphasized the organic closeness to nature of settler life, its immediacy, authenticity, vitality and practical roughness as opposed to the verbiose abstractness and idealism of metropolitan imperialism.

Already in 1907, in Gertrude Page's *Love in the Wilderness. The Story of Another African Farm*, 'the wilderness is likely to be peopled by men and women superior to those who have not left England. Stripped of non-essentials they have uncovered their true selves. They are more real... White Rhodesians are superior types to Englishmen... [They are] people at one with nature' (Chennells 1982: 185).[4]

As disillusion with the prospects of gold mining in Rhodesia grew, the colonialists became critical also of the British South Africa Company variety of imperialism: '... the individual settler opposed to the forces of capitalism is a recurring figure throughout the novels whether the capitalism be that of the Chartered Company itself or other large mining or agricultural companies...' Out of this disillusion with capitalism grows a populist 'myth of heroic self-reliance' (Chennells 1982: 235).

From early on the 'aristocratic' egalitarianism of colonial ideology in Southern Africa goes hand in hand with the idea of 'separate development' for Europeans and Africans. Like the landscape or the wild animals, the African is seen as part of the nature to which the

---

[4] The title refers back to Olive Schreiner's novel *The Story of an African Farm* (1883) and its very different representation of colonial existence.

settler is so close and must be kept there and only marginally attached to white society as labourer, servant or tool if he is not to degenerate or turn into a menace.

The distinction between healthy 'raw' Africans and those who have been contaminated by contact with white civilization, which is found already in the early 1880s in Olive Schreiner's *Undine* (cf. Kaarsholm 1985a: 79 and Marks and Rathbone 1982: 5), is elaborated again and again in the years following the South African War. Spectacular instances are John Buchan's rhetoric of a Roman imperial statesman in *The African Colony* (1903)[5] or the amateur anthropology of Dudley Kidd in his *The Essential Kafir* (1904):

> It would be an excellent thing if the natives could be left alone to some original and natural mode of civilization suited to their natures;... The natives must be more or less the drudges of the white men, owing to their inherent inferiority and incapacity. It is impossible to expect the Ethiopian to change his skin or the leopard his spots. I know an educated Kafir will occasionally come up and say, 'I have been watching my face in the looking-glass, and I really think I am becoming a little whiter.'... An educated native will try to make himself white; but we should be able to prevent that calamity... It is a thousand pities that we cannot banish all European clothing from native territories, and allow the Kafirs to evolve naturally, and form a society of their own, just as the Malays have done in Cape Town. Such a plan would be better for both black and white. Native manufactures would then develop naturally (Kidd 1904: 405f.).

The article will look at how elements of this imperialist legacy are administered and transformed in five Rhodesian novels published during the UDI period and more specifically at their treatment of thematic contrasts between 'decadent' and 'natural' societies and between men and women. Two of the novels, Robin Brown's *When the Woods Became the Trees* and John Gordon Davis' *Hold my Hand I'm Dying* are from the mid-sixties, the other three - Peter Stiff's *The Rain Goddess*, William Rayner's *The Day of Chaminuka* and Robert Early's *A Time of Madness* - from the early and mid-seventies.[6]

---

[5] '... to put it shortly, how to keep the white man from deterioration without spoiling the Kaffir, - this the kernel of the most insistent of South African problems' (Buchan 1903: 285; cf. Kaarsholm 1986: 11).

[6] The inclusion of William Rayner's *The Day of Chaminuka* may seem strange, since Rayner only lived a few years in Rhodesia, and the book was published in Britain

The same themes are then examined as they are represented in three Zimbabwean novels published after independence - Stanley Nyamfukudza's *The Non-Believer's Journey* (1980), Edmund Chipamaunga's *A Fighter for Freedom* (1983) and Garikai Mutasa's *The Contact* (1985). This provides an opportunity to assess how the tradition of imperialist ideology and colonialist culture has been confronted since 1980, and how the programmes that were formulated during the struggle for national independence for an end to cultural imperialism and for mental decolonization have been put into practice by modern Zimbabwean writers.

The cultural political aims of the nationalist movements were put forward from time to time during the war in articles in the journals *Zimbabwe News* and *Zimbabwe Review*, and there do not seem to have been great differences between the goals articulated in this field by the two main organizations, ZANU and ZAPU, that joined up to form the Patriotic Front. Or rather, if there were variances in the views of culture, they do not seem clearly to have followed party lines.[7]

Important general outlines of a revolutionary cultural policy were presented in two long articles on education in *Zimbabwe News* in 1978: Nathan Shamuyarira's 'Education as an Instrument for Social Transformation in Zimbabwe' and Dzingayi Mutumbuka's 'Foundation of a New Mentality' (Shamuyarira 1978: 61-4; Mutumbuka 1978: 54-60). The texts are interesting, because they emphasize different aspects of the nature of colonial oppression and

---

and in fact banned in Rhodesia, presumably because of its being slightly more explicitly pornographic in its sadism than the average. This, however, highlights some of the hypocrisy and self-contradiction involved in the dominating white literary culture. Further, Rayner is significant, like Wilbur Smith - whose *The Sunbird* (1972) might also have been included, because his novels illustrate how the Rhodesian literary circuit of production, distribution and readership was in fact a sub-system within the much larger worlds of literature of the Republic of South Africa, the Commonwealth and Great Britain. This is of interest also because the genre of the White Rhodesian war novel, which after 1980 has disappeared from Zimbabwe, lives on, not only in the Republic of South Africa (as exemplified by Wilbur Smith's *The Leopard Hunts in Darkness* (1984), but also internationally - cf. e.g. the Danish novelist Lars Bonnevie's *En grav i vinden* (1986).

[7] An early exposition of ZAPU cultural policies is contained in Mpofu 1969: 13-15, which calls for the resurrection of Zimbabwean culture from 'the abnormal influences brought about by British colonialism... The struggle is to reject foreign impositions in our systems and concepts of culture.' The text mentions spirit mediums as natural rallying points for a culture of resistance.

consequently give priority to different ingredients in the cultural development programme of the new socialist Zimbabwe.

Shamuyarira's essay opens by contrasting two quotations, one from a British colonial official, Lord Buxton, who in 1909 defined 'the civilized and responsible African' as one who has extinguished his cultural tradition, wears European clothes and speaks good English; and one from a ZANU policy document that describes cultural oppression:

> The imperialists have diluted our rich cultural heritage by way of films, literature, mass media, schools and Church[es]... They have plunged our people into a morass of emotional and spiritual confusion... They believe the Western culture is right and that ours is wrong and uncivilized. This is a mental process that has taken years of intense cultural aggression, and which has resulted in the loss of our cultural heritage (Shamuyarira 1978: 61).

Thus attention is centred on the need for 'mental decolonization' and liberation from 'cultural imperialism'. Colonialism is presented as cultural oppression inasmuch as it has 'westernized' Africans and alienated them from their original and authentic culture.

In Mutumbuka's well-written article, the point of departure is more complex. Colonial cultural oppression as exemplified in education was a double process, in which a small African élite was affiliated to white settler culture, 'westernized' and taught to 'internalize the enemy' in the way described in Shamuyarira's article. At the same time, however, the masses of the African population were scrupulously kept away from the benefits of Western culture, and indoctrinated with the idea that, as Africans, they should stay at the bottom of an extremely hierarchical and repressive social structure: 'Besides creating a colonial mentality, this system also creates a stratified society...' (Mutumbuka 1978: 56).

The central concern of a revolutionary cultural policy therefore, according to Mutumbuka, must be democratization and the development of 'critical independent thinking.' Education, taking over the schools from the enemy or persuading students to cross the border and join the struggle, becomes a main target: 'Instead of authoritarianism and passivity we encourage from the very beginning group work, group co-operation, group decision making, individual initiative, criticism and group self-criticism' (Mutumbuka 1978: 58).

In a schematic interpretation, it seems that here two basic positions on cultural policy are put forward: one which gives priority to the freeing of an oppressed traditional and authentic African cultural from the yoke of colonialism and could perhaps be termed 'romantic anti-colonialist', and another that sees tradition as having been not only suppressed, but also exploited, manipulated and put to use within the framework of the colonial hegemony. The latter position, which might be called 'critical modernist', therefore calls for and gives priority to the creation of a cultural life which is new - a free, but 'untraditional' African culture.

In the discussions of the Zimbabwean war novels it will be examined how these two different sets of priorities and basic conceptions are dealt with in practical writing and representation after independence.

Mythologies of War in Rhodesia

All five of the Rhodesian war novels that are dealt with here elaborate on a paradigm which was formed in 'classic' imperialist ideology, and which can be seen perhaps most clearly in Kipling. In his short story 'The Head of the District' (in *Life's Handicap*, 1891), for example, Kipling confronts not just the two poles of British civilization and Indian savagery, but creates a characteristic pattern of four complementary positions. On the positive side, we have not only Tallantire, the practically minded and realistic Assistant Deputy Commissioner, but also Khoda Dad Khan, his loyal helper from one of the warlike tribes. The negative side is represented by the fanatical Mullah, but also by the 'Very Greatest of All the Viceroys', the idealist and bureaucratic high imperialist who bases himself on 'principle' and ignorance of fact.

The point of this pattern is that as there are on the one hand both 'sound' and 'decadent' forms of civilization, so there are, on the other, also both 'natural' and 'unnatural' varieties of nature or wildness. This double contradiction is reproduced almost as a cliché in the Rhodesian novels.

In Gordon Davis' *Hold my Hand I'm Dying*, for example, the rough and hearty, masculine fraternity of the beer-swilling Public Prosecutor Joseph Mahoney and his faithful 'Matabele' servant Samson Ndhlovu is opposed by both the irresponsibility of the British government letting the Rhodesians down and by the barbaric forces of the communist guerrillas emerging out of and personifying the landscape of the Zambezi Valley (Gordon Davis 1967: ch. 11, 333 and 631f.).

Similarly, in *The Rain Goddess* by Peter Stiff, the Rhodesian policeman-hero Saul Jenkins is complemented by his elderly Sergeant Ndhlela. Contradictions are intensified and enriched by Ndhlela's son, Kephas, joining up with the opposing side of brutish and sadistic nationalists to emphasize the dimension of traditional authority being challenged by youthful and unnatural rebellion. The fourth pole of 'bad' imperialism is represented not so much by the British as by the disastrously naïve American missionary Abraham Hale, who pays a terrible price for his pacifism and support of the nationalists (Stiff 1973: 10, 61 and ch. 2).

In both novels, the stereotype of the loyal African follows a well-established Rhodesian literary convention by presenting him (for it is nearly always a he) as 'Matabele'.[8] The basic racism of their discourse is thus supplemented by one of tribalism, which opposes the aristocratic, warlike, respectable and, once they have been conquered, faithful people of Matabeleland with treacherous and effeminate Shona, as represented in *The Rain Goddess* by the evil nationalist Madziwa who poses as a mission school teacher (Stiff 1973: 72-4).

At the same time it is this history of division and irreconcilable difference that justifies the colonial conquest and the continuation of white rule. In *A Time of Madness* Robert Early writes proudly: 'The pitiful warriors of the Shona people... had taken the land from the little yellow bushmen, killing them or forcing them to flee into the arid, inhospitable desert of the Kalahari. The Matabele had done exactly the same thing to the Shona and only the arrival of the whites in 1890 had prevented their annihilation' (Early 1977: 236-8).

It is with these divisions among the African population that hopes may be placed for a white settler victory in the war: '...animosities of tribal difference and hatred still flourished and... had resulted in the Matabele formation of ZAPU, trained by the Russians, and ZANU, consisting mainly of Shonas and backed by the Chinese communists' (Early 1977: 237).

A 'natural' and organically coherent society, as envisaged by these authors, would obviously presuppose the separate development and controlled interaction of not only white and black

---

[8] Chennells 1982: ch. II, 'The Search for Allies: The Myth of the Ndebele'. In this very interesting chapter, Chennells follows a course, which to my mind is problematic, by tracing the White Rhodesian mythology of different Ndebele and Shona characteristics back much too simplistically to the different traditions of resistance to colonialism in the south-west and north-east of Zimbabwe. His references here are to Ranger 1970.

human beings, but also of the different 'traditional' or 'tribal' groupings.

The social and political implications of the relationship between fathers and sons are explored more fully in William Rayner's *The Day of Chaminuka*. The hero in this novel is a tough, elderly farmer, Ben Holt, who is contrasted on the white side with his recently dead artist son, 'Dear, diffident, charming James!', who moved to London, when he was not able to stand the pressures of increasing confrontation in Rhodesia.

The forces of rebellion on the other side are represented partly by the sadistic guerrilla commander Rufu, who poses as the medium of the spirit of Chaminuka, and partly by the pale-skinned and more reasonable nationalist Moyo, who is shocked by the traditionalist excesses of Rufu and tries to eliminate him. The turning point of the plot comes when it is discovered that Moyo is in fact the son of Ben Holt by a woman servant. Thus the positive elements on the two sides, the authoritarian father and the good son, are reconciled by their common blood in a way that is most unusual in Rhodesian literature.[9]

Most commonly, however, the disintegration of sound and natural values on the sides of both whites and blacks in the novels is represented as the result of the influence of missionaries or related forces of misunderstood enlightenment. This again is a stereotype which goes back to 'classic' imperialist ideology and probably has its most famous example in John Buchan's *Prester John*, where the educated African, Reverend John Laputa, turns out to be a dangerous leader of rebellion (Buchan 1910; Kaarsholm 1986).

The consciously or unconsciously malign effect of missionary efforts is a central and explicit motif in both *The Rain Goddess* and *A Time of Madness*, but there is a clear connection also between this motif and the representation of the influence of foreign communists. Thus the efforts of the wicked Hungarian KGB agent Stanislau in *A Time of Madness* is a perverted continuation of the work begun by the naïve Father Antonio. And in Merna Wilson's *Explosion* (1966), the unnatural endeavours of the churches are continued by the malicious liberal, Professor Granger, who fails those of his students who refuse to join his political demonstrations.

---

[9] On the treatment of 'miscegenation' in Rhodesian novels, cf. Chennells 1982: 378-420. Chennells also quotes texts that explain the decline of the 'Matabele' kingdom in terms of dilution with 'the blood of inferior tribes' (Chennells 1982: 91).

The most spectacular instance of the use of this Buchan-based stereotype is the account of the rebellious 'Black Messiah' movement in Robin Brown's *When the Woods Became the Trees* (1965). In this strange teenage novel (a kind of Rhodesian *Catcher in the Rye!*), however, there is also the attempt to differentiate between good and bad acts of Christianity, as Father Barry Geoghan, who is long suspected by the adolescent heroes, Rory and Duffy, to be the leader of the Messiah movement, shows his true colours. At end of the story, when Salisbury is under siege, and women and children have been evacuated to South Africa, Father Barry literally crucifies himself in the no-man's-land between Salisbury and Highfield and brings the murderous fighting to a mystical halt (Brown 1965: 254). The reconciliation which is really attempted in the novel seems rather to be that of the different groups within the white community under siege - old and young, fathers and sons, soldiers and believers, who should come together with their loyalist African friends in one big, naturally organic community under the sign of the cross.

The ultimate battle in the novels, ideologically, is not that of whites against blacks as much as one between different visions of society and the universe, between worlds that are 'natural' and in harmony with the great scheme of things and worlds which are 'decadent' and have 'misdeveloped' - moved away from certain unbreakable laws and principles. And both worlds are inhabited by both whites and blacks.

The image of 'decadence' is presented most directly by John Gordon Davis in *Hold my Hand I'm Dying*, when he describes a 'toga party' in Bulawayo in the early 1960s, which refers back directly to the last days of the dissolution of the Roman empire (Gordon Davis 1967: 236ff.).[10] Here urban society is described as over-civilized and sexually depraved, and the hero longs for a return to nature: 'I must get out of this way of life. I must get back close to the earth, I wish I could get back into the bush, to the [Zambezi] Valley...' (Gordon Davis 1967: 238).

Nature, on the other hand, is ideally free of human beings, a romanticized purity - 'pregnant and primitive and exciting and virgin' all at once - which impresses itself on the narrator as he watches a pair of lions making love. Animals are almost more human than

---

[10] This form of imagery also has its equivalent in the imperialist writing of the turn of the century, e.g. in the comparative analysis of the decline of the Roman and British Empires in G. W. Steevens: 'From the New Gibbon', *Blackwood's Magazine*, February 1899; cf. Kaarsholm 1985c: 186.

human beings in this vanishing Africa that is coming to rot in the conflict between the complimentarily decadent forces of white over-civilization and black nationalism (Gordon Davis 1967: 370 and 372).[11]

This is clear also from the change in the significance of the metaphor of the Kariba Dam, which opens and concludes the novel. At the outset, the flooding of the Zambezi Valley, the removal of the Tonga people and drowning of wild animals are represented as an image of the destructive consequences of white civilization, development and progress. At the end of the novel, which takes the reader back to the valley where the dam is threatening to burst, the coming flood is treated as a metaphor for the onslaught of the guerrillas which constitutes an equally great threat to the natural balance of Africa as does the blind progress of civilization (Gordon Davis 1967: Parts One and Ten). And now, after UDI, the white Rhodesians and their African loyalist assistants, who together form the only force to attempt to uphold the balance, have to fight to a bitter end that is seen to be approaching rapidly.

In Stiff's *The Rain Goddess* we also find an identification between the Rhodesian way of life and the natural order of things. In this case the manoeuvreing of ideological legitimation is particularly provocative, since Stiff attempts to argue through his novel that white Rhodesians are 'natural' Africans and in harmony with the traditions of the continent, while the black nationalists are an 'unnatural' intrusion.

Not only is the male fraternity of the Rhodesian soldiers at one with the landscape of the bush (Stiff 1973: 181), their brutal actions against the guerrillas are also sanctioned through the intervention of traditional African religious forces. Thus the drought which reigns throughout most of the plot is presented as nature's way of responding to the war and as an expression of the unhappiness of the spirits and the 'rain goddess' with the state of human affairs in general and with the upheavals brought about by the Moscow-trained nationalists in particular.

At the end of the novel, when the guerrillas have been humiliated and sadistically massacred, the rains break as a sign of the spirits' approval of the re-established natural hierarchy and order. As the

---

[11] A similar view of total authenticity in a natural world without pollution with human beings can be found in Buchan's *The African Colony* where he is reminded in parts of the Transvaal of a 'type of pure world before our sad mortality had laid its spell upon it' (Buchan 1903: 79).

last 'terrorist' dies, 'The Heavens opened... The Spirit of the Rain Goddess had received her sacrifice of blood, and was satisfied. The rain would now be released from the Heavens' (Stiff 1973: 255-6).

The break-away from decadence and the re-establishment of a natural order is a particularly clear pattern in the plot structure of Robert Early's violent *A Time of Madness* which is a double story of the manly Rhodesian police detective Richard Kelly, fighting 'terrorism' and communist infiltration, and of the rehabilitation and re-education of the white Johannesburg gangster Lance Koster through the experiences of the war and a natural life with fellow males in the bush.

The novel begins with a vision of urban decay as exemplified by the night-life of Hillbrow: drink, drugs, sex and even violence against the police are the order of the day. Having killed his best friend and partner in crime and buried his body in a mine dump, young Lance has to make a quick get-away and drives north on his motor-bike to join the British South African Police in Rhodesia.

The war against the incoming guerrillas and their communist backers and naïvely humanitarian fellow-travellers becomes the salvation of Lance and a much-needed cleansing and revitalization of the whole fabric of society. Lance dies the death of a hero, but Kelly and his compatriots live on to punish not only guerrillas, communists and homosexuals, but also unsympathetic foreigners, like the poor American tourist, Henry Clarkson, who gets beaten up - 'This is Africa, not Disneyland. The animals are wild' (Early 1977: 246; 191). Or, in a climax of unintended humour, a group of white Zambians ('That's where the whites pay taxes to finance the ters') who receive a much more severe beating for speaking disrespectfully to a waiter: 'Before you bugger off... just remember, there are no kaffirs in this country. Only Rhodesians' (Early 1977: 87f.).

'Nature' is used, then, in the Rhodesian novels to describe and justify a specific type of hierarchical society, based on racism and separate development, but it is also in these novels an ambiguous concept which is full of threats of mutilation, engulfment and extinction.

This has to do with the extremely *masculine* nature of the writing represented in the five novels, which are filled to the brim with images representing phallic narcissism and sadist aggression, ambivalence towards women and extreme fear of castration. In this respect, they once again come close to some almost petrified anxieties of 'classic' imperialists like Kipling.

In *The Naulahka* (1902), for instance - one of Kipling's worst novels - the fear of women and of the Indian landscape come together in the representation of a terrific gorge, into which the colonialist hero slips and slides: a magnificent *vagina dentata* with a crocodile hidden at its bottom - 'the darkness and the horror below' (cf. Kaarsholm 1989).

This situation is repeated in an almost stereotyped fashion at the end of Robert Early's *A Time of Madness* where Kelly and Stanislau fight out their final battle at the edge of Livingstone Island by an even more impressive gorge, the Victoria Falls, and where the communist mastermind eventually falls to a fate worse than is justified, even for him: 'With sudden, irrational feeling I knew I didn't want him to die. Not this way. A quick bullet, a rope, these he deserved. But not this. This was not just death, it was a hideous torture that no man should suffer' (Early 1977: 266).

And the situation reoccurs, with a monster very much more hideous than Kipling's, in the scene in *Hold my Hand I'm Dying* where the faithful Ndhlovu is caught by a crocodile and dragged under water through a hideous tunnel of slime and half-digested food to its lair (Gordon Davis 1967: 116f.). Samson is eventually saved by his white master and male comrade, for nothing besides death can come between the two of them, while the novel carries on for more than 600 pages without Joe Mahoney being able to make up his mind whether he will marry his beloved Suzie or not.

Consequently, what is under threat in the Rhodesian war novels is also a *male fraternity* which has to defend itself through acts of extreme violence that are represented as a release of natural energy, a return to the authenticity of primeval instincts. All the novels thus culminate in terrific massacres of black nationalists and guerillas, and in all cases these orgies of violence have to be prepared and justified by detailed and often pornographic descriptions of equivalent outrages, mutilations of children, rapings of missionary women, sexual harassment of white women on the part of the destroyers of the social fabric.[12]

---

[12] The most outspokenly pornographic of the novels is Rayner's *The Day of Chaminuka* in which the naked white heroine Beth is make to lick the boots of the traditionalist Rufu time and time again. Meanwhile he reminisces about his ultimate humiliation at school when he was made to play Olivia in Shakespeare's *Twelfth Night*. It is probably because of these scenes that the book was banned in Rhodesia - there is a limit to everything (Rayner 1976: 190ff.). Cf. the analysis of similar motifs in German right-wing literature of the 1920s in Theweleit 1987.

So also in this respect, in the treatment of sexuality and of relations between men and women, there is a continuation in the Rhodesian war novels of the legacy of imperialist ideology. But a continuation which is at the same time a letting loose and a dramatic transformation of ethical pretension into pornographic sensationalism.

War Novels of Independent Zimbabwe

I want to turn now to the selection of post-independence Zimbabwean war novels and examine how they deal with some of the basic thematic structures and contrasts that have been described - to what extent they continue them, change them or are able to do without them.

The tragic or comic tension between 'tradition' and 'modernization' is probably one of the most prominent themes in the modern literature of African countries generally - and probably nowhere more so than in Rhodesia and Zimbabwe, where, from the mid-1950s, the Southern Rhodesia Literature Bureau encouraged its exploration (Krog 1966). Partly because it could be used to promote a 'traditionalism' that the Bureau sought to encourage in its endeavours to support literacy and separate cultural development through the creation of 'indigenous' or 'vernacular' literatures, partly because it was seen as suitably unpolitical. And where at the same time, in an interesting dialectic between the intention and effect of the Literature Bureau's activity, the exploration of the theme led also to the writing of great texts critical of traditionalism like Charles Mungoshi's *Waiting for the Rain* (1975) or the novels of Ndabezinhle Sigogo.

That the theme was fraught with contradiction was obvious from the start, when the first novel published by the Literature Bureau, Solomon Mutswairo's, *Feso* (Shona edition, 1957, English version 1974), met with an unexpected double reception. Its representation of a heroic Zezuru past, where, in spite of wars between the vaHota and the vaNyai of the Mazoe Valley, the ancestors lived in an almost paradisical harmony with physical nature and sang hymns of praise to Nehanda Nyakasikana, could be read not only as a eulogy of quietistic traditional life, but also as an image of a glorious pre-colonial past to which nationalist speakers and activists could appeal. Whether it originally was intended to or not by its author, *Feso* created a stir, was removed from the curricula of African schools and went out of print (Mutswairo: 1957and 1974; Kahari 1980: 39-50 and Krog 1966: 149-152).[13]

The contrast between natural/traditional and decadent/modern worlds of experience has continued to be a prominent theme in the literature of Zimbabwe since independence in 1980, and features also in novels dealing with the war.

This is seen clearly in Edmund Chipamaunga's long and interesting book, *A Fighter for Freedom* (1983), which explicitly addresses the transformation of the social and cultural hegemony from the mid-1960s to the end of the 1970s in three parts entitled 'Under Authority', 'With Authority' and 'In Authority'.

At the outset of the story, the protagonist Tinashe is an adolescent boy torn between the influences of his father and his mother. The father, Mr. Gari, is a teacher and headmaster at a missionary school and is described as a tragic figure, who has lost his strength and self-respect due to the corrupting influences of cultural imperialism. He goes to pieces, drinks, loses his position and repetitively quotes Tennyson: 'Into the valley of Death rode the six hundred...' His education has led to his self-destruction, he 'despises the traditional way of life and regards it as common and vulgar... he [has] become a prisoner of foreign dominance and lost his self-respect' (Chipamaunga 1983: 84).

---

13 Another text by Walter Krog is worth quoting for its tone and its discussion of the publication history and reception of *Feso*: 'It was not until 1957 that the Bureau's first sponsored book was published, an event that was later to have minor political repercussions. This pioneer novel of Shona literature entitled 'Feso' was written by Solomon Mutswairo. It was approved as a set reader in schools for two years and went to three printings. African Nationalist politicians claimed that the book was a brilliant allegory and that between the lines could be read a slashing attack upon the 'oppressive' white-dominated Government. It was maintained that the Bureau officials responsible for the selection of manuscripts for publication had been cleverly hoodwinked into sponsoring propaganda against their own Government... Mutswairo admitted that he had no such intention when he wrote the story, which he copied from a Zulu book while studying at Adams College, Natal. The main theme, the oppression of one African tribe by another conquering tribe was taken to be a reference to conditions in Rhodesia by those whose political ends were thus served. When the book went out of print there were allegations that it had been banned, but it was the publishers, Oxford University Press [Cape Town], who decided not to reprint for a fourth printing, basing their decision on purely publishing economics. Shona literature, therefore, had a somewhat controversial start, and the Bureau made it known that its particular taboos were, broadly speaking, politics and religion' (Krog 1979: 67).

He decays further when the family is forced to move into town, to Harare Township, where they are robbed of their furniture, and the father 'comes home drunk, reciting Tennyson like a mad man most evenings. He is broke most of the month, and yet he finds money or ways to soak himself in drink almost every day of the week' (Chipamaunga 1983: 114). He loses himself among prostitutes and falls an easy prey to the influence of gangsters and agents of the UDI regime.

On the other hand, the mother, MaTinashe, represents family cohesion - she is a competent craftswoman, is closely linked to the traditional life of her relations in the countryside and holds out against all corrupting influences both at the mission and later in Harare (Chipamaunga 1983: 14ff.). It is with his mother's family, staying with Uncle Roro, that Tinashe both gets a notion of the African culture that used to prevail, based on family obligations and community values, and gets into contact with the guerillas.

The struggles against colonialism, for social transformation and for the re-establishment of the traditional family are thus inextricably linked throughout the novel. When Tinashe joins the nationalist movement, it is in order to move closer to nature, to reform society and bring together again his father and mother and resurrect the authority of his father, 'to restore dignity and respect to the many families in the country'. At the successful end of his quest, the father is reinstated as headmaster and his re-birth is described in an allegorical tableau, 'a beautiful wooden carving depicting a man and a woman, their right hands firmly gripped in a strong handshake and holding a rooster between them in their left hands' (Chipamaunga 1983: 203).

The development of the plot is accompanied throughout by elaborate sets of natural metaphors. The landscape is alive and provides a running commentary on the state of human and social affairs. Early in the novel, the natural scenery is full of dangerous traps and ditches, of animals ready to kill and of mysterious occurrences like trees moving (Chipamaunga 1983: 24 and 34-5). Later, Tinashe learns that the mobile trees are really guerrillas in disguise, and that the landscape, and nature more generally, through the mediation of ancestral spirits support the struggle against colonialism. The guerrillas 'have chosen to live with wild animals, to preserve and restore by force, dignity and self-respect' and know how to disappear 'in the form of the vulture, snakes, beetles, scorpions or just air. They are capable of changing into anything' (Chipamaunga 1983: 183 and 235).

On the other side, the settler forces are seen as destroying and literally poisoning the countryside in their attempt to eradicate the guerrillas, and the imagery is elaborated further through the introduction of a contrast between the 'unnatural' animals of the white soldiers (dogs, horses) and the 'natural' wild animals that are the allies of the nationalists: 'The animals which the forces in opposition employed quite often had had their nature debased by ruthless technological manipulation so much that the fighters had long classified them as machines' (Chipamaunga 1983: 208 and 192).

Tinashe's first act in support of the guerrillas is a direct attack on decadent white 'civilization', as he throws petrol bombs at a hotel frequented by Rhodesia Front members in Salisbury. The anti-modernist message of the novel is emphasized further through the successful attempts on the part of the guerrillas to employ alternative and traditional technologies in their campaign. This is most fully developed in chapter 11, where the freedom fighters are camping at Great Zimbabwe, enjoying the protection of the spirits of 'the clan of the Mugabes', and seek inspiration from the example of the original builders, wanting to be 'free of dependence on colonial material, technique or technology' (Chipamaunga 1983: 219 and 225).[14]

The treatment in the novel of the theme of sexuality and of relations between men and women is dominated at the outset by the contrast between Tinashe's parents, where his mother is clearly represented as an embodiment of 'dignity and self-respect' the novel sees as the essence of a traditional society free from colonial oppression.

But there is a contradiction between the description of the monogamous relationship between father and mother that Tinashe joins the guerrillas to strengthen and the polygamy of Uncle Roro's village, which is otherwise depicted as a traditionalist idyll. And there is perhaps an even more striking contradiction in the fact that though Tinashe sees his mother as the incarnation of social cohesion, it is the traditional power position and authority of his father that he seeks to re-establish. So the precise form of reconciliation between the sexes and social transformation which is arrived at towards the end of the novel, when Mr. Gari and his wife are remarried by Uncle Roro, is left somewhat unclear. And the very last scene of the novel is an image of massacres, 'an eternity of horror',

---

[14] On the use of Great Zimbabwe in Rhodesian literature, see Chennells 1982: ch. 1: 'The Search for an Origin: The Myth of Great Zimbabwe'. A late example is Wilbur Smith's *The Sunbird* (1972).

of the killings at Chimoio and a subsequent guerrilla victory - violence and counter-violence. What happens at war is clear, what follows is not.

A similar portrayal of the *chimurenga* as a struggle for an authentic, traditional form of society in correspondence with the forces of nature and against a depraved, colonialist white civilization can be found in Garikai Mutasa's *The Contact* (1985). The treatment of nature here, however, is different and self-contradictory. On the one hand emphasis is placed on the ambiguity of natural processes, on existence as a cycle of life and death, of love and cruelty, and the war is described as part of this cycle, as a violent explosion of purification which is necessary for the continuing reproduction of society and nature (Mutasa 1985: 28). On the other hand, war is seen as an unnatural intervention of brutality into the harmonious equilibrium of nature and of traditional society:

> ...they heard the ululating women far away in the village and the drums beating. A rhythm of history. Those drums were carrying the message to the people. The mujibhas must have seen the fighting of the people and reported.
>
> Then silence. A naked silence in the bush. A bush full of insects going about their daily routines of eating and releasing waste matter, of reproducing and gathering, of building nests and courting. Singing to the bright flowers, revelling in the sweet nectar and dancing in the formations of irregularity. Bees, ambling ants, doves and screeching woodpeckers filling the upper and lower reaches of the forest. An eco-system of equilibrium shattered by two minutes of the uncivilized violence of man; the only animal capable of such cruelty (Mutasa 1985: 32).

There seems to be a male and a female principle involved in the running of the natural cycle, and the novel does not know how to reconcile them. There is the brutal, violent and male nature of the lion, and the life-giving, reproductive female world of the insects and plants, and counting the images it seems to be the latter conception with which the voice speaking in the novel is in greatest sympathy.

Whatever nature is, though, the guerrillas are acting in unison with it. They seem to be 'at one with the jungle,' which makes the opposing army so confused that it fires at tree stumps, and the very act of revolt against colonial rule is compared to the earth recovering from a rain storm:

> A battle of the elements. Liquid and solid. Dividing and separating. A cleavage in the country, in the forest, among the animals, the people... Life pregnant with life... The revolt became a co-ordinated order with the green sprouting of life and foliage. Beautiful flowers from trees and shrubs, miniatures from the carnage. The lords and gods of the the earth were on seasonal strike, creating and re-creating what the gods of the heavens had destroyed. They filled the earth with life in vengeance of the rain. Rebellion. Revolt. The storm had destroyed only to strengthen its adversary; the earth. The earth; now flowing and growing with animals, insects and blossoms (Mutasa 1985: 92, 97 and 66).

Opposed to this pastoral of natural rebellion stands the urban world of colonial civilization, a society and a way of life of which - as in so many other African novels - the prostitute is a symbol: 'Suckers to the manhood of Zimbabwe, the women gathered in their multitudes to be picked up' (Mutasa 1985: 52; cf. Gaidzanwa 1985: 50ff.). A society of radical divisions in terms of privilege and power, between 'beautiful suburbs' and 'crowded townships', and in which African men and women lose their identities faced with the onslaught of Western influences - films, television soap operas, advertisements for commercial products, skin lightening creams - but 'when, Comrades, can we Zimbabweans ever be Americans?' (Mutasa 1985: 103 and 105).

Into this divided world, then, which is represented quite eloquently in the novel through its group of protagonists, representing different social types, bursts the war as a great leveller to prepare the ground for a situation in which people can revert to their authentic culture, in harmony with themselves and free of 'foreign ideologies' (Mutasa 1985: 106).[15]

Stanley Nyamfukudza's war novel, *The Non-Believer's Journey* (1980), is different in important respects from those of Chipamaunga and Mutasa. It does not attempt to describe the war through the eyes of a character directly involved on one of the two sides of the actual fighting, but chooses a person who gets caught in the cross fire, so to speak, and has to re-orientate himself. Secondly, its point

---

[15] The one-page postscript to the novel modifies its harmonious conclusion by briefly listing the fates of the main characters after independence and concludes: 'Not everyone was lucky' (Mutasa 1985: 125).

of departure is much more that of modern urban life than is the case in the two other novels - the main character, Sam, is a disillusioned and initially quite cynical secondary school teacher in Highfield. It is only when he embarks on a visit back to his rural home area near Wedza that he gets to experience the contradictions between town and country and between modernity and tradition as well as the war as confrontations he cannot escape. Thirdly, Nyamfukudza's novel is, of course, written at a time much closer to the events it describes, and this may account for the greater freshness and complexity of its presentation.

The first chapter contain some wonderfully vivid sketches of life in Salisbury's biggest black township in the late 1970s. Sam goes off on Fridays and Saturdays to what is now the Mushandira Pamwe to listen to the new music that is breaking through:

> The musicians were becoming slightly daring as the war steadily gained hold over larger and larger parts of the country. Most of their songs were based on traditional drum and Mbira rhythms and all the lyrics were laced with emotional, though muted, political protest. It was a heady mixture when one had had enough to drink and the size of the crowd each night showed how effectively it sold (Nyamfukudza 1980: 12).

With this 'heady mixture', we are far removed from any stiff and inflexible opposition between traditional and modern life. The music represents a new and original culture that amalgamates influences from several sides. But apart from this element of politics in his rather drab everyday life, Sam is full of scepticism as regards the nationalist struggle. He is opposed to the violence and generally misanthropic as to the idealism of political activism:

> Scattered amidst the rubble and ashes of property belonging to genuine traitors and collaborators had been much that had belonged to business, career, tribal and even love rivals... Freedom! Kwacha! Uhuru! Where had it all gone? Would they not be plagued again with violence and intimidation by thugs, all in the name of liberty? (Nyamfukudza 1980: 15).

He goes away from town to visit his family and attend the funeral of an uncle who has been killed as a 'sell-out' in an area near Mtoko and Wedza, where there is an escalation of war between incoming guerrillas and Rhodesian troops. On the bus, listening to two men playing the *mbira*, he experiences a longing for the lost life in the country:

> It was as if he and all those around him had been insidiously dissociated from the realities of time and place, and the multi-rhythmic pulsations of the traditional tunes were the throbbings of their hearts beating in unison in some land far removed from a hampering, shackled life under the white man's rule in the city... an illusion of freedom (Nyamfukudza 1980: 24).

Having been subjected to a brutal road-block check, Sam sees the aggressive Rhodesian soldiers take off in a helicopter in pursuit of an escaping bus passenger and catches a glimpse of the machine-gunner, 'holding fast to his weapon, the long fat barrel sticking out through the open doorway like an outrageous phallus' (Nyamfukudza 1980: 36). Immediately after, at Mrewa, where he has to spend the night, he experiences a night of love with an old girl friend, Raina, which is different from his normal one-night affairs at Highfield, because she is a girl he can suddenly respect. Not because she is a 'traditional' girl, but rather because she has made herself independent and is quite different from the way he remembers her from before 'the present troubles':

> She was no longer the patient, rural maiden, destined to be the loyal and obedient wife of an old man twice her age, and to bear him a long queue of kids... As he watched her walk up with the cup of coffee, what he saw was a restless, restrained impatience. 'She's gone to bad,' the old men would have said, and he liked that! (Nyamfukudza 1980: 41).

As Sam enters his family's home area, he finds a society falling apart under the strains of the war, but also due to traditional enmities and strife. He presents his own family story as one dominated by self-destruction, by aggressive males and petty enmities, of authoritarian extended family obligations and people wasting their earnings on witchcraft. In total contrast to Tinashe's endeavours in *A Fighter for Freedom*, Sam sees the dissolution of the traditional family as a blessing:

> He hated and despised it all. It was his view that the best thing that could happen to the Mapfekas was for them to put as much distance as possible between the various members of the family (Nyamfukudza 1980: 68).

But gradually, his perceptions begin to change. Nature, the rural landscape and the forest, which at first seem threatening to him change their significance, culminating in a dream of a cave in the forest, 'female, warm and suffocating', and of the women of the forest - a dream which is partly unsettling, but also in a strange way indicating the possibility of a different world from that of male, phallic aggression, and which makes him think of Raina: 'He had been thinking of her when he fell asleep. Not a bad woman at all, he decided' (Nyamfukudza 1980: 99-100).

Sam's cynicism begins to give way, and at a *pungwe* called by the guerrillas outside the village, he feels torn between a strong urge to join the new force and the different kind of community it seems to have a chance to bring about, and the scepticism he has grown used to. During the singing of *chimurenga* songs, he feels 'a horrible sense of dread' and has

> the most desolate experience of his life, the feeling of dissolution,... he felt wretched at being cut off by his inability to share in the fervour of his fellow men, to open up and sing out his problems, his hates and his hopes, dispelling, at least for the duration of the song, all the doubts and the mistrust which gnawed at his being (Nyamfukudza 1980: 105).

At this point, as Sam is just beginning to open up and get ready to change his life, the novel concludes tragically by his being killed in a meaningless quarrel with a guerrilla officer.

The Non-Believer's Journey is thus moving towards, though not reaching, a solution and a form of reconciliation, which is radically different from those presented in the other two Zimbabwean war novels we have looked at. It is critical of traditional society in a way that is reminiscent of the writings of Mungoshi and Sigogo (cf. e.g. Sigogo 1962 and Mungoshi 1975), but also radically opposed to the form modernity takes in the apartheid-like cities of Rhodesia under colonial rule, where the misery of the townships is set off by the absurd pseudo-aristocratic pretensions and the vulgar display of wealth in the white suburbs (Nyamfukudza 1980: 24-5). At the same time, it is unusual in presenting a demolition of male dispositions of aggressivity and dominance and a recognition of independent and self-reliant women as a necessary prerequisite for the liberation of society (Nyamfukudza 1980: 24-5). The need for a transformation of power relations between the sexes is also hinted at in Mutasa's metaphors of nature, but Nyamfukudza's writing is in this respect much clearer and less ambivalent.

There is a strong element of romanticism and idealization of the past in the novels of Chipamaunga and Mutasa, which tend to see the alternative to cultural imperialism as a liberation from oppression of traditional African forms of social life in harmony with nature. A romanticism, which comes close to the programme for post-independence cultural policies formulated in the article by Nathan Shamuyarira from 1978 quoted above, and which also, in its yearning for a pre-colonial pastoral, is strangely reminiscent of the romantic anti-capitalism, the critique of 'decadent' civilization and the quest for a 'natural' alternative which pervade Rhodesian mythologies.

In contrast, the double edge of the cultural criticism articulated in Nyamfukudza's novel is much more in line with Dzingayi Mutumbuka's insistence - in the other *Zimbabwe News* article mentioned - on a policy of 'critical modernization' and on the education and active promotion of independently thinking and socially competent individuals as a precondition for a genuine and thorough transformation of the structures of colonial society.

In its attack on the oppression and depravation of both urban/modern and rural/traditional life under colonial domination, *The Non-Believer's Journey* stresses the need for the culture of decolonized society to aim for something radically new. War is not celebrated as a 'purification' process, which will automatically sweep away the complexities of development - even if victorious, it will contribute tragedies and complications of its own. There is no authenticity to return to - the only hope lies with a future where independent men and women may come together in a democratic effort to master the patterns of power and domination that have controlled their lives for the past century.

References

Bonnevie, Lars (1986) *En grav i vinden*, Copenhagen.

Brown, Robin (1965) *When the Woods Became the Trees*, London.

Buchan, John (1903) *The African Colony. Studies in the Reconstruction*, London.

Buchan, John (1910) *Prester John*, repr. Harmondsworth 1981.

Catholic Institute of International Relations (1978) *Rhodesia: The Propaganda War - A Report from the Catholic Commission for Justice and Peace in Rhodesia*, London.

Caute, David (1983) *Under the Skin: The Death of White Rhodesia*, Harmondsworth.

Chennells, A. J. (1977) 'The Treatment of the Rhodesian War in Recent Rhodesian Novels' in: *Zambezia*, vol. V, no. 2.

Chennells, Anthony John (1982) 'Settler Myths and the Southern Rhodesian Novel', D. Phil. dissertation, University of Zimbabwe.

Chipamaunga, Edmund (1983) *A Fighter for Freedom*, Gweru.

Early, Robert (1977) *A Time of Madness*, Salisbury.

Frederikse, Julie (1982) *None but Ourselves: Masses vs. Media in the Making of Zimbabwe*, Johannesburg.

Frederiksen, Bodil Folke and Kaarsholm, Preben (1986) 'The Transition from Resistance to Establishment Culture in Zimbabwe, 1965-1985', paper presented to a conference on 'Culture and Consciousness in Southern Africa' at the University of Manchester.

Gaidzanwa, Rudo B. (1985) *Images of Women in Zimbabwean Literature*, Harare.

Gordon Davis, John (1967) *Hold my Hand I'm Dying*, London.

Herf, Jeffrey (1984) *Reactionary Modernism: Technology, Culture and Politics in Weimar and the Third Reich*, Cambridge.

Kaarsholm, Preben (1985a) 'Imperialisme og masochisme i Olive Schreiner's romaner' in: *Kultur & klasse*, no. 50.

Kaarsholm, Preben (1985b) 'Imperialisme som fin-de-siècle modernisme: Engelsk 'new journalism' i 1890erne' in: *Kultur & klasse*, no. 51.

Kaarsholm, Preben (1985c) 'Imperialism and New Journalism circa 1900' in: Eckhard Breitinger and Reinhard Sander (eds.) *Studies in Commonwealth Literature. Papers presented at the Commonwealth Literature and Languages Conference at Bayreuth University, June 16-19, 1983*, Tübingen.

Kaarsholm, Preben (1986) 'Monument of Empire: Aesthetics, Politics and Social Engineering in the Writings of John Buchan', paper presented to a conference on 'The Humanities between Art and Science, 1880-1914', Elsinore.

Kaarsholm, Preben (1988) 'The South African War and the Response of the International Socialist Community to Imperialism between 1896 and 1908' in: Fritz van Holthoon and Marcel van der Linden (eds.) *Internationalism in the Labour Movement, 1830-1940*, Leyden.

Kaarsholm, Preben (1989) 'Kipling, Imperialism and the Crisis of Victorian Masculinity' in Raphael Samuel (ed.) *Patriotism. The Making and Unmaking of British National Identity*, vol. III, London.

Kahari, George P. (1980) *The Search for Zimbabwean Identity*, Gweru.

Kahari, George P. (1986) *Aspects of the Shona Novel*, Gweru.

Kavanagh, Robert (1985) *Theatre and Cultural Struggle in South Africa*, London.

Kidd, Dudley (1904) *The Essential Kafir*, London.

Krog, E. W. (ed.) (1966) *African Literature in Rhodesia*, Gwelo.

Krog, W. (1979) 'The Progress of Shona and Ndebele Literature' in: *NADA, The Annual of the Ministry of Home Affairs*, vol. XII, no. 1.

Krog, Walter (1974) 'Rhodesian Literature. The Rhodesia Literature Bureau - Its Aims, Objects and Achievements' in: *African Research and Documentation. The Journal of the African Studies Association of the UK and the Standing Committee on Library Materials on Africa*, no. 4.

Marks, Shula and Rathbone, Richard (eds.) (1982) *Industrialisation and Social Change in South Africa. African Class Formation, Culture and Consciousness, 1870-1930*, London.

Martin, David and Johnson, Phyllis (1981) *The Struggle for Zimbabwe. The Chimurenga War*, London.

Maughan-Brown, David (1985) *Land, Freedom and Fiction: History and Ideology in Kenya*, London.

Maxey, Kees (1975) *The Fight for Zimbabwe. The Armed Conflict in Southern Rhodesia since UDI*, London.

Mpofu, Lazarus (1969) 'Pan-African Symposium. Zimbabwe Culture and the Liberation Struggle. Algiers, July 21st-1st August, 1969' in: *Zimbabwe Review*, vol. 1, no. 3, August.

Mungoshi, Charles L. (1975) *Waiting for the Rain*, London.

Mutasa, Garikai (1985) *The Contact*, Gweru.

Mutswairo, Solomon M. (1957) *Feso*, Cape Town, repr. Harare 1982.

Mutswairo, Solomon M. (1974) *Zimbabwe. Prose and Poetry* (including an English language translation/version of *Feso*), Washington D. C.

Mutumbuka, Dzingayi (1978) 'Foundation of a New Mentality' in: *Zimbabwe News*, vol. 10, no. 6, November-December (Maputo edition).

Nyamfukudza, Stanley (1980) *The Non-Believer's Journey*, London.

Pichanick, J., Chennells, A. J. and Rix, L. B. (1977) *Rhodesian Literature in English: A Bibliography (1890-1974/5)*, Gwelo.

Pongweni, Alec J. C. (1982) *Songs that Won the Liberation War*, Harare.

Ranger, Terence (1970) *The African Voice in Southern Rhodesia, 1898-1930*, London.

Ranger, Terence (1985a) *Peasant Consciousness and Guerilla War in Zimbabwe. A Comparative Study*, London.

Ranger, Terence (1985b) 'The Invention of Tribalism in Zimbabwe', Gweru.

Rayner, William (1976) *The Day of Chaminuka*, London.

Ridley, Hugh (1983) *Images of Imperial Rule*, London.

Shamuyarira, Nathan (1978) 'Education as an Instrument for Social Transformation in Zimbabwe' in: *Zimbabwe News*, vol. 10, no. 2, March-April (Maputo edition).

Sigogo, Ndabezinhle C. (1962) *Usethi Ebukhweni Bakhe* ('Sethi's Place of Betrothal'), Salisbury.

Sigogo, Ndabezinhle C. (1984) *Ngenziwa Ngumumo Welizwe* ('I was Influenced by the Political Situation'), Gweru.

Smith, Wilbur (1972) *The Sunbird*, London.

Smith, Wilbur (1984) *The Leopard Hunts in Darkness*, London.

Stiff, Peter (1973) *The Rain Goddess*, Salisbury.

Suyin, Han (1986) *... and the Rain my Drink*, London. First edition London 1956.

Theweleit, Klaus (1987) *Male Fantasies, vol. 1: Women, Floods, Bodies, History*, tr. by Stephen Conway, Cambridge.

Wilson, Merna (1966) *Explosion*, London.

Art in Zimbabwe: From Colonialism to Independence

Stephen Williams

> In order to be an artist it is necessary to seize, hold, and transform experience into memory, memory into expression, material into form (Fischer 1964: 9).

Introduction

The title of this paper might suggest a chronological, historical account of art over the last hundred years in Britain's last African colony and the new nation state of Zimbabwe. Although this task is a much needed one, the area of art history being a neglected discipline throughout Africa, the focus of this paper is of a more sociological nature and examines, with specific reference to the visual arts, the way in which culture[1] has responded to and helped promote social and political change in Zimbabwe. The paper looks at the effects of contact between traditional and colonial cultures and considers how this process of acculturation has contributed towards the creation of a Zimbabwean national cultural identity.

A people's history is reflected in its culture. Art and its institutions are the material embodiment of that culture, the visual arts symbolizing life experience and being a means of communicating and bequeathing cultural ideas and values. The sociology of art perceives artists as producers in society, differing from other workers only to the extent of their specialization. Accordingly, the artist is seen as an integral part of society, fulfilling a role in the sphere of cultural production, rather than in the liberal/romantic sense as

---

[1] Raymond Williams claimed that culture is one of the two or three most complicated words in the English language (Williams 1981: 87). Culture is used in this paper in the context of the opening quote from Ernst Fischer, i.e. as an objectification of human experience.

mystic, eccentric and peripheral to society (Wolff 1981). In other words, art is functional and thus by inference social in nature.

Zimbabwe: Historical and Social Background

The destruction of the traditional social formations of the Shona, Ndebele and other groupings was a direct consequence of military defeat. During the 1890s the British South Africa Company provoked the indigenous peoples of Zimbabwe into various situations of conflict with the Company's troopers, creating the pretext for the confiscation of land and cattle and leading to a considerable weakening of existing socio-economic systems. With the demise of the old political structures, the gradual introduction of hut, poll and other taxes, as well as a host of discriminatory and protectionist-based legislation, traditional economies ceased to function as they had in the past, blacks being forced into the money economy in order to subsist and meet fiscal demands.

Within a decade of the establishment of Fort Salisbury in 1890, the British South Africa Company had laid the foundations of capitalism by creating a class society, the basis of which was skin colour. The decimation of traditional support systems created a class of black workers who, in classical Marxist terms, had been separated from their own means of production and consequently forced to sell their labour on the white-owned farms and in the factories and mines of Rhodesia and South Africa.

The nature and extent of the proletarianization of blacks in Zimbabwe has been the subject of considerable academic debate. The labour reserve strategy employed by settler governments ensured a readily available source of cheap labour whilst at the same time serving to subsidize wages by providing a subsistence-type economy for dependants. Because of this, workers were seen to have 'one foot in the countryside', and consequently to be of migrant or peasant-worker status (cf. Malaba 1980:7-28). Irrespective, urbanization increased steadily along with industrialization, recent estimates being that twenty-three per cent of Zimbabwe's population lives on a largely permanent basis in the towns and cities of the country (Government of Zimbabwe 1987:1).

Of interest to this paper is the way in which art and material culture became transformed during the process outlined above. From the very beginning, the relationship between white and black in Rhodesia was structured around domination and exploitation.

Racist laws ensured the protection of white privilege and prevented competition from blacks in agriculture, business and the job market. The entire state machinery of the settler colony was geared towards maintaining this status quo. A fundamental part of the strategy of maintaining political and economic domination was the downplaying and denigration of indigenous culture in the face of an 'official' Eurocentric culture. This imposed culture was demonstrative of the values and interests held by the settler population and was seen to exemplify sophistication and superiority.

The new relations of production brought about by colonialism, shifts from rural to urban settings and of status from peasant to worker, was profound and touched every aspect of people's lives. Into the new milieu, blacks brought the most portable aspects of their culture such as music, dance, oral literature and traditions of basket-work, pottery production and other crafts. Cultural interaction in the form of new ideas, skills, materials and technologies occurred, resulting in some old art forms becoming modified and others ceasing to be practised.[2]

On one level this may be seen in a purely material sense, as the substitution of materials and technologies; plastic for grass or electric guitars for *mbiras* (traditional thumb pianos). Such substitution is, however, in itself highly symbolic of the broader changed conditions of life which people had adapted to, and reflective of an altered consciousness brought about by new roles within the new economic system.

New relations of production created new social formations to replace the old, traditional structures and to organize people in opposition to the oppressive and unjust colonial legal system. The first black trade union, the Reformed Industrial and Commercial Workers Union (RICU), was formed as early as 1927 and the first broad nationalist party, the Southern Rhodesia African National Congress (SRANC) in 1957. These democratic movements evolved through a series of bannings, detentions and general harassment as structures representative of black opinion and aspiration in the face of limited legal means of recourse. A mostly peaceful approach was followed until the early 1960s when the Rhodesian Front came into power on a racist manifesto. The rightward shift of white politics

---

[2] The most ubiquitous effects of acculturation occurred as a result of contact with European culture. An accelerated interaction of cultures between ethnic African groupings also took place however, as a result of their being thrown together in situations of work and township life.

brought about a radicalization of nationalist politics, the banning of the Zimbabwe African National Union (ZANU) and the Zimbabwe African People's Union (ZAPU) forcing them underground and into a situation of guerilla warfare.

It is in the context of this rapidly altering social milieu that cultural centres such as the Mzilikazi Art and Craft Centre came to play such an important role in providing a focus for shifting patterns of cultural expression.

Situated in Mzilikazi Township and opened in 1963, the Centre is a section of the Community Services Department of the Bulawayo City Council. Designed as a school leaver project, it has today developed into one of the major institutions for the training of visual artists in Zimbabwe.

Mzilikazi is particularly renowned for the distinctive style of social realist water-colours which have been produced over the years. As a body they represent a fascinating factual record of township life. The series of paintings by Justin Mtungwazi, for example, entitled 'Zhee Riot Series' (c. 1960), presents a detailed record of one of the first instances of popular urban resistance to colonial rule (Williams 1986). These paintings and other products of the centre, such as its ceramic sculpture, have over the years commented on daily life in the townships, often in a remarkably descriptive and objective manner. The scenes depicted show the struggles of the working people of Bulawayo during the 1960s and 1970s against colonial rule, the actions of freedom fighters and scenes of everyday township life. This tradition of social commentary has developed into a recognizable genre or school and has continued into the independence era with expositions of social themes such as the squatter problem, rural life, unemployment and depictions of the South African situation.

The prominence of the Mzilikazi Art and Craft Centre as a leading institution in the training of the visual arts is a position held almost by default, due to the fact that there is no formal art school in the country or the region. The Centre has nevertheless produced some of the region's most outstanding artists, this being all the more remarkable given its inauspicious beginnings and terms of reference.

Acculturation; Tradition and Change

In 1985 a wonderful and elucidating debate erupted in Bulawayo over the winning entry in a sculpture contest (Williams and Galbraith 1985). The contest had been initiated in an attempt to get local sculptors to create pieces of public art to replace colonial monuments removed at independence but never substituted with work more appropriate to the new social order. The first prize was awarded to the sculptor Adam Madebe for this welded metal piece entitled 'Looking to the Future'. Over five metres tall, it depicted a man gazing into the distance, his right hand shielding his eyes from the glare of the sun. The controversy centred around the fact that he was totally naked.

The debate was a public one which, fuelled by the local newspaper, the *Chronicle*, featured in front-page stories, two editorials, numerous articles, features, cartoons, photographs and over forty published letters from readers. The battle lines were initially demarcated between traditionalists and modernists, the major issue being whether nudity in art was offending and contrary to African culture. The matter never was satisfactorily resolved however due to the intervention of the Minister of Local Government who, after seeing the sculpture ordered it removed from public view. At this stage politics came to the surface and firmly supplanted any concerns of culture or aesthetics.

The most important aspect of the affair was the nature of the debate, waged and argued in homes, places of work, beer halls and bars. At the crux of the matter was the question of the nature of contemporary culture and the place of traditionalism within that culture. The controversy served to stir people to consider these issues and to examine their ideas and feelings about their culture.

A fundamental question raised by this sort of debate is whether there is such a thing as an authentic traditional culture or whether culture is a continuously changing and dynamic process.

Traditional art reflects a complex of social, political and religious issues in which usage and aesthetic appeal become merged qualities to a far greater extent than in First World easel art. As traditional political and economic systems adapted to new circumstances and evolved as institutions, cultural production became modified as a reflection of the changes. The fact that traditional art is so integrated into daily life suggests that the production of material culture is a very close indicator of societal shifts. To talk of an authentic traditional culture serves to isolate it in time and insinuates that traditional society was incapable of change.

Two differing views of the nature of acculturation are expressed by Ellert (Ellert 1984) and Fatuyi (Fatuyi 1986: 167-172). Ellert adopts a quasi-traditionalist position on culture shift:

> Indigenous cultural values were suppressed and through forced labour and urbanization people were exposed to western influences alien to their culture... The traditional industries and crafts that have survived, did so in a hostile climate in which much has been forgotten... The pressures of an alien culture were too great and time does not stand still. The younger generation, particularly those in the urban sector, is growing up ignorant of a vital aspect of their cultural heritage. The process of change and development into a new technological age is inescapable and necessary, but it is equally important to know and understand past traditions and their material culture.

Ellert's emphasis on traditional values can be contrasted to the argument put by the Nigerian art educator Rufus Boboye Fatuyi:

> Cultural contact and interaction permit learning and understanding, which may result in a change of behaviour or new ways of life... During such contact revolutionary tendencies are bound to occur. Culture contact transforms cultures... The critics of colonial life have always argued that this process has led to alienation, to the abandonment of traditions, ancestral origins and modes of thought. Despite this... it is my opinion that culture-contact leading to cultural interaction possesses greater advantages than disadvantages.

Fatuyi's argument points to the dialectical relationship which existed between colonizer and colonized, the suggestion being that the acculturation process was not entirely without benefit to colonized peoples. Certainly in the instance of Zimbabwe, changes in culture inevitably and somewhat ironically played a role in bringing about the eventual demise of white minority rule. The accumulation of different ideas, skills and technology, together with new types of social formation permitted new forms of opposition to the settler regime. Changes in social, political and economic life created a new consciousness which was both mirrored and influenced by culture.

Whilst Ellert's perspective does not entirely deny the process of acculturation, it views it in a negative manner and consequently excludes its dynamic element. Traditional material culture inescapably did decline with the advent of colonialism, but largely because of its inability to function in the way it was originally designed and its inappropriateness within the new milieu. Culture change must be perceived in the context of the altered economic base of society and the technological needs of that environment. The development of 'tourist art' is one example of the adjustment of art to the realities of a money economy, in some parts of Africa this being traced back as far as Portuguese trading in the sixteenth century (Bascom 1976: 309).

Art, Ideology and Policy

In itself culture is incapable of bringing about change. The liberation of Zimbabwe came about as the result of many diverse forces of which culture was just one. Culture does, however, share many similarities with ideology in that both aspire to shape and form the consciousness of man. Both set up suppositions of what is good and bad, beautiful and ugly and as such both are capable of mobilizing people to action (Lukin 1980).

The ideological value of culture has not been lost on the post-1980 government, a high profile having been placed upon the issue of a Zimbabwean national cultural identity since independence. Whilst a detailed policy statement on culture has never been presented, published interviews, speeches and other materials stress democratization of the nation's cultural institutions.

The *First Five-Year National Development Plan 1986-1990* (Government of Zimbabwe 1986: 40-41) devotes only a few hundred words to culture, the crux of which is that the promotion of culture is to be 'based upon the principles of democratization and decentralization of cultural facilities and services'. Practically this will mean the establishment of Culture Houses, 'whose components include local museums, galleries, libraries, arts and craft production and marketing, as well as recreation halls' at district level, District and Provincial Arts Councils and an increased emphasis on culture in schools.

'Culture' in ministerial terms has always been attached to larger ministries, such as 'Education and Culture' or 'Youth, Sport and Culture'. The move away from the coupling with education was much applauded given the size and overwhelming importance of the education component and the fact that culture was often relegated in emphasis. Of the many ministers who have been responsible for culture since 1980, Simbarashe Makoni has made some of the clearest statements on policy. In an interview in 1984 he emphasized that it was government policy to promote a national culture:

> A national culture does not mean a single cultural identity or pursuit or projection. A national culture is a culture which adequately and accurately reflects all the components of that nation. And in our situation we happen to be a multi-cultural nation and that culture must be one that reflects all the components of the nation. Also culture is not a static phenomenon. It is a dynamic experience. If we take the interaction between the two major ethnic groups in Zimbabwe since the advent of colonialism, it is not correct to argue that the culture of the indigenous people has remained unaffected by the culture of the foreigners and conversely it is not correct to say that the culture of the Caucasian race has remained unaltered during the period of interaction with the indigenous people (Makoni 1984: 9-11).

Makoni makes interesting links between acculturation, culture change and multi-culturalism as the constituent parts of a national culture. In the same interview Makoni explains the policy of developing Culture Houses in terms of making cultural facilities available to the people, 'because the people are themselves our strongest vehicle for cultural development' (Makoni 1984: 10).

Makoni was succeeded as Minister of Youth, Sport and Culture by David Karamanzira who at a function in the National Gallery of Zimbabwe in December 1985 made the following statement on cultural policy:

> The Government is fully aware that all cultures are subject to influences from inside and from outside, and that they change, develop and modify in response to these internal and external influences. But we also hold that there are enduring, worthwhile values in the souls of our major peoples, the Shona and the Ndebele, as well as in our smaller ethnic groups. It is the Government's belief that our National Gallery should be charged with special responsibility to the nation to reach back into the past to collect and to preserve for posterity the finest examples of our cultural landmarks. It should also record the way in which our arts have developed and changed to the present time (Karamanzira 1985: 1-2).

Karamanzira endorses the multi-cultural nature of Zimbabwean society as a fusion of traditional values tempered by urbanization and the colonial experience. In addition he emphasizes the importance of the visual arts in transformation and in helping establish a cultural identity symbolic of the character of Zimbabwe's nationhood:

> But our capital has so little in its wide and beautiful streets to indicate that we are in Africa, let alone Zimbabwe. Our capital could well be in Australia, or modern Europe, or Latin America. I challenge the National Gallery to help us change this image (Karamanzira 1985: 2).

Art Education and its Institutions

Education has always been a political issue in Zimbabwe. Successive colonial administrations, from the British South Africa Company to the Rhodesia Front, used education as a means of maintaining white domination in the economic and political spheres. The colonial education system was divided on a racial basis between 'A' group schools for whites, Indians and coloureds (people of mixed race) and 'B' group schools for blacks. The differences between the two systems were obvious, one being specifically designed to offer a high standard of education so as to reproduce a class of administrators and commercial personnel, whilst the other was vastly inferior and geared to producing a class of black workers who needed only rudimentary literacy and numeracy skills.

A paper by the Curriculum Development Unit of the Ministry of Education entitled *Art and Socialism* (30/9/86), states:

> Prior to independence art education, like all other aspects of education was used as a tool for ideological manipulation. Far from being a subject which led to enlightenment and self-expression it was used to reinforce cultural differences and further inculcate values of racism, sexism and colonial superiority into learners.

In general art was taught in the 'A' group schools, whilst craft was taught in the 'B' group schools. The division was based to some extent on economics, art materials generally being expensive (and therefore reserved for whites), but nevertheless this did conform to the general policy of black education being primarily geared towards the production of manual workers.

The rehabilitation of the education system became one of the most urgent tasks facing the newly elected government in 1980. Although the achievements in education made since independence have been impressive, the discipline of art education has been relatively neglected - despite the great emphasis upon culture generally. The problems of children not receiving an art education during their schooling extend, according to some writers, beyond mere aesthetics into the realms of the development of social consciousness (Read 1970). In Third World countries such as Zimbabwe the establishment of a national cultural identity takes on even more importance, both as a means of countering the worst aspects of colonial culture, as well as uniting disparate ethnic groupings for common developmental and other goals.

At the core of the problem is the lack of a formal school of art and design in Zimbabwe. Within the entire region, between Makerere University in Uganda and the polytechnics and university art schools in South Africa in fact, there is not one art school. The seriousness of this is that there are no training facilities for artists or art teachers and no facilities for research, the reason cited by several studies that art education in the area is in its infancy (Lancaster 1982: 295-307; B. V. Project Development Prode 1987).

The development of art training in Rhodesia approximated to some extent the route of education generally. In the same way that missions were responsible for much black education in the country generally (all of it up until 1940), the training of artists was left virtually entirely to missions such as Cyrene and Serima, up until the 1960s when centres such as Mzilikazi, Nyarutsetso and the National Gallery workshop were opened. At present the training of visual artists is still in the hands of the non-formal sector, although the Harare Polytechnic and the Bulawayo Technical College do run commercial art courses.

The *First Five-Year National Development Plan 1986-1990* places much stress on the expansion of aesthetic training in schools and other institutions:

> The teaching of music, drama, dance, art and crafts, as well as behavioural cultural aspects, is to be a crucial undertaking within the school system..... In order to democratize the acquisition of artistic skills and access to the arts by the greater masses of the people, facilities for training in and presentation of visual and

performing arts will be built, improved or re-oriented. Crafts Centres will also be established to facilitate the improvement and marketing of a rich diversity of crafts.

The centrality of the art school or institution is stressed by Janet Wolff:

> In the production of art, social institutions affect, amongst other things, who becomes an artist, how they become an artist, how they are then able to practise their art, and how they can ensure that their work is produced, performed, and made available to a public (Wolff 1981:40).

Currently planning is well advanced for the building of a Regional School of Art and Design in Harare (B. V. Project Development Prode: 1987) which will serve as a focal point for the training of art teachers and practitioners throughout the SADCC region encompassing the front-line states of Mozambique, Tanzania, Zambia, Botswana, Angola and Zimbabwe.

Genres; Stone and Paint

In Rhodesia cultural practice was consistent with other policies in that it was racial in character and served to segregate ethnic groupings through means such as separate arts councils, educational systems and facilities. Culture simultaneously but dialectically grew in two directions - the culture of the colonizer and the culture of the colonized. Genres of black visual arts that developed during the colonial era were often encouraged in informal institutions such as missions, council art centres and gallery workshops.

One of the best known of these is the genre of stone sculpture nurtured by Frank McEwen, the first Director of the National Gallery of Rhodesia, who in the the early 1960s encouraged gallery assistants to start working in steatite and other stone. A stylistic development emerged which became known as 'Shona Sculpture' and was celebrated throughout the world's art centres such as the Museum of Modern Art in New York and the Musée Rodin in Paris.

Because of the synthetic way in which it was engendered and the manner in which it was instantly turned into a commodity, its relevance as a genuine expression of Zimbabwean culture is perhaps most apparent as a reflection of capitalist modalities. A favoured theme of this type of sculpture is the spirit world, depicted in both anthropomorphic and zoomorphic form. This is reflective of and corresponds to the Shona practice of ancestor worship, but its relevance beyond that, to the man in the street, is questionable and raises the larger issue of whom art is produced for. Celia Winter-Irving articulates this sentiment in positing that:

> The implications of this taxonomic shift is that notions of the importance of function and use have gone into receivership and the values of these works lie solely in their artistic merit and commodity potential. Broadly this implies a lessening of interest in tribal structures of the past and near present. Such are the ways of cultural imperialism (Winter-Irving 1986).

It is worth noting that the misnomer of the title 'Shona Sculpture' has in recent years been corrected to 'Zimbabwean Stone Sculpture', this being a more (although still not totally) accurate description of the multi-ethnic background of the principal sculptors, some of whom originate from countries such as Mozambique, Malawi and Angola.

Whereas black visual art during the colonial era created an international reputation with sculpture, white visual arts centred on painting, but suffered more from the isolation of UDI and sanctions. An inward-looking vision focussed on the beauty of the veld and mountains, the genre of the 'Rhodesian landscape' becoming a favourite subject.

A feature of much of the painting produced by whites during the 1960s and 1970s is its total lack of social and political content, conforming to the notion of the artist described at the beginning of this paper, as being detached from the realities of society. In itself this is a comment upon the divided nature of Rhodesian society and the effectiveness of the Smith propaganda machinery, but nevertheless this consciousness can be directly contrasted to the style of social realism being pursued during that period at Mzilikazi Art and Craft Centre and other similar centres such as the Nyarutsetso Art Centre in Highfield Township, Salisbury.

Conclusion

Colonialism inevitably led to a destruction of traditional economic systems and the modification of society and the cultural practices which embodied it. Processes of urbanization and other forms of culture contact created an altered consciousness and brought about new social formations and mediums of cultural expression. Throughout the twentieth century the people's culture has served to both describe these developments and at the same time to inspire the pursuit of a more egalitarian society. Accordingly, the struggle for Zimbabwe was waged on political, economic, military as well as ideological and cultural fronts.

An immediate task of the Zimbabwe Government after independence was to begin to democratize cultural institutions so as to make them accessible to all of the people of Zimbabwe as vehicles of their cultural expression. As with other matters, the government has adopted a pragmatic approach to change, largely following a policy of adapting colonial cultural legacies to serving the new demands.

Not surprisingly, after just a decade of independence a national cultural identity is still emerging from amidst the many diverse influences of the past and present eras. Colonialism, the quest for social and economic transformation, internal politics, and the realities of the South African situation, all serve to shape the character of the national consciousness and the way in which it is manifested culturally.

The state cannot however, either through intervention or policy, create a national cultural identity. The state may be able to formulate and influence cultural policy, but it can never directly produce culture, the dynamic of culture existing on a plane which transcends the machinations of state, resting ultimately with the people themselves. Culture reflects the relationship of the people with the state, articulating the way in which people live, work and die and serving to seize, hold and transform that experience into form.

References

Bascom, W. (1976) 'Changing African Art' in: N. Graburn (ed.) *Ethnic and Tourist Arts*, Berkeley.

B. V. Project Development Prode (1987) *Feasibility Study. The Establishment of an Art and Design School in Zimbabwe*, Tilburg.

Ellert, H. (1984) *The Material Culture of Zimbabwe*, Harare.

Fatuyi, R. (1986) 'Cultural Interaction and Cultural Change: The Effects of Acculturation on Traditional Societies' in: *Journal of Art and Design Education*, vol. V, nos. 1 and 2.

Fischer, Ernst (1964) *The Necessity of Art*, Harmondsworth.

Government of Zimbabwe (1986) *First Five-Year National Development Plan 1986-1990*, Harare.

Government of Zimbabwe (1987) *Quarterly Digest of Statistics. September*, Harare.

Karamanzira, D. (1985) 'Policy for the Future' in: *Insight*, no. 2.

Lancaster, J. (1982) 'Art Education in Zimbabwe: A Review of the Present Position and Suggestions for Development' in: *Journal of Art and Design Education*, vol. I, no. 2.

Lukin, Y. (1980) *Ideology and Art*, Moscow.

Makoni, S. (1984) 'Interview. Towards a National Culture' in: *Moto*, no. 21, 9-11.

Malaba, Luke (1980) 'Supply, Control and Organisation of African Labour in Rhodesia' in: *Review of African Political Economy*, no. 18.

Read, Herbert (1970) *Education Through Art*, London.

Williams, Raymond (1981) *Keywords*, London.

Williams, S. (1986) 'Artists in the Community: The Mzilikazi Painters' in: *Insight* no. 1, Harare.

Williams, S. and Galbraith, D. (1985) 'Bulawayo Nude Statue Causes Storm' in: *Moto*, June.

Winter-Irving, C. (1986) 'Contemporary Stone Sculpture from Zimbabwe' in: *Craft Arts*, February/April.

Wolff, J. (1981) *The Social Production of Art*, London.

Culture and the Tasks of Development in Africa: Lessons from the Kenyan Experience

Kimani Gecau

Introduction

Towards the end of his book *Not Yet Uhuru* published in 1967, soon after Kenya's independence, Jaramogi Oginga Odinga was to write that:

> Kenya's problems in the age of *Uhuru* are formidable. We have to deal with landlessness, combat unemployment, give the children more schools and the people more hospitals, push up living standards of the poor in a world where the gap between the rich countries and the poor is daily growing wider... We have come to understand that *Uhuru* is a matter of dealing with poverty (Odinga 1967: 314 and 310).

Coming so soon after independence, Odinga's sobering words might have appeared alarmist to those who were still luxuriating in the euphoria of independence. Across Africa other voices, particularly on the literary scene, were being raised in the same sober appraisal of the meaning of *Uhuru*. In 1966, Chinua Achebe published his scathingly satirical novel *A Man of the People*. And in the same year of publication as *Not Yet Uhuru*, Ayi Kwei Armah was to publish his *The Beautyful Ones Are Not Yet Born*, surely one of the most bitter and angry artistic expositions of the new regimes and ruling classes in Africa. Back in Kenya, Ngugi wa Thiong'o's *A Grain of Wheat* appeared also in the same year as Odinga's book. Ngugi's work, whose setting and point of departure are the four days before

Uhuru in Kenya in 1963, is prefaced with the following comment:

> Although set in contemporary Kenya, all the characters in this book are fictitious.... But the situation and the problems are real - sometimes too painfully real for the peasants who fought the British yet who now see all that they fought for being put on one side (Thiong'o 1971: vi).

These works, by different authors from different countries unknown to each other, were making the same essential point: that we needed to pause, re-examine where *Uhuru* had so far failed the ordinary person, and correct it accordingly in order to meaningfully consolidate the gains of independence.

Today, twenty years after these authors raised their voices in warning, not even those who brushed and still continue to brush aside the message in these works would deny that Africa is in a crisis and that our very survival, let alone independence, is in jeopardy. Indeed there has been so much piling up of, and so much talking about, Africa's problems over the years that, to paraphrase Brecht, they have become invisible.

The general African problems might appear peripheral in Kenya especially to those who believe the story that Kenya is a 'showcase' of capitalist development in Africa. Contrary to appearance, however, Kenya shares most of the general African problems. If the per capita Gross National Product is any indicator of a nation's wealth, then according to the 1984 *World Development Report*, Kenya is in the category of the low-income or poor economies. With a GNP per capita of $390 in 1982, it is the twenty-seventh poorest country in the world, in the same rank as Sierra Leone, and much poorer than either Sudan or Mauritania. For comparison's sake, Zimbabwe with a per capita GNP of $ 850 is an above-average lower-income economy standing at number fifty-one in the World Bank hierarchy (World Bank 1984: 218). According to the official Kenyan Statistical Abstract, only one per cent of the population earned over Shs. 1,200 (about US$70) per month, in 1972 (Leys 1975: 260). In 1983, only 16,000 women and 86,000 men earned Shs. 3,000 and over per month (about US$190) (*The Weekly Review*, January 24 1986: 5). These figures might not obviously prove the point, but there is a great inequality in incomes which continues to get bigger.

In spite of the limitations of the World Bank's 'economistic' prescriptions, the report by and large echoes the fears voiced by Odinga and others. The crucial question posed by the report, however, is whether there are sufficient 'administrative and political skills' present among those who formulate and implement policies to avert the looming developmental crisis. In 1967, Odinga and Ngugi were already casting doubts on the economic management abilities, ethics and the political make-up of those in power. Odinga put it this way:

> When we hang out the national flag for *Uhuru* meetings and rallies we don't want the cries of *Wapi Uhuru* (where is *Uhuru?*) to drown the cheers. Our independence struggle was not meant to enrich a minority. It was to cast off the yoke of colonialism and poverty. It is not a question of individuals enriching themselves but of achieving a national effort to fight poverty in the country as a whole. Kenyatta's cry to Kaggia before a vast crowd at a public meeting, 'What have *you* done for yourself?' is a sign of the depths to which our spirit of national sacrifice for *Uhuru* has sunk. Is there no need for national sacrifice? Has *Uhuru* given the people what they need? The landless don't think so, nor do the unemployed (Odinga 1967: 310).

Already in 1967, Odinga was pointing at the social stratification within the country which has been the single most important factor in determining the course that Kenya's economic and social life would take. Clearly, then, the necessity for developmental strategies to overcome the present and future crises and to remove the limitations imposed by the existing political and social relations is much more than an academic question. If our people are now and in the future not to be reduced to the level of bare survival, if they are to live at all as human beings in a humanized world, those who are genuinely concerned and with the ability and skills need to pool their resources as a matter of urgency. It is our view that though labour and productivity are the essence of life, development is more than these. It is a process in which man collectively and, above all, qualitatively improves his spiritual and cultural well-being in the course of the production of his material life.

It is in this context that we believe culture as the ideological manifestation of the material and historical reality of a people is *the* measure and indicator of a people's level of development at every stage of their history. In this presentation, we shall take a sweeping look at those factors which have influenced the development in Kenya of the present cultural situation and in conclusion suggest likely areas in which the cultural worker could continue to make meaningful interventions in aid of development.

Colonialism and Underdevelopment

In his seminal work, *Underdevelopment in Kenya: The Political Economy of Neo-Colonialism* published in 1975, Colin Leys was to provide us with a deeply analytical and yet lucid study of how the new ruling class in Kenya has become a participant in the process of underdevelopment. We cannot, therefore, talk about Kenya's development unless we also address the question of underdevelopment and the socio-economic formation within which it takes place. Leys pointed out that:

> ...underdevelopment theory is - or should be - precisely a theory of history [of Third World countries], a theory of the contradictions in the development of their modes and relations of production under colonialism and imperialism. Contradictions which are expressed today in the growing polarization between authoritarianism on the one hand, and revolution on the other (Leys 1975: 7-8).

We shall not here discuss how the pre-capitalist, pre-colonial societies in Africa responded to what seemed to them the wilful authoritarianism of natural forces over which these societies had little control due to the low level of productive forces. There was also the implicit 'authoritarianism' of traditions gone archaic. And though class formation was either non-existent or at a very low level, there were individuals who, because of the division of labour, were angling to lord it over others.

Suffice it to say that in the culture of our pre-capitalist societies we find attempts to make rituals and magic, in the absence of science, the tools which were used to 'tame' nature, and to prepare and strengthen society in the struggle for production, reproduction and survival. And in the many folk-tales, proverbs and songs is reflected the democratic world view of these societies. Thus apart from being the ideological reflection of the particular mode of production, these were also artistic expressions of a society which was purposefully and consciously striving to know and define itself and to assert its mark of social organization and harmony on nature. By so humanizing nature, man was affirming his freedom.

This polarization between authoritarianism on the one hand and the struggle for freedom on the other, was to become glaringly manifest after colonial conquest. Colonial conquest, in Kenya as elsewhere, was to play its now well known contradictory role. It was at once both 'destructive' and 'regenerative' (Marx and Engels 1976: 82). It either destroyed or set into motion the process of destruction of the pre-capitalist mode of production and laid the material basis for the emergence of modern societies integrated into world capitalism. It is now common knowledge how colonialism went about its business: political domination, heavy taxation, forced labour, and, in countries where there were settlers, the expropriation of the bulk of productive land and the prevention of Africans from growing cash crops. These measures had the intended effect of forcing Africans to stop producing for themselves and for their own development in order to produce for the settlers. This is the basis of the consequent development of underdevelopment which is the main cause of our present crisis.

Through the ideology of nationalism, articulated through such concepts as Negritude, Pan-Africanism and the African Personality, people were mobilized in anti-colonial and anti-imperialist struggles. However, as Leys observes, decolonization came at a time when the local strata and classes 'with an interest in sustaining the colonial economic relationships' had become 'powerful enough to render direct rule by metropolitan powers unnecessary' (Leys 1975: 9). Thus though nationalism played, and continues to play, an important role in the development of political consciousness and in mobilizing the people for national liberation, it has within it two opposing ideological and political tendencies. On the one hand, there is a pro-bourgeois tendency mostly associated with the social strata discussed above, and on the other hand, a revolutionary-democratic tendency, associated with the masses of the people.

The development of social stratification within the Kenyan people was to be accelerated and become a deliberate policy in the mid-1950s. At this time, political consciousness had developed to the point of armed struggle for national liberation. Through the Swynnerton plan and other measures, land was transformed into a commodity which could be used for capital accumulation, and social stratification developed further.

Economic policies pursued immediately after independence had the net impact of consolidating the stratification of society which had been developing before 1963. And though not overtly obvious then, this stratification and the consequent class struggle was implicit in the politics leading to independence. The economic policies, for example, came in the wake of the Mau Mau war for independence, a war which had in-built within it a class struggle between the emergent social strata:

> The squatters and the Nairobi 'crowd' who finally supplied the majority of the forest fighters epitomized the impoverishment and frustration of the lowest paid and least secure sections of the African population. By the same token, there were others who were relatively secure, and a few who were comparatively affluent. As the emergency wore on the violence that occurred was increasingly between the uneducated and landless Kikuyu, from whom the forest fighters were overwhelmingly recruited, and the educated and landed families, who preponderated in the ranks of the 'loyalists' and the 'Home Guard' units. In many respects it must be seen as a civil war, or rather a series of civil wars, which accounted for a major part of the 13,000 African deaths which were due to the Emergency (Leys 1975: 50).

At the time of the declaration of the Emergency, the British, who had already detained the more militant trade unionists such as Markhan Singh and Chege Kibachia, also detained the political leadership of the Mau Mau. Aware of the possibilities of the war leading to a radicalization of the post-independence situation, they encouraged economic measures such as those discussed above which would lead to a wider spread of those who had property interests in the maintenance of the status quo. They also began to groom a new crop of political leaders. Therefore, unlike in Zimbabwe for example, neo-colonialism in Kenya is more than 'a particular mode of imperialist *policy* applicable to [all] ex-colonies...' - it is

> a characteristic form of social and economic life - or of class struggle - [because] the transition from colonialism to independence permitted the relatively efficient transfer of political power to a regime based on the support of social classes linked very closely to the foreign interests which were formerly represented by the colonial state (Leys 1975:27).

It is this history of continuing polarization and class struggle which has given birth to present-day Kenyan culture - a culture which is at once an ideological reflection of the struggle and an influence on the contending forces. This is what we shall look at in the rest of the paper.

Education and Neo-Colonialism

Education and the school are, of course, the most important cultural institutions for development. In fact we could say that if colonialism took over the people's land and either kept them ignorant or gave them a highly selective education, national liberation aimed to liberate the land and through access to less selective and more relevant education, free the mind, the human resources. Before independence, in the 1940s, independent schools were built by the people to this end. Many songs were sung exhorting children to study hard in order to take part in the liberation and transformation of their country. In other words, to transform education from being an instrument of domination to its being one of liberation.

It was necessary, therefore, that after independence, government should respond to this hunger for education. Significantly, the government encouraged people to build schools on a collective self-help basis - *Harambee*. This method of development had a lot of positive aspects in it. It mobilized the people around concrete development tasks and tapped their collective will and energies. It also made people rediscover their organizational skills and creative talents. It therefore had the potentialities of leading to the people identifying and confronting their needs and becoming the authors of their own development. However, the potential mass democratic character of the movement did not, and could not, develop in the existing political and economic context. *Harambee* lost its collective mass participatory character and became a vehicle for furthering the political interests of those who can contribute more than others. The logic of the movement was, in other words, turned upside down as it were. Instead of the movement becoming a mobilizing force, the initiative has been taken over by the petty and 'auxiliary' bourgeoisie. Indeed, it is not unusual for the people to be coerced to contribute towards a *Harambee*.

However, under this movement and with government encouragement, the number of schools in Kenya has increased phenomenally as has the enrolment. Enrolment in secondary schools, for example, rose from 37,000 in 1963 to 465,000 in 1983 (*The Daily Nation*, 3 October 1984: 11). In 1986 there were 460,000 students in the standard seven class alone. Government has also in theory eliminated primary school fees. However, this democratization of access to education has obvious costs in terms of availability of teachers and materials. As the 1984 *World Development Report* noted: '... in the urban areas of Malawi and Kenya, class size frequently exceeds sixty students. Combined with a lack of teaching materials large classes make learning difficult' (World Bank 1984: 85). The situation in some rural area schools is worse than this, given the usually favoured position of urban areas.

The quid pro quo to education is that meaningful employment be available at the end of schooling. This is particularly so in a system of education such as Kenya's which is, like a pyramid, broad at the base and quite narrow at the top in terms of entrance to tertiary institutions. Only a pitifully few, roughly one per cent, of those who enter primary school, find their way into a university, polytechnic or other tertiary institution. It is imperative, therefore, that the economy expands enough to provide the needed jobs for the increasing numbers of school-leavers. However an optimistic estimate is that only about 60,000 jobs are available per year.

It is in order to confront this employment crisis that government has instituted commissions of enquiry, the latest of which recommended the present education system with its bias towards technical and handicraft subjects. However, in a situation in which those who work by the hand are not accordingly remunerated, in which there are glaring inequalities and the bourgeois ethos is strong, it is doubtful that school-leavers will be satisfied to eke out a living as self-employed carpenters and blacksmiths. Apart from the need for capital to start them off, it is also likely that the school-leavers will come to realize that they are not being trained to participate meaningfully in the development of the country, but only as peripheral petty artisans and producers in the so-called informal sector - the *Jua Kali* people - within economic relations in which they are the most exploited. They over-work themselves in order to subsidize the mainstream capitalist economy by providing 'cheap goods and services designed for the poverty life-style of those whose work makes the "formal sector" profitable, and enables them to live on their [low] wages' (Leys 1975: 268). In other words, they join the grand design of neo-colonial economic relations in perpetuating self-exploitation and the exploitation of other labour.

The new education system seems to be based on only one of the recommendations of the ILO mission which visited Kenya in 1972. The ideological limitations of the reformist measures recommended by this mission seen in the context of the realities of the Kenyan economy are analysed by Colin Leys. The mission warned that:

The frustration of younger people in search of opportunities - frustration instilled by their present preparation for life -

may lead to alienation and intolerable tensions.... (Leys 1975: 263).

The ILO mission's warning was soon to become a reality. Student unrest in schools which began in the seventies, even as the ILO was warning of 'intolerable tensions,' had reached a chronic level in the eighties. Statistics about this unrest are hard to obtain, but a few facts will illustrate its scope and character. In the seven months between March and September of 1974, there were strikes in seventy secondary schools, one teacher training college and one Roman Catholic seminary (*Viva Magazine*, April 1985). In February 1985, students at a Harambee school set fire to their school and stood guard to ensure that the fire did as much damage as possible (*Weekly Review*, 22 February 1985). Three years later, in February 1988, students 'burnt down several buildings, including a store and a laboratory, and critically injured a teacher as a result of rage' (*Daily Nation*, 19 February 1988). Student unrest at the University of Nairobi has become a well-known, almost annual, occurrence. Since 1969, there have been about twenty demonstrations and closures of the University, the latest in November 1987.

The situation described here would seem to warrant a more conclusive study of the teaching and learning situation. Such a study would ascertain whether beyond the quantitative changes in education, there has been a discernible philosophical transformation aimed at moulding out of the children a new Kenyan person - someone who moves into the ideal that we would have wanted to be; one who is armed with skills and attitudes to wrestle with underdevelopment. In other words, we need to find out whether our suspicions are right that under neo-colonialism education is still an alienating instrument of domination by the bourgeoisie, not one that liberates by integrating the learners into their environment as active participants and agents of change and development and by so doing develops the personality and the national productive forces.

Popular Music and Cultural Struggle

Difficult to discuss briefly, but an exciting area of study, is the contribution of popular music in commenting on and analysing the post-independence situation, and in the expression of a collective world-view and consciousness. Taken as a whole, popular songs have been a chronicle of the changing social situation and the relations thereof. Singers have, in an ideologically uneven, but enthusiastic and creative manner commented on the popular subject of the commoditization of all that was previously sacred, including love and sex: 'You buggers a thing given to you free by God and now you put it up for sale!' The spirit of these songs is recaptured by the following verse from a song which Ngugi quotes in his *Petals of Blood:*

This shamba girl
Was my darling
Told me she loved my sight.
I broke bank vaults for her,
I went to jail for her,
But when I came back
I found her a lady,
Kept by a wealthy roundbelly daddy,
And she told me,
This shamba-lady told me,
No! Gosh
Sikujui
Serikali imebadilishwa[1]
Coup d'état 66
      (Thiong'o 1977: 277-278).

Much earlier than this, the singers had already protested at the commercialization of the dowry system. A young man, without the means, would be asked to pay an exorbitant amount of money plus new items like high-grade cows and a water tank, which in the rural areas became symbols and actual sources of social differentiation. The songs expressed the rebellion of the youth against this practice:

A raw youth straight from school,
Where will he get a water tank from
And two high-grade cows?
It is better to stay single.

And the girl said,
If I won't marry this one,
I will not come back after I go to Maiko's.
I will begin my own hunting.

---

[1] 'I do not know your government has been overthrown.'

Equally the dominant consciousness of self-seeking and selfishness to the point of fratricidal conflict has been commented upon:

> Who is that wondering how conflict arises
> Between a man and his brothers.
> It is those who already have that continue to grab selfishly
> And employ their young brothers to milk their cows for them.

> I have travelled from Mombasa to Kisumu
> And have not heard anyone in tears for the sake of another.
> All are saying 'Iiya, I must get rich some day.'
> One would think you are a sharpshooter from your talk of getting rich.

Social stratification and class struggle have been expressed in characteristic metaphors and imagery drawn from the lives and experiences of the people. Thus one song, in very subtle language, complains that the existing situation, in which some people have been left to perish or survive on their own, is unnatural because even a goat 'when it gives birth to twins, it nurtures both of them'. Twins in this case is an obvious reference to the rich and the poor, and the goat is a metaphor of the whole country - which unlike the goat has not been able to nurture and feed its twins.

But there are also songs whose reflection of the social disparity is more overt. For example, in the early seventies there were two or three songs whose similar message was that when we are walking along the streets, the only thing that makes us appear to be the same is the fact that we are wearing more or less the same form of clothing. But behind this, there are those who dine and wine at the big hotels, others are satisfied with fish and chips, while yet others spend their lunch hour sleeping in the park unable to buy food. In the same vein of reflecting the inequalities, a singer was to sing that:

> If God had a telephone,
> I would surely phone him up and ask him,
> 'Did you shake some people by the hand?'

The institution of borrowing from banks, which became widespread after the change of the land tenure system, has also been sung about:

> I know well money is hard to borrow,
> And some are born in a family of twelve.

His sole collateral is his wife and children,
There'll be some ending up like a castrator of the donkey.[2]

For obvious reasons, overtly 'political' songs have not been many,
unless one takes into account the propagandistic ones which are
sung in praise of one thing or another that a government notable
has done. In the early days, there were many songs celebrating the
coming of independence and looking forward to the expected federation of East Africa and of Africa as a whole. The optimism in
these songs was soon to turn into either disappointing silence or a
warning expressed in proverbs and metaphors as happened after
the murder of J. M. Kariuki:

Leaders, now that Kariuki is dead
With even his fingers cut,
Did he graze on forbidden pastures?
If you don't watch out, we shall catch up with you.[3]
There'll be some dying before their flocks reach the pastures.
The antelope hates the one who shouts at it,
But the one who cut off parts of his body,
The one who took him to the wild beasts,
Must one day be rolled down a hill in a bee-hive
In the presence of all the masses of Kenya.[4]

These are only a few examples from a very rich genre of artistic expression which has not been studied thoroughly. Such has been the
wave of expression in popular songs that even the church produced
songs which commented on the social situation and, as could be expected, concluded that the trouble with the rich and the poor is that
their hearts and souls are starved of the word of Jesus. But, as has
become the fate of the church, this standard Christian prescription
to a social situation did not find favour in the ears of the powers
that be. The two songs we have in mind - 'Maai ni Maruru' ('The
Waters are Bitter') and 'Ng'aragu yaNgoro' ('The Hunger of the
Soul') were banned straightaway.

---

[2] Obviously a castrator of the donkey would end up with such a severe kick he
would be lucky to be alive afterwards.

[3] Another translation would be 'if you don't watch out we shall become locked in
battle.' This is the actual literal meaning.

[4] Traditionally, witches and other anti-social elements were killed by rolling them
down a hill in a beehive after communal verdict had been passed and in the
presence of everybody.

At the same time other forms of protest arose at the way in which the struggle for independence was being misrepresented. Odinga's *Not Yet Uhuru* was the first of a series of publications whose intention was to negate the thrust towards reaction and the obfuscation of history. Steadily in the 1970s there arose a literature and other cultural activities, which were to emphasize the history of Kenya from a positive point of view, and to also look critically at the present reality in the country. Well-known among these are Ngugi's works written in the 70s and early 80s - including some of the stories in *Secret Lives, The Trial of Dedan Kimathi* (co-authored with Micere Mugo), *I Will Marry When I Want* (co-authored with Ngugi wa Mirii), *Petals of Blood, Devil on the Cross* and *Detained: A Writer's Diary.*

Gakaara wa Wanjau published his *Mwandiki wa Mau Mau Ithamirio-ini* in 1983 with youth in mind. This book, which was to share the 1984 Noma Award with Njabulo Ndebele's volume of short stories, is actually a diary of events from the day of Gakaara's detention on 20 October 1952, the day when the emergency was declared, to his release in 1960. The old KCA members with whom he was detained were emphatic that if ever the events in detention camps were lost or forgotten, they would blame it on Gakaara. And so he wrote his diary in exercise books, which he hid in the false bottom of his wooden box, as a duty and responsibility to the collective history.

Gakaara is himself a remarkable literary figure. He is one of the 'group of the 40s', those who were young in the 1940s, who went to fight in the Second World War and became politicized. After the war, from 1946, he began writing books and songs to protest against colonialism and to promote the cause of struggle. In detention, he took a correspondence course in short story writing. He also continued to compose songs, very much like those in Maina wa Kinyatti's collection (Kinyatti 1980), and taught the other detainees. He wrote at least two books which he was to publish afterwards.

He was in fact detained because of his writings which were 'brave, educative, inspiring and mobilizing' (Wanjau 1983: xi). For the same reason he was chosen to be the chronicler of events in the camp in which he was detained. On the face of it, the style of the diary is painstakingly factual and unemotional. But the book is a testament to the bravery of the people who endured numerous forms of humiliation and indignity without breaking. Adversity seemed to bring out the best in them. They collectively boycotted work and went on hunger strike. They smuggled out numerous letters and telegrams, organized their own committees, educated themselves and, above all, kept their spirits high through dance festivals, foot-ball competitions and debating.

The book is a testimony of the detainees' dignity, which they had to constantly struggle to maintain, and of their unity and great love for each other. Gakaara, like Maina wa Kinyatti before him, published his book with the obvious aim of teaching the youth of Kenya its history - 'a nation without its history is a dead one,' he says. Thus in his introduction he gives a brief history of the Mau Mau which ends with an enumeration of the selfless virtues of the Mau Mau leadership and a clear discussion of what it means to be a traitor to one's country - to sell one's country for money. This becomes an explicit condemnation of those who support neo-colonial economic relations. Gakaara ends his book with a reminder of the great pain when, after independence, goverment policy was to 'forgive and forget,' and those who had fought found that those who had abused, humiliated and tortured them had to be forgiven. The need for revenge passed away over time. What did not pass away was the impoverishment of the fighters and their inability to buy land (Wanjau 1983:166).

A National Theatre Movement

Perhaps the most notable cultural trend in the post-independence period and one with a particularly high social profile has been the development of theatre. A good over-view of this development from pre-colonial times up to around 1981 is offered by Ngugi wa Thiong'o in his *Decolonising The Mind: The Politics of Language in African Literature*. As he observes, theatre during the colonial period became disconnected from its popular roots and brought under the patronage of missionary schools and well-meaning non-African individuals like Peter Colmore and Graham Hyslop.

The development of Kenyan theatre in the post-independence period has been characterized by the struggle to break away from this historical legacy of patronage. In the 60s, the thrust of theatre, as in other spheres of life, was towards the 'Africanization' of the existing content - in itself an expression of the dominant nationalist consciousness. More and more African schools entered the annual School Drama Festival. At first these performed a hotch-potch of plays most of which were non-Kenyan in themes and content.

However, such plays as Ngugi's *The Black Hermit, The Rebel* and *A Wound in The Heart* were also to be performed in the 60s. By the end of the decade, dramatists were beginning to probe more sensitively into the current social relations. Ngugi's *This Time Tomorrow* is a good example of this trend. Towards the middle of the 1970s a theatre rooted in the history and the realities of Kenya was to come into its own with the production at the National Theatre of Francis Imbuga's *A Game of Silence* and Ngugi's and Micere Mugo's *The Trial of Dedan Kimathi* in 1975. But it was not until *Ngaahika Ndeenda* was performed at Kamiriithu in 1977 that a conscious attempt was made, in both form and content, 'at reconnection with the broken roots of African civilization and its tradition of theatre' (Thiong'o 1986: 42). With *Ngaahika Ndeenda*, therefore, Kenyan theatre entered a new stage of development.

However, the dominant trend has been, as with Kamiriithu, to find a form and content which would reflect the lives and experiences; the hopes, frustrations and dignity of the majority working and peasant classes - a form, therefore, which would be rooted in the aesthetic and social history of Kenya. This trend is clearly seen among community-based and school-based theatre groups. In May 1983, a commentator identified six community-based groups operating in the working-class surburbs of eastern Nairobi. Other groups were operating from Ngong, Mombasa, Nakuru, Eldoret and Kisumu (*Sunday Standard*, 8 May 1983: 6). In March 1986, about ten such groups staged a four-day festival of drama, song and dance at the Nairobi City Hall.

The groups are made up of young men and women, usually out of school and unemployed. They are hardly reported about in the local press, yet they are involved in the development of a new theatre at grass-roots level. Their plays are either original or published ones with an appeal to the intended specific audience. Yet, as was noted in a commentary, members of these groups are regarded as ruffians and anti-social elements and are either denied licences to perform or given one day licences, because they are at the mercy of those 'who fight against a national or a true people's theatre' (*Sunday Standard*, 8 May 1983: 6).

Notable among these groups is the Black Angels Dogmatic Club which around 1985 hit the streets of Nairobi with the original play *Kinyonga Bar and Restaurant*. With this play the group competed for audiences and money with the many itinerant preachers, jokers and charlatans who liven up the streets of Nairobi during lunch-time. Members of the group were unemployed high-school graduates, who made their livelihood out of street theatre, and who hoped one day to be able to build an open-air theatre.

Equally illustrative is the emergence in 1987 in the industrial town of Thika of another drama club made up of workers in the town's water supply department. They travel to outlying areas performing to schools (in English), to peasants in churches (in Gikuyu) and to fellow town workers (in Kiswahili). According to an eyewitness report in February 1988, this group's performance of *Who is to Blame* made audiences both laugh and weep. One man from an appreciative peasant audience said that the play's 'greatest asset' is that it 'showed the picture itself, as it should be'. The adult audience generally agreed that the play was educative and should be seen by more people through national television (*Sunday Nation*, 21 February 1988:19).

Side by side with this development of community-based theatre is the even more vibrant and widespread school- and college-based theatre. From inter-house competitions, plays go on to compete at a district, provincial and, finally, national level. Thus, only a tiny fraction of the plays that enter the competition reaches the finals. Since 1982, the schools' festival has included dances as well as plays, and the venue for the final competitions has been rotating around the provinces. From 1986, the festival further includes the dramatization of poetry. This goes together with a national music and recitation festival involving both primary and secondary schools.

Colleges and primary schools have annual theatre festivals as well. In fact, one of my most memorable experiences in the theatre was the acting of a little girl from a Mombasa primary school in 1980. She played the role of a mother whose son had been captured and sold off to slavery in a play which was, indeed, a total theatre experience. Though the schools' festival is the best known, all these festivals constitute what is a veritable national theatre movement. In 1986, there were 1,800 finalists in the schools' festival and in 1987, forty-four schools from all corners of the country competed in the finals.

The Kenya Schools Drama Festival has brought to the fore 'classics' such as *Makwekwe* (1981), *Kuna Kilio* and *Visiki* (1982), *Manamba* and *Mwanadamu* (1983) and *The Dream* (1985). Most of the plays presented have been original - in 1983 *all* the plays were original - and have been mainly in Kiswahili and other national languages. They have also artistically integrated song and dance and drawn heavily on present and past historical experiences and the myths of the Kenyan peoples. In 1986, for example, the winning play in Dholuo, *Lwanda Magere,* celebrated the mythical hero of that name. Mention should also be made of the indomitable Onsondo Onsondo whose 'Majitu' plays made stark, highly creative and dramatic use of folk-lore to critically comment on the contemporary situation.

Thus through the efforts of the organizers who are teachers, supported by government, the Kenya Schools Drama Festival continues the trend set in motion by the University Free Travelling Theatre and Kamiriithu - to produce theatre which attempts to 'reconnect with the roots'.

Though the festival continued to feature high-quality plays up to 1986, censorship and the prevailing 'anti-dissident' political climate might have negatively affected the 1987 festival. According to a review of that festival, the quality of the competing plays was not impressive. There was not enough maturity, analysis and sensitivity in the treatment of reality, and the artistic standard was not high enough. The reviewer was also concerned about 'the decline of original plays in Kiswahili and the mother tongues' (*Sunday Mail,* 27 March 1988: 9).

Conclusion

In conclusion, it is necessary to remind ourselves that neither nice words, nor the performance of a play or the writing of a novel will by themselves solve our immense development problems. We agree with Oginga Odinga that there is no alternative to the total mobilization and development of our human resources and the proper management of our natural wealth, if we are to break out of the vicious cycle of poverty. The raising of the level of education, skills and mastery of science and technology among the masses are prerequisites in the development of the productive forces and increased productivity. But so is the inculcation in the people of a scientific world-view, and the belief that the world can be changed by the purposeful actions of people and not the wilful activity of nature or fate.

The few examples we have highlighted of cultural development in post-independence Kenya do show that art, itself arising from and reflecting a given material situation, can play a role of justifying, distorting and turning the people away from meaningfully addressing the reality in which they live. This, in effect, conserves the status quo and is the culture of the ruling class in any given situation. On the other hand, there is an art which has played the traditional educative and mobilizing role. This is an art that has drawn on positive images from people's history, instilling confidence and, in the words of Wole Soyinka, having themes which point out 'the worlds' many dilemmas, in re-directing the consciousness of societies and mobilizing the responses of people towards eventual changes' (Leys 1975: 18). It is this impetus towards change which the cultural worker should strengthen in order to speed up the process of development.

References

Kinyatti, Maina wa (1980) *Thunder from the Mountains: Mau Mau Patriotic Songs*, London.

Leys, Colin (1975) *Underdevelopment in Kenya: The Political Economy of Neo-Colonialism*, London.

Marx and Engels (1976) *On Colonialism*, Moscow.

Odinga, Oginga (1967) *Not Yet Uhuru: The Autobiography of Oginga Odinga*, London.

Thiong'o, Ngugi wa (1971) *A Grain of Wheat*, London.

Thiong'o, Ngugi wa (1977) *Petals of Blood,*, London.

Thiong'o, Ngugi wa (1986) *Decolonising The Mind: The Politics of Language in African Theatre*, London.

Wanjau, Gakaara wa (1983) *Mwandiki Wa Mau Mau Ithamirio-ini,*, Nairobi.

World Bank (1984) *World Development Report*, New York.

Marechera in Black and White

David Caute

Introduction

The writer Dambudzo Marechera died in Harare on 18 August 1987, at the age of thirty-five. A brilliant light, flashing fitfully in recent years, was extinguished.

He once wrote: 'It's the ruin not the original which moves men; our Zimbabwe ruins must have looked really shit and hideous when they were brand-new.' The manuscript containing this sentence has never been published; indeed the evidence suggests that - despite his international reputation - almost half of his major work remains unpublished.

Marechera grew up in Rusape, midway between Harare and the Mozambique border, one of nine children of a long-distance lorry driver and a nanny. Despite the grim poverty he later described, the boy Charles (his real name) was soon reading:

> I obtained my first [book] - Arthur Mee's *Children's Encyclopaedia* - in the local rubbish dump where the garbage from the white side of town was dumped everyday except Sundays... One brilliant blue morning I found what I thought was a rather large doll but on touching it I discovered that it was a half-caste baby, dead, rotting (*Mindblast*).

He wrote of his parents with a virulence never forgiven by his family - shortly before his death he complained that he had been forbidden to attend his sister Tsitsi's funeral - but a true writer wins his laurels by the most intimate of betrayals. In *Mindblast* (1984) he described his mother, who worked as a nanny for white families:

> ...she would invariably give me a long sermon about how girls are 'easy' and 'why don't you get on with laying one or two?... 'There is nothing to it,' she said. 'You stick it in the hole between

the water and the earth, it's easy... You strike like a fire and she'll take you and your balls all in. Right? Up to your neck.'

...mother, so soon after father's death, became a prostitute to keep the family going. I felt it keenly and was all of eleven years old... It was then that I hated all notions of family, of extended family, of tribe, of nation, of the human race. There was also within me an active sexuality directed at my little sister who a few months ago paid me back in brutal coin.

An Escalator of Outrage

In 1973 he arrived at Oxford as a refugee from the University of Rhodesia. Like the majority of his country's writers, he side-stepped the liberation struggle, the guerrilla war, the deadly camps in Mozambique. Other pupils of his old school, St Augustine's, tore up their 'O' level certificates and crossed the border by night, and many of them did not survive.

He had been in 'the Struggle' and seen death at close quarters. There are a lot like him around. Youngsters who have tasted death and who will not flinch from firing at you if they think you are the enemy. I hope I am not an enemy (*Mindblast*).

Marechera conducted his own war in universities, at literary gatherings and against television directors whose attention he was quick to interpret as exploitation. According to legend he was sent down from Oxford after attempting to set fire to New College, but the dons who remember him deny it; he had failed to attend tutorials and behaved so erratically that in 1976 he was offered a choice between psychiatric treatment at the Warneford or expulsion. He landed in a London tenement via a jail in Cardiff.

Screams from the other cells
Deafened me from my own cries
There were policemen gumshoeing in my blood
I woke up dead in Southall
There were policemen investigating themselves
There was the Queen admiring a pig at the Sussex Agricultural
Show
        Miss Piggy squealed with
        Exquisite pain

> When love thy neighbour
> Went against the grain
>> (*Portrait of a Black Artist in London*).

Dambudzo was an escalator of outrage; he would eat steadily from the hand that fed him until he realized that he must bite it to remain true to himself. He attended the *Guardian* fiction prize ceremony in extravagant costume and displayed his gratitude by tossing saucers at the chandeliers. He enjoyed the tender bohemian muddle of an artists' tenement commune near Euston Station - metropolitan encounters, Nigerians, Senegalese, fellow-writers, editors, bars, bizarre hats, failing to turn up for appointments with various literary editors. He borrowed, begged, stole, bummed; his publisher was driven to such despair by Marechera's raids on Bedford Square that the receptionists were put on permanent 'red alert' and on one occasion the police were called.

But what of British racism? It was real enough; his unpublished works, *The Black Insider* and *Portrait of a Black Artist in London,* comprise a brilliant evocation of the uprooted black anarchist at large in racist Britain. Yet the racism of police and population was something that Marechera could live with on terms of distant irony; indeed he thrived on its absurdities and petty crimes. (Punch-ups with Nigerians were a more pressing problem, but the bandages he wore were the result of hurling *himself* through the plate-glass window of the Africa Centre in King Street.) He was a supremely comic writer and his very black baby features were often splashed with laughter. Of course solemn acolytes and amanuenses reinforced his tendency to self-importance, but no sooner was he reminded about worlds and stages than he nodded, showed his irregular front teeth, and put on the mask of comedy.

Art and anarchy were the ideals of this black Steppenwolf; drink and debilitation his fate.

> I am against everything.
> Against war and those against
> War...
>> (*Mindblast*)

(This wasn't strictly true: Marechera was never a nihilist, indeed his instinctive humanism was irrepressible).

As the following passage indicates, it is tempting to view

Marechera as situated, or trapped, 'between' two worlds:

> Thus he lies between the worlds of Africa and Europe, between
> the experience of physical poverty and cultural wealth, between
> colonialism and racism and the rebellion against them. Further,
> he is caught between the idea of pure, true love and the loathing
> of earthiness and sensuality impressed upon him for so long at
> his mission school... (Flora Wild, 'Write or Go Mad', *Africa Events*,
> March 1986, p. 59).

Tempting, but probably a mistake. If one takes these separate and
contradictory 'moments' in Marechera's upbringing and experience,
what is most striking is the way this highly receptive, imaginative,
egotistical and mendacious talent absorbed one into the other, deliberately played off one against another while 'refusing' any fixed
cultural identity: 'You talk of the culture I come from how come you
know I got a distant culture...,' he'd say.

He also invented, fabricated, fantasied. The 'Oxford' accent he acquired and retained was in a league of its own among Zimbabweans. He turned up in Bedford Square, outside his publisher's,
wearing full horse-riding regalia, including cap, satin coat, jodh-
purs, high boots - all he needed was five pounds for the taxi. 'I can
hardly travel by public transport dressed like this!' he protested. He
was a magpie. He saw and felt everything; he was the most 'aware'
person I have ever encountered. He was too dedicated a conductor
of the Marechera orchestra ever to find himself stranded between
drums, strings and woodwind. And this vast curiosity, this appetite
for mimesis, drew him to Europe, to the 'great' cultures. He denigrated his own Shona language and those who wrote in it; he
despised what he regarded as the narrow provincialism of those
who made a fuss about Great Zimbabwe. Unlike the white women
he slept with, he had no time for cultural relativism.

The following passage is taken from his unpublished autobio-
graphical novel, *The Black Insider*. The setting is the Africa Centre in
King Street, Covent Garden, where (as he puts it) 'once more we felt
safe and together':

> Afterwards, when the beer had settled in that tender spot in my
> deepest gut where I am one grim knot of pessimism, I looked
> around, at the bar where a few blacks in national costumes were
> standing, at the dining tables where the smart black faces were
> eating impeccably African food recommended by the *Guardian*,
> and at the side seats where little groups of black and white faces

sat talking and drinking in an unmistakably non-racial way. Here then was the womb into which one could retreat to nibble at the warm fluids of an Africa that would never be anything other than artificial. A test-tube Africa in a brave new world of Bob Marley anguish, Mowtown soul, reggae disco cool, and the added incentive of reconceiving oneself in a friendly womb.

The Return of the Free Artist

In 1980 independence (genuine this time) brought thousands of Zimbabweans (exiles by necessity or choice) back to their native land within the space of a few months. Freedom, dignity and the immense expansion of job opportunities for educated blacks encouraged this massive return; homesickness and family bonds, sentiment and *sadza*, also played their part. But none of these factors carried magnetic force for Dambudzo Marechera. Nor did the 'liberation struggle' - indeed one of his first actions, when he joined the TV crew making a film version of *The House of Hunger*, was to insult an ex-guerrilla working on the project in the Park Lane Hotel, Harare. It was a white television director who had lured him home and it was not long before they bitterly fell out. Marechera recoiled from the familial roots he was now invited to rediscover; he also recoiled from the heroic tribalism of the ZANLA and ZIPRA armies, the raw populism of nationalist politics, the demagoguery of commissars and 'shefs' - the conformity demanded by power and preferment.

One may speculate further about this quarrel early in 1982. If Dambudzo recoiled from his actual roots he may also have shrunk, when it came down to it, from leading a television crew into a personal history partly of his own invention. It's unlikely that any biographical episode related in any of his writings is entirely accurate or even wholly in accordance with his own sober recall - as I have pointed out in 'Marechera and the Colonel', the fictional motifs are too repetitive, obsessive, 'automatic' in the surrealist sense, to be faithful mirrors of differentiated reality. The 'loathing of sensuality and earthiness' at the St Augustine's School, Penhalonga (referred to by Flora Wild) was largely a fiction of Dambudzo's invention. There were always plenty of girls at the school, though Marechera had departed long before the ZANLA guerrillas arrived in 1977-80, bringing their own version of 'earthiness'. Teachers at St Augustine's recall Charles Marechera as not popular with his fellow pupils (or with his own brother) on account of his vivid pretensions. On the other hand, when I asked two St Augustine's sixth formers in 1984 whom they regarded as Zimbabwe's most exciting writer, both of them said, without hesitation, 'Marechera'.

In 1982, finding himself 'home' in Harare, for better or worse, he quickly established himself as *enfant terrible*, scene-stager extraordinary, rootless and roofless. He interrupted lectures, heckled ministers, abused Party functionaries, sabotaged national book fairs, and derided the literary programme of a socialist government - 'They say I must write my books from the front page of the *Herald*.' (He was referring to Nathan Shamuyarira, Minister of Information at that time). Publishers dropped him. (Government departments, particularly Education, operate a patronage commercially indispensable to African book publishers - no need, therefore, for the iron fist of overt censorship).

Marechera sheltered behind the myopic optimism of the artist who writes for himself yet demands a large, rent-paying audience. (Asked who he wrote for, he was liable to snap back: 'Not for you.') Never too shy to claim a niche in the pantheon of the global avant-garde, and never reluctant to complain of political persecution (a badge of honour), Dambudzo likened his own predicament to Mayakovsky's. I said: 'You mean they'll erect a statue to you in Rusape [his home town] after your death?' He giggled and haggled with the waiter about payment for the beers he was ordering four at a time. 'All that Shona sculpture hype, David, it's just shit.' (He had the colonial habit of dropping one's name into sentences like lumps of sugar into a tea cup).

The image of the free artist became an alibi for self-indulgence; Dambudzo remained a Peter Pan whose large, saucer eyes would grow wider as he spun anecdotes out of fact and fantasy in almost equal measure. The child in Dambudzo remained father to the child, destroying the flesh and sustaining the spirit until finally drink, cigarettes, drugs and self-imposed malnutrition brought him to the end. He was his 'own worst enemy', of course, but an inspired enemy capable of painful self-scrutiny:

> The Eumenides are not behind the curtains but are the spots of dirt on my spectacle lenses... Steve Biko died while I was drunk and disorderly in London... Soweto burned while I was sunk deep in thought about an editor's rejection slip (*The Black Insider*).

Censorship and Socialism

In 1985 Marechera gave an interview to the Parisian left-wing daily, *Libération*. In its introductory thumb-nail sketch the paper romantically suggested that he had been *contraint de prendre le maquis* ('constrained to go underground') during the period of white rule. Marechera recalled:

> There was an enormous gap between life at school, an education in the English style, and the life which awaited us after school, extreme poverty, the horror of waiting for the next meal without knowing if there would be one... The opposition between the brutal reality of our lives and the idealism engendered by the English novels one could read at school.
>
> Before 1980 I wrote out of an indispensable need for intellectual evasion, to escape the surrounding horror by listening to my interior imagination. Living in my head, the rest counted for less.
>
> Is it more difficult to write since independence? The visible absurdities [of the colonial era] have departed... Now I am more preoccupied by individual liberty than by national liberation, the defence of those who cannot defend themselves. Now that we are independent I write, for example, about prostitutes, because all the African revolutions have taken it out on prostitutes and beggars, on those sections of the population who have never had the capacity to defend themselves...
>
> ... certain people now think that a writer like myself is irrelevant, that I ought to become a teacher, to struggle against illiteracy, etc. They say to me, 'Comrade, we have won the struggle, what are you disturbed about...' The writer becomes a problem. To criticise this or that is unpatriotic. My writings were considered subversive by Ian Smith before independence, and they still are. A book of mine was banned in 1981 and I was thrown into jail during last year's Harare Book Fair. During those six days in prison I made friends among the crooks and petty thieves who were my cell companions. They asked me why I was there. I replied: 'Books.'

In fact Marechera had been arrested because he had been overheard giving an interview to two very beautiful young women journalists, Kaess and Tjong, from Netherlands Radio at the Meikles' Hotel during the posh awards ceremony which accompanies each annual book fair. Dambudzo had been speaking loudly and critically and flamboyantly - a provocation to the plain-clothes men from the Central Intelligence Organization who haunt these occasions. (So clumsy were they that they arrested the Dutch journalists as well, confiscated their tapes, and never returned them. I have explored this episode, its antecedents and consequences, in 'Marechera and the Colonel').

Marechera told me about his cellmates the day after his release from Harare Central Police Station in September 1984. For a few days he proudly retained strands of red prison blanket wool in his vaguely dreadlocked hair. Spooning strawberry yoghurt, he recounted his ordeal. 'They put me in with a gang of con men who reckon they've pulled off the perfect fraud. In six days with them I learned more about making money than in the rest of my life! They laughed at me - that a person of my respectability should be in gaol! A writer! And don't forget I was arrested wearing my Book Fair suit.'

He lit another cigarette. 'As a matter of fact they called me a "balance". It comes from the Shona *baranzi*, meaning a straight guy, a fool, who always obeys the law and keeps his nose clean. If I tried to sleep during the day they'd say, "Hey, look, Half-past-Four wants to sleep, hush hush." A Half-past-Four is someone who works a regular day and stops work on the dot of half-past-four.'

He laughed in delight, his smooth, cherubic face alight with the effortless intercourse of life and art.

Musaemura Zimunya, the dean of Zimbabwean writers, who led the successful fight against the Censorship Board's banning of *Black Sunlight*, has written of Marechera: 'For the first time in our history, people had a view of what a writer could be, something which more developed countries are used to.' (The writer as unrooted saboteur, iconoclast, bohemian; the writer broken free of tribal bonds, national pride, political cant, podium rhetoric). Marechera, continued Zimunya, 'lived as he wrote and wrote as he lived.'

Yet Marechera privately dismissed most of his Zimbabwean colleagues as cowardly opportunists who failed to be counted whenever he was in trouble with the police. Deep in beer he would weave malicious but humorous tales about Zimunya, Mungoshi, Hove, Nyamfukudza - his friends, colleagues and fellow-artists. Aggressive and cheerfully paranoid in his chosen role as outcast, he nevertheless craved recognition, invitations (to lecture, to travel, to booze) and the company of the very careerists whose antics on the greasy pole he mercilessly derided in flashes of coruscating wit as novelist and dramatist. In the bars and hotels of Salisbury he sought out and provoked the Special Branch heavies who had wisely decided to combat subversion where whisky flowed rather than in the remote bush of Matabeleland.

Marechera was a radical certainly, and he had bravely faced up to white thugs when a student at the University of Rhodesia in the early 1970s, but socialism bored him and he despised the people, the *povo*, just as he scorned to use the Shona language. The rule in Zimbabwe is that you can ignore the official collective values in practice but not ridicule corruption and commissarial pretension in print. He was the only Zimbabwean writer who could have suggested that the Zimbabwe ruins must have 'looked really shit and hideous when they were brand-new'.

Life among the Progressives

Clearly Marechera's preference, both in fact and fiction, was for white women. Since independence Zimbabwe has been a happy hunting ground for large numbers of progressive young people, male and female, British, German, Scandinavian, Dutch, Canadian, Australian, American and, indeed, South African. They have come to radical Zimbabwe as students, as teachers, as aid workers, as researchers; and most of them, one way or another, as determined Friends of Zimbabwe.

Despite the noticeable erosion of the 'charisma factor' previously associated with the 'heroic guerrilla' image so popular among New Left students in the 1960s, nevertheless each generation of young intellectuals will develop reservoirs of romantic idealism in restless search of an outlet: somewhere to go, somewhere to be, somewhere to express solidarity and commitment. Third World countries or colonies engaged in forms of armed confrontation with imperialism (Nicaragua, for example) exert a special attraction. Zimbabwe clearly fits into this category; indeed Zimbabwe was the front-page liberation struggle of the late 1970s (with an astonishingly swift 'happy ending' against all the odds). Equally swift was the dramatic alteration in the kind of white people who made a bee-line for Zimbabwe before and after 1980. The young mercenaries, soldiers of fortune, sunbathers, racists and Texas Evangelists who arrived in the 1960s and 1970s, attracted by segregated land lots, easy gun laws, 'culling gooks' and laying down the law to 'kaffirs' - they were abruptly displaced in 1980 by the Greens and Reds of the young

European intelligentsia. The white artisans moved out, the white PhDs moved in.

Before independence, during the bitter years of the 'bush war', the bars and dance floors were crowded with boys and girls from the suburbs: hearty, muscular young men, executives, apprentices, mechanics, electricians and salesmen drinking huge quantities of Lion or Castle lager, brimming with bravado about the on-going war; sleek, carefully made-up young women called Lynn, Trish and Sharon, secretaries or nurses or beauticians, whose knowledge of blacks was largely confined to the 'cook-boy' and the 'garden-boy' plus a few 'cheeky' characters encountered at work.

In the suburbs of Salisbury, Gwelo, Umtali and Bulawayo, every educated black was a kaffir at heart. As the saying goes, 'You can take a kaffir out of the bush but you can't take the bush out of the kaffir.' There would have been no room for Dambudzo Marechera among the Fireforce commandos and Selous Scouts relaxing in the Park Lane, the Oasis or the Holiday Inn. (And yet, most paradoxically, he got equally drunk in the same bars when his time came).

The young white people who headed for Zimbabwe after 1980 came in quest of the reverse adventure: to be called comrade by the comrades. By tendency intellectual, or scholarly, or at least engaged in higher education, they spoke of 'colonialism' and 'neo-colonialism' - whereas the young Rhodesians had spoken of 'Communist terrorism'. Eager to get to know black people, to learn some Shona, to travel to remote country areas, they hitched lifts into Botswana, Mozambique, Zambia, delighted to discover that the civil war had left behind it little or no legacy of racial bitterness. Unlike Rhodesia's Lynn, Trish and Sharon, who dressed sexily and entered beauty competitions or show-jumping competitions caked in make-up, the new intellectual women wore the relaxed, subdued colours and the unvarnished faces of the counter-culture. The blacks, meanwhile, needed rubber necks to keep track of this coming and going of the white tribes.

The new whites were often media-conscious and eager to publish black poetry and short stories or to make films about the new re-settlement schemes, the ex-combatants' cooperatives financed by the Zimbabwe Project, and - always - the lives of black women. The name of Dambudzo Marechera became well known to these students of the humanities after 1982. Although the new white women were strong feminists and Marechera was a little prince of chauvinism, he was nevertheless a celebrity and a challenge for cultural headhunters looking for sexual adventure.

What was sought was a romance in the widest, Conradean, sense of the term, a journey into the interior. Sexual liaisons between educated blacks and whites most easily occur when one or the other party is a temporary visitor, or in transit. There are obvious reasons for this. The very impermanence of one partner offers a relationship 'without consequences'. The absence of the parents and family of at least one partner allows the couple a greater social freedom. Thirdly, the Zimbabwean male and the European female enjoy what might be called 'the emotional bond of familiar strangers' - that is to say, they share many elements of a common culture but without the grim legacy of hostility which often separates blacks and whites born 'downtown' and 'uptown'.

The vast majority of such 'charter flight' relationships are between black men and white women. (Perhaps the psycho-sociological typology advanced twenty years ago in Eldridge Cleaver's famous *Soul on Ice* is still relevant). Not one or two but three of Marechera's white girlfriends have explained to me how, in the bars and hotels of Harare, single black women regard single white women as 'competition' rather than as sisters. 'Superior' competition, too: 'They think of us as prostitutes,' one of them added.

I discussed this with Marechera at his flat in Sloane Avenue. I didn't take verbatim notes but, paraphrased, his comments were broadly as follows:

> But, David, the white women are the opposite of prostitutes. If money passes hands it is likely to be out of, and not into, their handbags (or shoulder bags). They are not selling themselves but buying an adventure, a romance, a journey of the whole being. The currency of purchase consists of 'class', social connections, an international frame of reference, a broad culture - and, perhaps most important, their freedom. No *lobola* is required, no uncles have to be bargained with, no children need be taken care of (usually).

He grinned at the thought of it all.

Marechera himself was a prize catch: celebrated, romantic, an artist. Very few of these transitional women actually read much of what he had written, though they varied from stranded girls he'd 'rescued' in the Playboy Club to the well-read daughters of Lutheran missionaries. For example, one woman described to me the grief, the despair, that Marechera expressed in August 1986 when he abruptly received by post a large parcel of rejected manuscripts from a London publisher (see below).

'Dambudzo told me he was finished. It was the end. He was quite shattered.'

But did she know anything about these manuscripts? Did she ask to read them? Wasn't she curious to discover what this famous writer - her lover - had been writing? No; no. A relationship with Dambudzo did not involve anything as time-consuming or tranquil as reading.

This young woman, by her own account, had hunted Marechera down in the bars he haunted, having been introduced to him some months earlier. But once the relationship was established it was he who became insistently demanding, begging her not to go away and pursue her volatile itinerary (the young Europeans who love Africa are often extremely restless; they consume dirt roads like spaghetti and there are usually foundation grants or funds - Scandinavian, German, Dutch, Canadian - to refuel their adventure). 'You must make your own life,' she comments by way of apology for having left Marechera a year before his death.

In *Mindblast* the poet tells us a little about 'Dagmar', the woman he'd loved during his brief, hectic, passport-less visit to West Berlin in 1979. He later confided that Dagmar remained important to him because, on that single occasion, it had been he who had waved farewell to her rather than the other way round. Normally it was his white women who flew away over the flat plain of Harare towards the Zambezi Valley to the north or the Limpopo Valley to the south. Yet 'out of sight, out of mind' was Marechera's own, unstated, rule of life. Once they'd gone he brushed them out of his mind. Marechera's needs demanded instant gratification: the last woman was about as significant as the last Castle lager.

Marechera dedicated some poems to women but he might as well have been signing a napkin for an admirer in a restaurant. The poems themselves contained whatever was in the poet's head and only rarely offered more than a hint of the particular mistress's profile. But the imagery was striking, as the following extracts from three (as yet unpublished) poems, all dedicated to the same woman, may indicate:

Nuclear tests of underground love!

Brief acquaintance, dredged by shared experience,
Is now a harbour for the biggest tankers
Of the human spirit...

Through windowpanes I view the wide vistas
Of improbability become possible, hugging each to
Other in heartrending love; ...

Aftermaths

We cannot do anything about Marechera's death but we can do something about a lesser tragedy - the fact alluded to earlier in this essay, that at least two of his major works remain unpublished. In conclusion, I want to give a brief account of how and why this happened.

Marechera's *House of Hunger* and *Black Sunlight* had both been reprinted by Heinemann Educational Books (African Writers' Series) when, in September 1984, I discovered two unpublished works, *The Black Insider* and *Portrait of a Black Artist in London* in HEB's files, both of them apparently forgotten by author and publisher alike. At that time HEB was undergoing a painful upheaval under new ownership and morale was low. Not until the spring of 1985 did I feel able to make a fresh approach and re-submit the two typescripts to Heinemann.

At that time I received a letter dated 21 May 1985 from Marechera (scribbled on the back of one of mine in a restaurant and handed for typing to Flora Wild, a German scholar resident in Harare since 1983, an expert on Zimbabwean literature, the author of several articles about Marechera, and now his principal literary executor). Wild had taken the roofless poet into her house in 1983-84. Marechera wrote:

> You know how things are down here - I should have written to you long ago but what with my rather Bedouin existence I tend to put things off for another day - London seems so far away!

After a touching profession of friendship, he went on:

> I have, in the last few days, received (more) bad news, i.e. College Press ... have rejected two MSS, a novel BURY ME TO THE DEPTHS OF DIAMONDS, and a new collection of poems AMELIA: SONNETS AND OTHER POEMS. These are now gathering dust on my desk. I don't know, David, but I feel as though I've been sucked into the centre of an unnameable vortex - turning, turning - not knowing which way to turn.

However, all was not lost and life sparked more prosaically in a P.S. He was due payment on an article:

Tell INDEX ON CENSORSHIP to urgently send me... my remuneration of 36.00 Pounds in the form of a Barclays Bank International Money Order.

Two months later, in Harare, he handed me his new novel which, despite Dambudzo's own confusions about its title, is clearly named *The Depth of Diamonds*. 'Please take it to London.' He mentioned his old editor at Heinemann (who had long since broken off relations out of cumulative exasperation) as if they had only yesterday parted the best of friends. Marechera's memory was a strobe light.

The title of this last work is taken from a poem, 'Junk', by Richard Wilbur. 'Then burnt, bulldozed, they shall all be buried to the depth of diamonds.' Very short, unworked, elliptical, often obscure, politically sacrilegious, sometimes brilliant, and entirely self-indulgent, the novella desperately needed more work. Two years of his life remained but - so far as I know - he never touched it again.

He also showed me the letter from College Press, publishers of *Mindblast,* rejecting the new novel:

Publication in its present form would be suitable for a small circle of erudite literary figures captivated by the author's undoubted brilliance as a writer. As a novel for the ordinary reader it is unreadable for reasons stated above [dense references to Greek mythology, no story-line, etc.]. Though not libellous, there is a possibility of the censor having doubts about allowing its publication because the ms. is saturated with four-letter words and lurid descriptions of sexual intercourse.

In July I sent *The Depth of Diamonds* to Heinemann Educational Books, with the suggestion that it be published in a single volume alongside the two earlier works. In October Heinemann wrote to Marechera that they were not interested in publishing *Portrait of a Black Artist in London* [a verse 'choreodrama' dating from the late 1970s] but would like to consider further the two novels.

By December 1985, Heinemann decided that they would not publish *The Black Insider* which was considered vitiated by 'difficult' literary allusions and 'a little boring', though there were some 'flashes of brilliance'. (In my opinion, *The Black Insider* is a fascinating commentary on Britain in the late 1970s, a work of dazzling Catholicism, graced by a wit distinctively Marechera's at the height of his powers.) Tom Engelhardt of Pantheon (American publishers of *The House of Hunger*), having read *The Black Insider* and *The Depth of Diamonds* was once again struck by 'the incredible energy' of Marechera's writing. Describing both works as 'more like first drafts of two novellas than finished works of fiction,' Engelhardt expressed willingness to 'reconsider' if Marechera did further work on the two texts.

On 8 January 1986, I wrote to Marechera, explaining that I was in agreement that *The Depth of Diamonds* needed more work. Although I got a written message from him dated 26 January, he never responded to this point. I suspect that Marechera was simply incapable of tackling any situation at a distance: entering into correspondence with a British editor about alterations to his text was beyond him, even though his entire literary future hinged on it. On 30 June 1986, Heinemann wrote to Marechera in terms remarkably similar to those in which College Press, Harare had rejected *The Depth of Diamonds*. The classical allusions, the publisher said, did not seem to fit in the novel at all and were not of interest to 'the general reader'.

… we have to publish books that people will enjoy reading and will not cost them too much in terms of time and effort!

Exclamation marks commonly denote surprise or paradox. Both might be in order when one remembers that Heinemann's African Writers' Series is the imprint, with a world-wide reputation, which has published Chinua Achebe, Ngugi wa Thiong'o, Kwei Armah, Christopher Okigbo and Sembene Ousmane.

Heinemann's final letter and the returned typescripts reached Marechera in August 1986, exactly one year before his death. Clearly this disaster weakened his will to struggle within (I don't say 'against') the coughing, the weakening lungs and general emaciation brought on by AIDS, by heavy drinking and smoking, and by self-inflicted malnutrition. (AIDS was diagnosed in February 1987). I am reminded of a passage from the television film of *The House of Hunger* where Dambudzo recalled how, on being thrown into a British prison, he had been asked to name his next of kin.

'None,' he replied.

But, they explained, someone had to bury him if he died. He chuckled: 'Heinemann then - fancy being buried by Heinemann!'

Only a few German admirers and patrons now kept faith with him (*Mindblast* had been published in German translation by M. Krumbeck Verlag, though not in England.) Marechera - who had a wonderful ear for historical allusions from other cultures - once said to me, 'My Germans are good Germans.'

In August 1987 his mother sat keening at the graveside of her little Rimbaud (or Rambo), oblivious to the large crowd of 'shefs', white liberals, media people, genuine friends and journalists who had gathered to salute a writer whose books were more talked about than read. Dambudzo's mother had lost two of her children within a couple of months. His sister, married to an activist of the South African ANC, had been killed in Harare by a bomb planted in a television set.

References

Dambudzo Marechera's *The House of Hunger* (1978) and *Black Sunlight* (1982) were published by Heinemann Educational Books. *Mindblast* (1984) was published by College Press, Harare. Marechera's *The Black Insider,* edited by Flora Wild, was eventually published by Baobab Books in Harare in 1990.

David Caute's 'Marechera and the Colonel' appeared in *The Espionage of the Saints: Two Essays on Silence and the State* which was published in 1986 by Hamish Hamilton.

'Marechera in Black and White' has been shortened by the editor of the present volume. Copyright 1988 David Caute.

Part Two

Nationalist Struggles, Popular Culture and Democracy

The Peasantry in Zimbabwe: A Vehicle for Change

K. D. Manungo

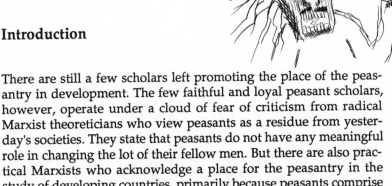

Introduction

There are still a few scholars left promoting the place of the peasantry in development. The few faithful and loyal peasant scholars,
however, operate under a cloud of fear of criticism from radical
Marxist theoreticians who view peasants as a residue from yesterday's societies. They state that peasants do not have any meaningful
role in changing the lot of their fellow men. But there are also practical Marxists who acknowledge a place for the peasantry in the
study of developing countries, primarily because peasants comprise
a majority of the populations in these countries. In view of this reality I have, over the years, become interested in the plight of the
peasantry - also because I was born and brought up in a peasant
household.

The majority of Zimbabwe's population is rural - about eighty per
cent. Critics may argue that 'rural' is not necessarily synonymous
with 'peasant', admittedly so, but in the Zimbabwean case, as I will
shortly illustrate, the majority of the rural dwellers are peasants.
Before more confusion besets us, a definition of the peasantry in
Zimbabwe would be appropriate.

Peasants are mostly rural dwellers working on a piece of land as
family members, with external relations to powerful non-peasants
who expropriate their 'surpluses' through tax, rent or through the
market economy. Peasants are highly differentiated: they include
the small-scale farmers who own the land they farm with their families or sometimes with seasonal labourers; the small traders with a
variety of businesses, but still claiming a piece of land where their
families continue to farm; the teachers in the rural areas who teach,
but still hold a piece of land to farm; the landless rural people (or
rural proletariat) who move seasonally between communal lands,
the commercial farms or the cities to earn a few dollars to meet the

demands of life sustenance; or even the worker peasants who own pieces of land in communal areas, but are employed in the wage economy in the urban centres. Peasants further include the farm labourers on the commercial farms, who, although they work on the farms, till small pieces of land and keep one or two cows for milk to supplement their meagre wages. Also traditional chiefs, although they were instruments in the settlers' control and domination of the peasants, sometimes view themselves as peasants.

While this is a lengthy definition of the peasantry in Zimbabwe, it will be useful in understanding the role of the peasants in the struggle for the liberation of Zimbabwe.

These segments within the peasantry of Zimbabwe may be different from those found in other countries, but the essential point that will be made in this article is that when the issue of freedom and national liberation was at stake, all these segments came together to support the guerrillas, albeit each in its own fashion, and came together to assist in removing colonialism.

The article seeks to examine the role of the peasants in the struggle for Zimbabwe and consequently to suggest a developmental programme for independent Zimbabwe that befits this group of outstanding actors in the struggle for Zimbabwe. It is my submission that peasants played a crucial role in the liberation of Zimbabwe and therefore the rewards of emancipation should alleviate the plight of the peasantry. Up to now I am pleased to say that the government has promulgated and implemented policies in line with bettering the lot of the peasants. Yes, the pace is too slow, but the 'spirit is willing'. An examination of the plight of the peasants before 1980 set against their present condition will reflect that a lot more has been done for the peasants in the few years after independence than was the case with settler governments during the preceding ninety years (Arrighi 1973: 180-234; Frederikse 1983; Machingaidze 1976; Moyana 1984; Ncube 1987; Palmer 1977; Palmer and Parsons 1977; Phimister 1974: 217-25; Ranger 1985; van Onselen 1976). A thorough knowledge of the plight of the peasantry under colonialism is the key to understanding the role the peasants played in the liberation struggle. The liberation struggle that reached its intensity in the 1970s was only an extension of a tradition of peasant resistance that had begun in the 1890s.

Peasants and Guerrillas

Several studies have recently come out on the liberation struggle in Zimbabwe, some more specific than others (Caute 1983; Chater 1984; Davidson 1981; Kriger 1985; Lan 1985; Martin and Johnson 1981; Maxey 1975). In most of these studies, authors try to bring out what they see as the salient features of the struggle. Motivated by different reasons each author comes out with his or her thesis. The studies by Norma Kriger (1985) and Terence Ranger (1985) have been central in influencing my research on peasants and the guerrillas in the struggle for Zimbabwe.

Ranger's study of peasant consciousness and guerrilla war in the Makoni district approximates the reality that I found in Murewa and Chiweshe. Ranger's study draws on history, the essence of a meaningful understanding of peasant behaviour in the liberation war in Zimbabwe. Peasant grievances played a major role in deciding who was to be supported, when the peasants were confronted by the Rhodesian forces on the one side and the guerrillas on the other.

Of great interest to me and my findings is what Ranger terms a 'people's war' to characterize the Zimbabwean struggle. Ranger argues that:

> ...in many significant ways the Zimbabwean war was pre-eminently a people's war; ...the balance of the equation of consciousness between peasants and guerrillas in Zimbabwe was very different from that in Mozambique, allowing for a more direct input by the peasantry into the ideology and programme of the war. In Zimbabwe, peasant demands for their lost lands were part and parcel of a developed consciousness of the mechanism of their oppression; of an understanding of the ways in which the state had expropriated them to the direct advantage of settler farming... (Ranger 1985: 14).

While I agree entirely with most of Ranger's findings and conclusions, I see Ranger, however, as isolating the guerrillas from the peasantry he was studying. Having admitted that the Zimbabwean liberation struggle was a 'people's war', separating the guerrillas from the peasantry is a mistake. My study leads me to see the guerrillas as an extension of peasant resistance to colonial rule. Admittedly, the guerrillas were coming in from external bases in Zambia and Mozambique, but the peasants viewed them as their 'children' who had come to assist them in removing the burden of colonialism. The words *vakomana* or *vana vedu* ('boys' or 'our children') were terms of endearment. There was a feeling of being one with the guerrillas among the peasantry. I believe it is the same mistake the Smith regime made in viewing guerrillas as outsiders which is now creeping into studies on the liberation struggle in Zimbabwe. At one point Ranger refers to the guerrillas as 'young strangers' arriving in districts to find that peasants had already become radicalized (Ranger 1985: 189). This may have been the case but in trying to stress the radical nature of the peasants before the arrival of the guerrillas there is a likelihood of viewing the guerrillas as outsiders. My contention is that this was just a homecoming - the guerrillas were themselves peasants coming back to confront the settlers with newly acquired technology: the gun.

While my disagreement with Ranger is a mild one, it is not so with Kriger's conclusions. Kriger's findings amaze me, to say the least. Given that Kriger's research area was contiguous to mine, I fail to comprehend how anyone could find evidence so heavily anti-guerrilla. I grant that the peasants were not a homogeneous class that behaved in one single way or another, as our definition shows. But given the history and experience of the peasantry under settler rule in Zimbabwe, I find it illogical to accept that there could have been a portion of the country where there was an overwhelming rejection of guerrilla goals of freedom for the peasantry.

Guerrillas, according to Kriger, had no material incentives with which to attract peasants - if anything the guerrillas preyed on the peasants. Kriger accuses other researchers of downplaying issues of social conflict in guerrilla wars. The Zimbabwean conflict was not just a 'guerrilla war', it was a war of total liberation from decades of oppression, subjugation, impoverishment and suffering under colonial rule. As Ranger points out, that was a consciousness the peasants did not need an outsider to tell them about.

My research and interviews with peasants show that a specific type of relationship seems to have developed between peasants and guerrillas. There were times when the Selous Scouts came into villages and pretended to be guerrillas. In the initial stages, the Selous Scouts managed to fool the peasants, but it was not long before they saw the difference. Guerrillas usually took time to reveal themselves to everyone in the village. They worked firstly with one trusted individual who was then used as a link with the rest of the community. When they were sure of the peasants' support, mobilization took place in the evenings at *pungwes*. There could be no confusing the guerrillas with the Rhodesian forces. The Rhodesian forces did not have the time to sit with the peasants and discuss grievances.

Kriger's central argument stems from the premise that guerrillas were unable to disrupt the coercive powers of the Rhodesian state, 'consequently violent tactics overshadowed other techniques used to try to create mass-based party organizations' (Kriger 1985: 13). Kriger states that guerrillas failed to establish military control and had no popular support. It is misleading to suggest that the guerrillas were out to effect military control. I would suggest that the guerrillas were out to wear down, stretch and exhaust the settler forces until negotiations for a transfer of power could be achieved. It was never guerrilla strategy 'to shoot their way' into Harare.

Kriger correctly identifies the segments within the peasantry in the rural areas. That is, the traditional leaders (chiefs), the teachers, businessmen and small-scale farmers in the purchase areas. She then draws the wrong conclusions about the aspirations of these groups. Kriger asserts that settler policies had assimilated much of the African élite into government employment and the market economy. She argues that because traditional leaders were state employees, they were therefore anti-guerrilla in their objectives, that the purchase area farmers were divided from the majority of the people by the land tenure system, and therefore their aspirations were to be assimilated into the white society. The non-agricultural élite in rural areas (presumably teachers and extension officers), Kriger states, were divided from the mass of subsistence oriented cultivators and therefore wanted assimilation into white society. Kriger's conclusions are totally misinformed.

Based on interviews with many teachers, shop-owners and chiefs, my conclusions differ strongly from Kriger's. The definition of teachers I presented does not separate them from the peasantry. Teachers, just as much as the peasants, felt oppressed and discriminated against. They had pieces of land to supplement salaries which they knew were much lower than those of their European counterparts. They produced grains which were bought cheaply by the Europeans because they were produced by Africans. The purchase farmers also felt discriminated against, as they did not get extension services the way Europeans did. Their crops were not treated equally with those of the white farmers. The loan and credit facilities were not as generous to the African farmers as they were to the European farmers. Instead of aspiring to become assimilated into colonial society, the small-scale farmers supported the guerrillas so that they would get better terms from a post-war government.

119

Kriger's conclusion that the divisive nature of settler rule complicated guerrilla efforts at establishing effective control, is again misinformed. Each of the classes within the peasantry had its own form of grievances against the settler system, and they therefore saw the guerrillas as representing a new hope of changing the system.

Kriger treats these groups as if they had no history. Yet it is common knowledge that all these groups had experienced settler rule with all its oppression. They had been suppressed by a system which used race as a cover for exploiting them. If the guerrillas could change that, then, well and good, they had to be supported. It is therefore surprising to read throughout Kriger's thesis about the 'coercion of the peasantry by the guerrillas'. Yet, in her own words, Kriger states that 'coercion is insufficient to elicit sustained participation' (Kriger 1985: 23). How is it, then, that the peasants stuck it out, through thick and thin, and sacrificed all, in order to remove colonial rule? One can only hope that the right questions will be asked so that a more accurate picture of what really happened can be produced.

Peasant Life during the War

It is evident from the interviews I have conducted that no matter how hard I try to summon that high quality of objectivity expected of researchers, I fail to come up with enough evidence to support the thesis that the guerrillas exposed the peasants to coercion during the armed struggle.

The overwhelming evidence presented to me in the interviews, states peasant grievances against the settler regime as the prime motive behind their support for the guerrillas. I conducted more than two hundred interviews over a period of four years at Chiweshe, Murewa, Chivhu and Shurugwi, and the views of peasants describing their support for the guerrillas overwhelmingly outweigh the reports of incidents of coercion.

When I asked an ex-combatant, Mike Nyanshanu, how the guerrillas dealt with opposition from the peasants, his answer was revealing:

> What did you expect us to do? After carrying those heavy landmines all the way from Mozambique, then plant them where we knew soldiers would pass, then to have a 'sell-out' inform the enemy! How did you expect us to deal with him?

I had no answer. Nyanshanu went on to describe how the suspected 'sell-out' would be given time to 'repent', but if he was observed to be continuously 'selling out', there was no option except to kill him. His reason for doing that, Nyanshanu said, was that it was better to sacrifice one person than sacrifice the struggle.

This type of evidence comes out time and again from ex-combatants and even peasants who witnessed some of these killings of the 'sell-outs'. In another interview, Stephen Mugwamba told of an incident at his school in Shurugwi where one teacher was visited by a friend. The friend stayed for a week and by the end of the first week, Mugwamba states that they had observed from his movements that he was a 'sell-out'. They handed him over to the 'boys' who were based in the area. After much interrogation he was found to be an undercover soldier who had used his friendship with the other teacher as an excuse to spy on the guerrilla movements in the area. They killed him, but Mugwamba says they pleaded for the teacher-friend to be spared as they believed he too had been hoodwinked. So it seems that the guerrillas tried hard to investigate cases brought to them by other peasants. Mugwamba states that whoever reported others had to be sure he was telling the truth, as otherwise the guerrillas would also beat him up.

I am inclined to believe these testimonies, as the number of civilians who were killed in this manner seems to have been very low in most villages where I conducted interviews. This is by no means suggesting that there were no atrocities or violence committed by the guerrillas on the peasants. But when you compare the massacres and atrocities the Rhodesian forces committed on the peasantry, it is hard to imagine that 'our' studies should stress guerrilla violence over that of the security forces.

The Catholic Commission for Justice and Peace catalogued massive materials on the Rhodesian forces' violence against the peasants throughout the war, but it seems that some of our colleagues try hard to ignore such vital sources when writing on the plight of the peasants during the struggle.

The protected villages set up by the Rhodesian security forces disrupted the lives of the peasants quite seriously. Suggestions that the peasants were better off in the protected villages is far from the truth. Almost all the interviews from protected villages suggest conditions of torture by security forces and the District Assistants who guarded these villages. Peasants speak of crowded conditions that were unfit for human beings.

Despite being moved into protected villages, the peasants risked all to support the guerrillas. The villages were guarded twenty-four hours a day, and peasants had to use one entry point where rigorous searches were carried out. Still, they took out food to the 'boys'. They devised all known tricks to take food out. Mrs Marangwanda of Chiweshe says in an interview that some peasants would use an ox-cart pretending that they were carrying manure to the fields - yet they had already put food under the manure securely tied in plastics. Women would wrap themselves with food and then put clothing over the food.

The Post-War Situation

Having said all that in defence of those of us who see the relationship between guerrillas and peasants differently from Kriger and others, I must state that peasant aspirations have not been fully realized after independence. The present position of the peasantry cannot be explained by emphasizing the conflict that is supposed to have existed between the peasants and the guerrillas. National liberation was so important a goal that it had to be achieved by all the oppressed forces of Zimbabwe. There had to be an alliance of all the disgruntled forces to remove the minority settler rule.

To look for reasons for the failure of peasant programmes in the seven brutal years of the armed struggle is to be misinformed. It is the whole history of colonial rule and what effects it had on the peasantry that has to be examined. Researchers should look at the classes that exist within Zimbabwean society.

The government has tried to alleviate the position of the peasantry. In agriculture land has begun to be redistributed to the landless - albeit slowly. There are problems associated with these initiatives, but debate is continuing. Here again research should find out why there are problems in land reform. Education has been extended to the masses. Statistics bear me out in this regard. Health has been extended to the rural masses. Primary health care and preventive methods have become the objectives of the Ministry of Health. A lot of discussion is currently going on in the media over the best means of resettling the peasants in the country. Villagization programmes have been started and these may solve the problem of amenities for the rural masses. It seems that political scientists like Kriger should try to understand history better so as to emphasize the issues which could assist in the development programmes of Zimbabwe.

We need researchers like Kriger, however, because there is a danger that human tendency may lead the new rulers of Zimbabwe into laxity and thereby allow the bourgeoisie to hijack the revolution. At the 1987 special congress of ZANU (PF) which ratified the unity accord with ZAPU, President Mugabe stated that the Leadership Code would be pursued vigorously. You see, in Zimbabwe, 'the spirit is willing'. That 'spirit' must continue to get support from researchers, but one is not saying the Krigers should be silenced. They are the goads which should urge on the ruling classes of Africa in the right direction. There would be no task too hard for the leaders, if they could mobilize the peasantry in the way they did in the struggle.

K. D. *Manungo*

References

Arrighi, G. (1973) 'Labour Supplies in Historical Perspective: A Study of the Proletarianization of the African Peasantry in Rhodesia' in: Arrighi and J. Saul *Essays on the Political Economy of Africa*, New York.

Caute, D. (1983) *Under the Skin, The Death of White Rhodesia*, London.

Chater, P. (1984) *Caught in the Cross-fire*, Harare.

Davidson, Basil (1981) *The People's Cause. A History of Guerrillas in Africa*, London.

Frederikse, Julie (1983) *None but Ourselves. Masses vs. Media in the Making of Zimbabe*, Harare.

Kriger, N. (1985) 'Struggles for Independence: Rural Conflicts in Zimbabwe's War of Liberation', Ph.D. thesis, M.I.T., Cambridge, Mass.

Lan, David (1985) *Guns and Rain, Guerillas and Spirit Mediums in Zimbabwe*, London.

Machingaidze, Victor (1976) 'The Development of Settler Capitalist Agriculture in Southern Rhodesia, 1903-1963', Ph.D. thesis, University of London.

Martin, D. and P. Johnson (1981) *The Struggle for Zimbabwe. The Chimurenga War*, London.

Maxey, K. (1975) *The Fight for Zimbabwe. The Armed Conflict in Southern Rhodesia since UDI*, London.

Moyana, Henry V. (1984) *The Political Economy of Land in Zimbabwe*, Gweru.

Ncube, T. V. (1987) 'Peasant Production of Grain Crops in Zimbabwe 1890-1986: An Overview', Henderson Seminar Paper No. 72, Department of History, University of Zimbabwe.

Palmer, R. (1977) *Land and Racial Discrimination in Rhodesia*, London.

Palmer, R. and Parsons, N. (eds.) (1977) *The Roots of Rural Poverty in Central and Southern Africa*, London.

Phimister, Ian (1974) 'Peasant Production and Underdevelopment in Southern Rhodesia' in: *African Affairs*, vol. XIII, pp. 217-25.

Ranger, Terence (1985) *Peasant Consciousness and Guerrilla War in Zimbabwe*, Harare.

van Onselen, Charles (1976) *Chibaro. African Mine Labour in Southern Rhodesia*, London.

Popular Struggles in Zimbabwe's War of National Liberation

Norma Kriger

Introduction

This article is about the mobilization and participation of peasant communities in Zimbabwe's guerrilla war of national liberation. Seminal studies of mobilization and participation in twentieth century revolutions have been pre-eminently about peasants (Barrington Moore 1966; Migdal 1974; Paige 1975; Popkin 1979; Scott 1977: 267-96; Skocpol 1979; Wolf 1969). Despite contending approaches, these studies agree on the importance of co-ordinating peasant action and address the conditions under which it is most likely to occur. Some argue that the effects of capitalism on agrarian class relations and agrarian institutions make peasants potential revolutionaries, but to be politically effective, they need outside alliances and organization (Barrington Moore 1966; Paige 1975; Scott 1979; Wolf 1969). Others place more emphasis on the role of organization and leadership in mobilizing peasants to participate in national revolutions (Migdal 1974; Popkin 1979).

The different approaches and findings of these studies have stimulated lively debate (Skocpol 1982; Cumings 1981; Van Luong 1984), but a number of important similarities might profitably be highlighted. Firstly, these studies all focus on the mobilization and participation of male peasants, and neglect how gender conflicts and generational conflicts with unmarried youth might complicate co-ordinating peasant action. Because they regard peasant collective action as a *sine qua non* of revolution, they agree that conflicts inside peasant communities interfere with peasant mobilization and participation. Preoccupied with peasant collective action, they seek the causes of peasant participation in common grievances against the state or landlords. With few exceptions, they are concerned with how revolutionary organizations can use local peasant grievances for their broader, national goals and in this sense adopt the perspective of the organization. Finally, they rarely rely on peasant voices about their experiences in revolution.

Two detailed studies of peasant mobilization and participation in ZANU's guerrilla war, like the general literature on peasant revolutions, address the question of how peasant collective action in support of the guerrillas became possible (Lan 1985; Ranger 1985). Consequently, even though they rely on oral evidence for the war period, and conceptualize the peasant community as internally stratified and differentiated according to gender and generation, they are ultimately interested in how these differences lose political importance in united action. Both maintain that ZANU guerrilla appeals to African cutural nationalism were effective in mobilizing peasants.

This article relies on oral data collected in interviews with peasants, youth, and the African rural élite who supported ZANU's guerrillas. These interviews were conducted in Mutoko district in north-east Zimbabwe in 1981-2 with the assistance of an interpreter. Without denying the importance of peasant grievances against the state and white settlers, I argue that conflicts internal to peasant communities provided compelling motives for many to participate in the war. At the same time, these conflicts undermined the guerrillas' efforts to organize and unite support. From the perspective of peasants and youth, the civilian organizations in which they participated to provide the guerrillas with logistical support, and the guerrillas themselves, were useful resources that empowered them in their local internal struggles for political and social change. Finally, I argue that local agendas were more radical than the guerrilla programme. I turn now to a discussion of four conflicts inside peasant communities that inspired peasants and youth to participate in the guerrilla war of national liberation: youth's revolt against rigid age-based hierarchical relations, expressions of resentment by the least well off against socio-economic differentiation in villages, women's attempts to transform their domestic lives, and stranger lineages' efforts to break the royal lineages' monopoly of specific village powers.

Generational Conflicts

Civilian organizations established by the guerrillas to provide for their logistical needs respected a major generational division in peasant society. Married peasants, or 'parents' as they were called, elected committees and were organized separately from unmarried youth over fifteen years old, referred to simply as 'youth'. The division of civilian organizations into 'parents' and 'youth' wings laid the organizational basis for young people to challenge the authority of their elders. They were aided by the personal influence they sometimes developed with the guerrillas. In the long hours that 'youth' were obliged to spend eating and sleeping with the guerrillas at their base after *moraris* (morale-boosting political sessions), they had an opportunity to develop personal relationships with them. Like 'youth', most guerrillas were young and single and the low status they shared in Shona society helped to strengthen the bonds between them. The different duties of elders (which required much less interaction with the guerrillas) and their generational differences in an age-stratified society were barriers to their developing close ties with 'youth'. At the same time, the relationship between 'parents' and 'youth' changed. 'Youth' became less dependent on their families for food and shelter because they ate and slept with the guerrillas. 'Youth' used the power they acquired from their duties in the support organizations to challenge 'parents' ' authority and control over their lives. The opportunity to alter oppressive constraints imposed by elders on their daily life, I argue, provided an important impetus that helped sustain 'youth's' participation in the guerrilla war. At the same time, their zealotry was costly for elders and interfered with the smooth running of the civilian organizations.

When collecting food and money from the chairmen, 'parents' dwelled on how 'youth' often defrauded them. They produced counterfeit letters requesting money and food from the guerrillas, masqueraded as guerrillas demanding food and money from elders and even held *moraris*, and appropriated money they were supposed to transfer to the guerrillas. 'Youth' confirmed elders' allegations but were largely unconcerned about them. It was elders, deeply disturbed by the 'youth's' abuse of their organizational power, who volunteered information about 'youth's' behaviour. The following comments by war chairmen describe such abuses by 'youth'.

> You might get a letter asking for $100 with a signature of a comrade known to you. Then the same day, or soon after, another letter might arrive with the signature of the same comrade. You get suspicious and take it to the comrades. They could sometimes kill youth who were doing this.

127

Four G. youth disguised themselves as comrades. They went to K. and other villages, carrying wooden guns that looked as if they were comrades' guns. The war was still young and we'd not had much experience of it. That night they collected $15 from parents in K. They even held a *morari* at a parent's home in K. and the parents cooked for them. It was late in the night. Two days later they were arrested and had to give cattle to the villages from which they had taken money. After two days, they wanted to do it again. M. youth arrested them. They were carrying wooden guns. One youth managed to flee that night. The other three were taken to their village chairman. He took them to their parents. Over fifty youth from the affected villages went with them. Their parents were made to each pay three cattle to each of the villages which had been affected. .. About two weeks later, the G. parents went to complain privately to comrades. They said: 'This is what our children have done. But we have been overcharged.' 'What overcharged,' said the comrades. 'Your children have been using our name to cheat the people.' And they then beat the youth at a *morari*. Then comrades told parents that youth would carry letters but the chairman and secretary would carry money to them. The youth would only accompany them.

Youth could forge letters or demand more than the comrades were asking and take the difference. Comrades could beat youth in public at *moraris* for this.

In the guise of executing guerrilla instructions, 'youth' sometimes challenged established social strictures. 'Youth may want to see a girl youth,' said a female 'youth'. 'They would tell the parents that comrades had come and wanted to see the girl. Parents would know it was a story and would say no. Youth would then beat parents.' Providing another example, she continued:

A youth might come and ask for *sadza* [mealie meal porridge]. There'd be some girls in the house and the parents would think the boy youth is just trying to take advantage. Parents could refuse *sadza*. He could beat them. Some youth were cruel.

Perhaps pointing to gender-based differences, a male 'youth' leader empathized with 'youth' and lambasted 'parents' for not letting their daughters stay with them in the mountains.

> They feared that their daughters would become pregnant. But we had our rules not to touch women. We would have to beat the parents sometimes before they let their daughters live in the mountains.

'Youth' repeatedly exceeded guerrilla instructions. When the guerrillas instructed 'parents' to avoid using roads they had landmined, 'youth' on occasions tried to stop 'parents' from using all roads. Also, the guerrillas had requested that neither they nor 'youth' be fed okra, certain vegetables and certain groundnuts. 'Youth' might stretch this order, demanding that 'parents' stop growing these foods for themselves too, and dig up their gardens or stand in their fields killing the plants. 'Youth' sometimes interpreted guerrilla orders to limit beer drinking as an instruction to outlaw it. A village party official and an elected member of the recently introduced village courts described how 'youth' found his brother at a beer-drink, and although 'there was nothing illegal about drinking... they took him to his house and beat him thoroughly with clubs and thick sticks.' When he himself was brewing beer one night, and 'youth came and spoke offensively', he told them it was not an offence and they left him. 'Youth' would sometimes beat 'parents' who refused to attend *moraris* although this violated their disciplinary code. Even when 'youth' merely informed elders of a *morari*, the latter found the imperiousness with which they did so offensive.

Many 'youth' defied guerrilla instructions that prohibited them from killing or beating alleged 'sell-outs' - their duty was merely to report and take them to the guerrillas, who would investigate the case. A village head who survived to tell the story of how he had been called an informer and assaulted by 'youth' illustrates 'youth's' heavy-handed abuse of power.

> Youth came once and threatened to kill me. They called me a sell-out. It was night and very dark. They knocked on my door and took me to where there was a *kurova guva* [the ceremony a year after a funeral at which the deceased's assets are distributed]. They'd been drinking. I could not see them clearly because it was so dark. I thought they were comrades because they'd made themselves guns like comrades' guns. At the *kurova guva* they beat me hard. They blamed me for being a sell-out because I was always being seen with the soldiers. It was the time the Guard Force engine had been stolen and soldiers were daily taking me

to the keep for interrogation. I couldn't explain this to them. They gave me no chance to talk. They just beat. I think this happened in the year the war ended. Someone else reported it to the comrades. I didn't. I thought that they were comrades.

'Youth' might even inform against their parents. Kersten England hints at conflicts between female *mujibas* (young people acting as messengers for the guerrillas) and their parents. According to a 1978 report, 'many women have been beaten to death... after they had been reported to the guerrillas for practising witchcraft... daughters have been indirectly responsible for the deaths of their parents' (England 1982). 'Youth's' challenge to their parents was summed up in their assertive claim: 'We are not your sons. We are the sons of Zimbabwe.'

Although critical of the speed with which guerrillas resolved cases involving 'sell-outs', elders depicted them as judicious, reasonable and less cruel when contrasted with 'youth'. When 'youth's' violations of their rules of conduct were reported to the guerrillas, they would intervene and punish the offenders, as the village head's tale reveals.

> ...I learned it'd been youth, and comrades had beaten them for their behaviour. That same day they beat the youth, they (comrades) came to my home and held a *morari*. Only people from G. village were here. That night they just said: 'Old man, can we see you.' Privately they asked me what had happened. They understood my story about the soldiers always calling to interrogate me about the engine. There was another old man whom the youth had reported to the comrades for selling beer to the Guard Force. But there was nothing wrong with it. Comrades listened privately to his story and understood.

Three weeks later, though, the 'youth' had their revenge.

> They said comrades had sent them to beat me. They broke into the house and beat me and my wife so hard that we were ill for three weeks. I never reported this because they said they'd been sent by comrades. They accused me of being a good farmer and using medicines that enabled me to farm better than others.

A black Catholic father also stressed the role of 'youth' in unnecessary killings of villagers and how guerrillas sometimes tried to intervene.

> *Mujibas* would use personal hatred to identify sell-outs. Many people who were innocent were killed by *mujibas*. *Mujibas* would condemn sell-outs before the comrades. Comrades might trust their version and kill innocent people. *Mujibas* themselves killed people. Many *mujibas* were killed by comrades for killing innocent people.

Too often, according to a war chairman, the guerrillas' intervention was belated.

> Sometimes people would get beaten as sell-outs when they weren't really. It was just hatred... Some days later it'd be discovered that you were innocent. There was nothing that could be done. You'd been beaten. Comrades could apologize to you.

A headmaster described how he would deliberately try to leave *moraris* before alleged 'sell-outs' were publicly beaten. On the other hand, 'youth' were very interested in this. They'd usually find the traitor and then join in beating the person. Why 'youth' were so prominent in killing and reporting 'sell-outs', according to a black civil servant in Mugabe's government, had to do with their low status in Shona society.

> The *mujibas* were very poor. They usually came from the fifth class in African society. They had no cattle or animals of any kind. They were essentially implementing vendettas against rich people in the community. Class one are businessmen; class two are employed people - teachers and government officials; class three are people with cattle and a plough; class four are people with cattle but no plough; and class five are people without any animals.

Yet if 'youth' were depicted as the ultimate villains, they were paradoxically also seen by elders as the real heroes of the war. Like many others critical of the 'youth's' cruelty, a teacher still paid tribute to them.

> In fairness to the youth, they were very important. They were like a telegraph system. They worked harder than many

131

comrades. While the comrades ate good food and slept at the base, they'd run messages all night, often going hungry. They slept in caves. With their few grenades, they killed many. They were more effective and daring than comrades.

Elders' greater respect for the role of the 'youth' during the war may reflect their continuing personal links to village 'youth', whereas guerrillas left the villages after the war. Also, the praise of 'youth' may have been influenced by the widespread perception after the war that they had been unfairly treated. While ex-guerrillas were integrated into the army or received government money to retrain and enter the civilian sector, 'youth' were not compensated for their sacrifices during the war, including the disruption of their schooling.

'Parents' and the rural élite were concerned about the reversal in the authority relationship with 'youth'. Denying any problem with 'youth' in his area, a war chairman offered a commonly held prescription for retaining control.

A chairman should have control over the youth, the children. Some lost control. If the youth did something wrong the first time, he should question them. Otherwise they keep doing more and more things wrong.

He goes on to suggest why 'parents' often let their authority slip: 'Maybe the reason for the chairman not asking the youth in the first place is that they were frightened of them.' Even after the war, the arrival of a former 'youth' leader could intimidate a group of elders. Later my interpreter inquired: 'Did you notice how frightened they were of him? They all became quiet and hardly looked at him.' On another occasion, he contrasted the lack of aplomb of 'youth' interviewees with their self-assurance and ability to inspire fear in elders during the war.

If you had seen the girl youth leader from my village during the war, you would not believe it were the same person today. Today she is useless. But then! You would have been scared of her. She was frightening. People who were very good in the war are useless today. If people came from town, the rural people could make them look silly with the way in which they would interrogate them, because all townspeople were suspected of being UANC supporters. Now the townspeople come with the cars and the rural people feel silly.

Another device of elders to retain some control of 'youth' was to try to develop personal ties with the 'comrades' and have them confirm instructions passed on from 'youth'. A teacher described their efforts to establish 'a direct relationship with comrades, so when youth would come and say: "Close schools, burn books, no religion - there's no God," we'd say: "Let's go to the comrades." ' Those adults, notably missionaries or teachers, who tried to establish a relationship with the guerrillas often managed to retain control (Ranger 1983; Linden 1979). If a chairman was suspicious of guerrrilla demands conveyed by 'youth', he could take them to the guerrillas to try to authenticate the messages.

I have argued in this section that one of the reasons motivating 'youth' to participate in the war was the opportunity that it gave them to challenge elders' tight control over their daily lives. It kept their enthusiasm for the war high, but it also injected considerable random violence into the day-to-day functioning of the civilian organizations. Anticipating the discussion of gender conflicts, it is instructive to contrast the behaviour of 'youth' and women - both oppressed groups but divided by education, religion, and other variables. Rather than engage in violent acts themselves, women relied on guerrilla violence to express their anger towards their husbands.

If one accepts that 'youth' targeted 'parents' because they were protesting their low status and strict parental control, then one must acknowledge that one of their central grievances was not part of the guerrilla programme. Had ZANU been concerned with changing African social relations, it would have attacked the lineage organization of Shona society that is at the heart of generational relations.

Stratification-Related Conflicts

The organizational features of support work not only coincided with pre-existing generational tensions but also with socioeconomic divisions. 'Parents' and 'youth' in the Tribal Trust Land, where communal land tenure was practised, were organized according to villages. Their organizations were independent of freehold farmers and their children in the Purchase Areas where the lower population density and the individual farmers' greater food supplies reduced the need for cooperative 'parents' committees found in the Tribal Trust Land.

Also, teachers, missionaries, storekeepers, nurses and others who constitute part of the rural élite were not part of the committee system, but contributed as occupational collectivities at their work place. The organization of civilian logistical assistance entrenched socio-economic divisions among rural Africans and gave an organizational basis for the expression of existing socio-economic tensions.

Guerrilla appeals to Africans to withdraw from participating in European institutions also directed attention to Africans who were usually better-educated and/or better-off than most rural Africans and made them vulnerable to being stigmatized as government collaborators. The duty of civilians - especially 'youth' - to report 'sell-outs' to the guerrillas provided an opportunity for those at the bottom of society to unleash their resentments against the better-off and better-educated. In the hunt for 'sell-outs', villagers were advantaged over the guerrillas. They lived among their co-villagers and could observe them day and night whereas the guerrillas interacted with villagers only at night. Consequently, they came to exercise a considerable power in identifying and reporting 'sell-outs' to the guerrillas.

An examination of the behaviour of 'parents' and 'youth' in the guerrilla support organizations in the Tribal Trust Land and how those better off interpreted this behaviour suggests how these socio-economic conflicts were expressed. I argue that a desire for a more even distribution of wealth in the villages was a compelling motivation for many of the poorest and least educated to sustain their interest in the war. The guerrillas, preoccupied with appeals directed at redressing racial inequities, did not address these local concerns for more egalitarian villages.

'Youth' and 'parents' defied guerrilla instructions to raid only white farms for cattle, and stole from African Purchase farmers especially in those parts of the Tribal Trust Land that lay close to Budjga farms. An elected councillor of the post-war district council in Mutoko Tribal Trust Land related how the guerrilla strategy of raiding cattle on white farms 'went wrong'. 'Individuals began to steal from black farmers and ordinary people and sell the meat.' A Purchase Area farmer described how 'initially, people in the reserves gave us a hard time. They stole our cattle, chopped our trees, and were eating so much meat that they called it meat cabbages.'

Better-off farmers were also likely victims of trumped-up charges. The African Farmer's Union, a national body of Purchase Area farmers, reported that 'prominent African farmers are being killed simply because they are better off than most of the people' (African Farmers' Union 1979). A village head in the Tribal Trust Land described how he and his wife had been beaten by 'youth' who accused him of 'being a good farmer' as well as using medicines - witchcraft was prohibited by state law and the guerrillas - that enabled him 'to farm better than others'.

Teachers and headmasters saw some clustering of opinion according to socio-economic background on the issue of school closures among 'parents' and 'youth'. According to one headmaster, 'not all parents wanted the school open. Those whose children weren't at school and were jealous, and ignorant ones, wanted the school closed.' Another noted that 'parents who could not afford to send their children to school or who were having trouble paying school fees would support the idea of closing the schools. Others would want it to stay open.' Some poorer parents, according to one of the headmasters just cited, 'associated education with the enemy. The only educated people whom they knew were blacks in the government - Guard Force, police, soldiers.'

A black Methodist missionary claimed that the key targets were 'teachers, ministers, businessmen... people would make up stories against them.' In the words of a headmaster: 'Parents resent us and businessmen. They see us as having worked with the previous regime. Parents would ask at *moraris*: "What can we do about teachers getting pay from Muzorewa?" ' Teachers resented and scoffed at the memory of 'youth' (and guerrillas) telling them that they had 'come to teach them politics'. They saw in 'youth's' intimidating approach to them a generational and socio-economic challenge.

Villagers often envied those who had jobs in town. A 'special messenger', who was given this position to test his loyalty after being reported as a 'sell-out' claimed:

> People who sold me out to the comrades and told them I was cooking for the army in town were just jealous that I had a job in town. When you stay with people here, they feel that you are the same as them, and then they are happy.

Tensions between employed migrants and rural residents surface in the following account of what happened when members of a migrants' family sought refuge with the head of their household who worked in Harare.

> When we returned here, everything had been taken from the home - even the cement in the kitchen. Only six of the twenty-seven cattle were left. And someone was using our land. It was just hatred because my father was the only man of that age from

K. village working in town. Even today, if we all leave the home, we come back to find sugar and flour all mixed together.

Envy of better-off people operated among resident villagers too. The following observations were made by other villagers about why certain individuals were killed as 'sell-outs':

Some would go privately to the comrades and complain. For instance, if you were jealous of someone who had a lot of cattle...

People might hate you because you have a lot of property; or maybe because you are cruel.

It was just hatred. Maybe you have money to drink beer; maybe you have the same girlfriend; maybe you have a lot of property in your house.

Relatives also sometimes 'sold-out' wealthier or better-educated family members. A man who had been detained under martial law during the war, and who taught from the time of his release until his election as a district councillor forced him to resign his job, drew attention to the ways in which relatives would abuse their powers to name informers:

...if relatives were against you, they'd make it difficult for you by reporting you to comrades. Relatives could be against you because you are wealthier than they are. You must not get too far ahead of them or else there'll be jealousy.

The experience of a 'youth' base commander illustrates how jealous family members might endanger one's life.

One girl reported to comrades that I was bad and intimidated youth and I was nearly killed. But comrades said: 'We know S. He's worked with us for long. He's a very good man.' They beat the girl publicly in front of the parents. The girl was a relative. She'd failed Grade Seven and was just jealous of me because I was educated and the comrades liked me very much. They gave me grenades and later even a gun...

Like the assault of 'youth' on elders, the attacks on better-off people occurred without any formal organization. Rather they were piecemeal, individual acts apparently chiefly by low-status single, unmarried youths, but also all those at the very bottom of the socio-economic hierarchy who used the opportunity presented by the war to vent their anger and envy. While some of their anger may have been motivated by the perception that these groups were collaborators, in the targeting of better-off people there does seem to be a sense that they were acting upon a vision of a more just distribution of wealth. Perhaps theirs was a defensive action to try to restore pre-capitalist norms whereby the rich were responsible for redistributing some of their wealth to the community so that subsistence for all was guaranteed (Scott 1976; Wolf 1969). Their goals were more radical than the guerrillas' in that, unlike the guerrillas, they were concerned with issues of redistribution within the African community.

Gender Conflicts

ZANU and others have pointed to the participation of women and girls in the war as carriers for the guerrillas, and as guerrillas and *chimbwidos* (girl 'youth') as evidence of its commitment to changing gender relations (ZANU Women's Seminar 1979: 15; ZANU(PF) 1984). At the same time, ZANU has been criticized by women within the party and others for the limitations of its programme of transforming gender relations (Ranger 1985; Anon. 1979; ZANU Women's Seminar 1979). Depictions of married women as more conservative than young women fighters, 'youth' and aspirant fighters in the refugee camps and the emphasis on party and guerrilla appeals has resulted in the important individual initiatives of married women to change gender relations being overlooked (England 1982: 134-5; Davies 1983: 82-3, 105). I argue that guerrilla appeals to families to be united and to men to stop beating their wives and drinking excessively originated with married women who saw in the guerrillas potential allies. Their initial success in wining the support of guerrillas gave them a strong motive in continuing to provide support for the guerrillas. However, the guerrillas backed off from promoting their agenda when there was a backlash from married men. Again, demands for changing African social relations were ultimately abandoned by the guerrillas, whose central platform was against racial discrimination and whose views about women were closer to those of their husbands.

According to villagers, guerrillas stumbled upon women's grievances against their husbands. 'Comrades could come through a village at night, hear a woman crying and find her husband beating her,' said a woman. From all accounts, the guerrillas then punished the husbands by beating them. Men felt threatened, and 'husbands would be afraid to do or say anything to wives,' said a primary school headmaster. 'They [the wives] could even call you a sell-out and have you killed.' With the guerrillas as their new allies, women felt empowered and reported to the guerrillas whenever their husbands beat them. Men were not only afraid, but they resented young people intervening in their private lives and constraining them from wife-beating which they perceived as their unquestioned right. A village head found the women's behaviour and the guerrillas' intervention on their behalf unacceptable.

> ...women could purposely refuse to listen to husbands. They knew that if they got beaten, the comrades would beat their husbands. Then husbands wouldn't easily get angry when their wives refused to listen to them.

A primary school headmaster pilloried women during the war, evincing his resentment towards their alliance with the guerrillas.

> Women were asked: 'How are you living with your husbands?' 'We are being harassed,' they answered. 'Would you like us to beat them now?' the comrades would say. 'Yes, yes,' the women would say. ... Comrades were pressing for equal rights in the home, especially as the war drew to an end. Comrades promised equality but they never explained whether they meant equal pay - which we are for - or equality in the home - which we oppose. If a letter comes to a woman, does the man still have the right to open it? 'Yes,' they say.

For a brief period, wives acquired control over their husbands. Without a trace of remorse, a woman said: 'Comrades would beat the husbands publicly. This pleased wives a lot. It brought an end to beatings of women.' And for a while, when 'men complained that comrades were interfering in their private lives' the comrades said, 'We know what men are doing: they go to beer-drinks, get drunk and go home to beat their wives.'

Over time, though, the pleas of men prevailed. A war chairman reported how men in his area negotiated an arrangement with guerrillas:

> We said to them: 'In your home areas, did you ever settle cases between husband and wife?' The comrades then relented. They told women they'd be beaten if they ever brought complaints about their husbands to them. They would deal only with cases relating to the party.

It is difficult to imagine the guerrillas executing effectively a policy of family unity and new standards of morality - prohibitions on adultery and divorce, and mandatory marriage to women who bore one's illegitimate children. The guerrillas displayed obvious contempt for their own prohibitions against sexual intercourse on duty. A teacher said:

> Comrades... became sexual. They took other people's wives and slept with them... They were tempted by money, young girls and women with husbands in Mozambique. They called these women 'their' women. ... They ['youth'] would have to go and get women for the comrades, yet they were told not to touch women.

A female guerrilla's report about the attitudes of her male comrades to birth control also raise questions about the depth of their commitment to changing gender relations. In her words, 'some of the male comrades did not like contraceptives because they thought it was murder, but really it was our duty and we female comrades were ready to defend it' (Davies 1983: 105). In a novel on the war, the Zimbabwean author Stanley Nyamfukudza captures the attitudes of guerrillas themselves to women when he relates how a guerrilla leader dismissed the ineffectiveness of 'fat politicians' who negotiated with the Smith government: 'They are all women, I don't want to hear about that!' (Nyamfukudza 1980: 108).

I have argued that married women initiated efforts to change the behaviour of their husbands towards them, and competed with men for the ear of guerrillas in their campaign. After initial success, the guerrillas withdrew their support from women and were won over by husbands' protests that they stay out of their personal lives. To appreciate why women participated in the war, one must take into account their efforts to take advantage of the war situation to try to improve their domestic lives.

Stranger/Royal Lineage Conflicts

Hilda Kuper's ethnographic survey of the Shona states that the division between members of the chief's patrilineage (*mucinda*) and commoners/foreigners/strangers (*vatorwa*) does not imply political or social subordination, but simply a distinction of origin between the lineage of the chief and others. She claims that no member of the chief's patrilineage, unless he occupies a position of authority in the tribal structure, ranks higher than a stranger (Kuper 1955: 28). Yet there is evidence that during the colonial period the perception grew that the incumbent rulers, through their policies of favouritism toward family members, had turned the chief's patrilineage into a local ruling class and strangers into a socially and politically subordinate group. Unable to compete for hereditary positions of chief and headman, strangers sought political influence on school committees, in nationalist party politics and independent churches (Garbett 1969: 307-326; Day 1980: 85-109).

During the war, the opportunity arose for strangers to usurp hereditary 'traditional' leaders' pre-colonial rights to hear court cases and allocate land. The war offered them two resources with which to compete against 'traditional' leaders: the war committees and the guerrillas whose fears about 'traditional' leaders being potential government informers they could exploit. Strangers' interests in eliminating the right to rule based on birth into a ruling lineage gave them a powerful motive to participate in supporting the guerrillas. Their interest in democratizing village politics was not part of the guerrilla programme, although the guerrillas were responsive to them when they represented a majority in their wards. In two of the four wards I worked in, the challenge mounted by strangers was unambiguous, and I describe below what occurred in these two wards. What happened in the other two wards is more complicated and space does not permit a discussion here.

In Nyamatsahuni and Nyakuna wards, war committees were dominated by strangers who in these wards were people who did not belong to the ruling Shumba (lion) totem. How did they come to occupy a virtual monopoly of the committee positions? On the one hand, they repeatedly claimed that the 'traditional' rulers and other potential ruling families of the Shumba totem eschewed positions and 'pushed' them into committee work, upholding a division of labour in which strangers did all the undesirable tasks.

> It is true that the war jobs were done by us. We are the *varanda* or *tonga* [slaves] of the Shumba. Traditionally, the difficult jobs are done by us. The Shumba only lead when the jobs are easy.

> Yes, the Shumba were afraid to die during the war. They could just give their sons-in-law and nephews the jobs. You could hardly refuse. The father-in-law could just say: 'Son- in-law, you take the job.' (Intra-clan marriages are unusual, and most of the men in his village were married to Shumba women.)

> I could not have refused. I am a Nhari [totem]. If I had refused, the people would have reported me to the comrades as a sell-out. The Shumbas could refuse and not be reported. It was their right to refuse, because they are Shumba.

> Don't think it was a position given to me out of respect. They pushed these jobs on to us. They were cowards. Traditionally, in Mutoko people who were not Shumba were called *varanda*. They were given a little land by the Shumba. The land would be smaller than the plots given to Shumba and usually less fertile too. We were never given gardens. They were reserved for the Shumba. At *dares* [traditional court hearings], we could not participate. But after the *dare*, they might send us to skin a goat for them to eat. We used to do their dirty work. The messengers of the headman were always *varanda*. How had the district commissioner's office made the mistake of registering the Rukau people as one of the families amongst whom the headmanship rotated? Because the messenger was from the Rukau family, and he was always going to the district commissioner's office, so that the people there thought that he was the headman himself! We sweep the ancestral graves of the Shumba; we collect the wood to make the fires for traditional beer-drinks, the *munga* [bulrush millet] or *rapoko* [finger millet] to make the beer, and we cook it. Then the Shumba drink the beer and clap hands to the spirits. The following morning, when they have already had lots to drink, they will give us some beer and tell us to disperse. We cannot go into the chief's *dare* where the Shumba drink. Since Nehoreka [the Shumba founding father] and Makati [a chief who once occupied the land] fought and Nehoreka won, this has been going on. Before the war, if they did not like us, they could chase

us off their land. But during the war we were building our homes near to their houses and using land we were not supposed to. They were too scared to do anything. Today, they are starting again.

Shumba were happy not to do the jobs in the war because they were dangerous.

Shumba were afraid to die... The Shumba didn't respect war leaders.

But strangers were not passive as Shumba 'pushed' them on to war committees, and by collective action tried to use the war committees to take control of local politics from the Shumba ruling families. 'Maybe other totems used the war as an opportunity to choose other people as their leaders,' said a stranger who was on a war commit-tee. 'Shumba are proud and they claim they are the owners of the land.' To cite another committee member: 'The whole village com-mittee was not-Shumba. We deliberately left Shumba out because they were always so proud. When they'd go to listen to a case at their headman, they'd not tell us.' Another justification for con-sciously excluding Shumba ruling families from committees, in ac-cord with a desire to wrest power from them, was that they were collaborators or potential traitors.

For sure there were no Shumba on war committees. Most of the kraalheads [village heads] etc. were Shumba and were being re-ferred to as sell-outs. That's why they weren't chosen. Take this village. The kraalhead is Shumba. You can't elect his children. They are not kraalheads, but they are his children.

Once strangers had control of the committees, they behaved in ways that suggest that they intended to take power from 'traditional' rulers. Although the exercise of power over civilian affairs was lim-ited by the war, chairmen sometimes tried to redistribute unused land that village heads had appropriated unfairly for their 'unborn children and unmarried sons' to those who had no land or insuffi-cient land. More frequently 'strangers' simply took the initiative and began to plough land wherever they liked, realizing that the Shum-ba leaders generally had no effective civilian powers during the war. War committees also tried to assert power by settling disputes. With the war, Shumba rulers' judicial powers were increasingly eroded by martial law and the guerrillas' involvement in disputes ranging from divorce and adultery to punishing alleged informers. Through negotiation with guerrillas, committees carved out a space where they could assert power: the settlement of disputes that arose in the context of the support organizations.

The perspective of Shumba from non-ruling families adds credence to the perceptions of strangers. They acknowledged that 'traditional' rulers were not interested in committee positions and disregarded committee work. A Shumba villager explained that headman Nyakuna had not been involved in committee work 'partly because he was a government servant, so if he took up such a position, he might get into trouble from the government'. Implicitly condoning the hierarchy of power relations, he continued: 'Also, people respected him as a headman and didn't want him to run risks running back and forth to the comrades.' When asked why the Shumba did not choose a person they respected to be a war leader, he answered that 'the headman had enough to do as headman'. Another Shumba denigrated committee work and confirmed the strangers' view that it was 'pushed' on to them.

> During the war we chose other totems to lead the people. Shumba had other positions: kraalheads, headmen and chiefs... We thought it was just a position for organizing things in the war... The other totems also did not want Shumba to have positions because they said that we already had positions. People don't like Shumba - they say we are proud.

A Shumba teacher drew attention to the old age of 'traditional' leaders that made them unsuited for physically demanding work, but also alluded to the impropriety of 'traditional' rulers doing menial support work.

> Kraalheads were not usually elected to committees. They were important people and often old. They couldn't be expected to move around much. Also, it was dangerous work.

The Shumba ruling families also supported the strangers' account of how they came to control the war committees. In both Nyamatsahuni and Nyakuna, ruling families were quite content to let strangers take control of the war committees, perceiving them as temporary organizations that would cease to exist after the war and fully anticipating a restoration of the status quo. This expectation was strengthened by the respect the guerrillas showed the ruling

Shumba, calling on them to offer prayers to the spirits at the beginning and end of *moraris*. Over time, the responses of the ruling families in each ward diverged. In Nyamatsahuni, the ruling families continued to ignore the committee's challenge; in Nyakuna, the ruling families fought back and reasserted control.

How can one explain their different responses? Two factors seem pertinent. Firstly, in Nyakuna ward strangers were a numerical minority. If the Shumba acted collectively and rallied around their rulers, they could stymie an assault from strangers. By contrast, strangers were a majority in Nyamatsahuni ward and even if the Shumba ruling families had assumed a leadership role, the power of numbers was against them. Secondly, headman Nyakuna had a history of being anti-government and a member of nationalist parties, whereas the former headman Nyamatsahuni had a history of government collaboration. Headman Nyamatsahuni had angered even villagers from the ruling clan shortly before the war by reporting the authentic medium of their ancestral spirit to the government as an impostor. What happened when the guerrillas visited him in 1976 unfolded slowly, in 'dribs and drabs', because members of his family who had been there were too intimidated to report the incident. Apparently, he was accosted by 'a gang of terrorists' who stripped him of his badge of office, symbolizing the removal of his powers, and some cash. 'They told him they would probably visit him at his kraal the next day. Although not clear, it appears they did so and this time took a pair of handcuffs and a muzzle loader.' They instructed him to call a meeting of his village heads and inform them he was no longer 'chief' and that they were no longer rulers in the area. One day later, he committed suicide of which there was some history in his family (Saunders 1976). Nobody was willing to fill the headmanship after his death, and so the most important political position of the ruling lineage in that ward remained vacant during the war.

The competition between strangers and ruling lineages in Nyamatsahuni and Nyakuna wards may be interpreted as the first opportunity in the colonial period to subject 'traditional' institutions and individual rulers to majority opinion without the government intervening. Although the guerrillas intervened, they tried to do so with due regard to public opinion. By organizing on the basis of lineage to wrest control of the war committees, strangers used the existing pre-colonial lineage organization, but in an innovative way: for the first time non-ruling lineages united in an organized assault on ruling lineages in two wards. The availability of lineage as a basis for organization made the challenge against the ruling lineage the only organized rural civilian protest during the war.

The revolutionary initiative to reconstitute local politics in a more democratic way came from rural people themselves. The guerrillas opposed 'traditional' rulers because of their involvement with government, but never challenged the institution of hereditary offices. When they killed incumbent rulers or encouraged committee members to take power from them or share power with them, the intent was to punish individual 'traditional' rulers for collaborating with the government and give some status and power to the new committees. The guerrillas' agenda never included eliminating the lineage-based, hereditary precolonial political system and broadening the basis for political competition for local power. It is worth recording that the only land redistribution that occurred in the district during the war was within the Tribal Trust Land under the auspices of stranger-dominated war committees. Constrained by the need for popular support, ZANU guerrillas never challenged the oppressive lineage-based, hereditary political institutions, the survival of which owed much to colonial policies. They might follow majority opinion on the issue, but opposition to hereditary rule was not part of their platform.

Conclusion

Theories of revolution correctly regard conflicts within peasant communities as obstacles to collective action. However, they are incorrect to dismiss peasant conflicts as debilitating for revolutionary mobilization and participation. On the contrary, the Zimbabwean case illustrates that conflicts within peasant communities spurred some groups to participate in the war. From the perspective of various local groups, the war was an opportunity to openly express grievances. Formerly powerless, they used their positions in the civilian organizations established to provide logistical assistance to the guerrillas and the guerrillas themselves as resources to press their own agendas. Guerrilla appeals for national liberation were mediated by the different interests of peasants and their children. Subsistence-oriented villagers and poor, uneducated 'youth' rejected socio-economic stratification, and their actions are consistent with a desire for greater egalitarianism within the villages. Strangers belonging to different totems united in two of the four wards studied to end hereditary political rule in the villages. Women tried to improve their marital relations and 'youth' their social status and lack of autonomy. Women and 'youth' lacked the social coherence of strangers, but they sought ways of expressing protest through individual acts and in the case of women, appealed to the guerrillas to intervene on their behalf. The state, settlers, and capitalist imperialism all shaped local conflicts and created grievances, but these and the guerrilla appeals were mediated by the interests of groups within peasant communities. As Anthony Wallace has suggested, human beings 'generally reserve their settled fears, suspicions, and hatreds to those closest to them: kinsmen, neighbours, and colleagues' (Fried et al. 1968: 177).

References

African Farmers' Union (1979) Report of 13 February 1979, Catholic Commission for Peace and Justice Files, Harare.

Anon. (1979) 'ZANU Women Meet', *Southern Africa*, July/August.

Barrington Moore, H. (1966) *Social Origins of Dictatorship and Democracy. Lord and Peasant in the Making of the Modern World*, New York.

Cumings, Bruce (1981) 'Interest and Ideology in the Study of Agrarian Politics' in: *Politics and Society*, vol. 10, no. 4, pp. 467-495.

Davies, Miranda (1983) *Third World - Second Sex. Women's Struggles and National Liberation: Third World Women Speak Out*, London.

Day, John (1980) 'The Insignificance of Tribe in the African Politics of Zimbabwe Rhodesia', *Journal of Commonwealth and Comparative Politics*, vol. 18, no. 1, pp. 85-109.

England, Kersten (1982) 'A Political Economy of Black Female Labour in Zimbabwe, 1900-1980', B.A. thesis, University of Manchester.

Fried, Morton et al. (eds.) (1968) *War: The Anthropology of Armed Conflict and Aggression*, New York.

Garbett, Kingsley (1969) 'Prestige, Status, and Power in a Modern Valley: Korekore Chiefdom, Rhodesia' in: *Africa*, vol. 37, pp. 307-326.

Kuper, Hilda (1955) 'The Shona. Ethnographic Survey of Africa' in: Daryll Forde (ed.) *Southern Africa*, Part IV: *The Shona and Ndebele of Southern Rhodesia*.

Lan, David (1985) *Guns and Rain. Guerrillas & Spirit Mediums in Zimbabwe*. London.

Linden, Ian (1979) *The Catholic Church and the Struggle in Zimbabwe*. London.

Migdal, Joel S. (1974) *Peasants, Politics, and Revolution: Pressures toward Political and Social Change in the Third World*, Princeton.

Nyamfukudza, S. (1980) *The Non-Believer's Journey*, London.

Paige, Jeffrey M. (1975) *Agrarian Revolution: Social Movements and Export Agriculture in the Underdeveloped World*, New York.

Popkin, Samuel L. (1979) *The Rational Peasant. The Political Economy of Rural Society in Vietnam*, Los Angeles.

Ranger, Terence (1983) 'Holy Men and Rural Communities in Zimbabwe, 1970-80' in: W. J. Sheils (ed.) *The Church and War. Studies in Church History*, vol. 20, Oxford.

Ranger, Terence (1985) *Peasant Consciousness and Guerrilla War in Zimbabwe and Mozambique. A Comparative Study*, London.

Saunders, J. F. (1976) Letter from District Commissioner, Mr J. F. Saunders, to Provincial Commissoner, Mashonaland East, 16 September, PER 5/HM/MTK.

Scott, James C. (1977) 'Hegemony and the Peasantry' in: *Politics and Society*, vol. 7, no. 3, pp. 267-296.

Scott, James C. (1976) *The Moral Economy of the Peasant. Rebellion and Subsistence in Southeast Asia*, New Haven.

Skocpol, Theda (1979) *States and Social Revolutions. A Comparative Analysis of France, Russia and China*, Cambridge, Mass.

Skocpol, Theda (1982) 'Review Article: What Makes Peasants Revolutionary?' in: *Comparative Politics*, vol. 14, pp. 351-375.

Van Luong, Hy (1984) 'Agrarian Unrest From an Anthropological Perspective: The Case of Vietnam' in: *Comparative Politics*, vol. 16.

Wolf, Eric R. (1969) *Peasant Wars of the Twentieth Century*, New York.

ZANU Women's Seminar (1979) Women's Liberation in the Zimbabwean Revolution. Materials from..., Maputo.

ZANU(PF) (1984) *Speeches and Documents of the First ZANU(PF) Women's League Conference*, Harare.

Religion and Witchcraft in Everyday Life in Contemporary Zimbabwe

Terence Ranger

Introduction

I had better begin by defining what I mean by 'everyday life'. I do not take this expression to mean private religious experience as opposed to public, microcosmic as opposed to macrocosmic. I take it to refer to the actualities of individual interaction within society, so that we are looking at the complex pluralities of religious ideas and practice rather than artificially isolating one set of ideas or one religious denomination. In this article, I shall take as my unit of study Zimbabwean society as a whole since I shall argue that religious experience in contemporary Zimbabwe has been shaped partly by political, social and economic developments affecting the whole country.

The weight of recent scholarship on Zimbabwean religious experience has fallen, not on describing the 'ordinary' in post-colonial Zimbabwe, but on narrating what happened to the country's various religious traditions during the 'extraordinary' upheavals of the 1970s guerrilla war. It has already become a truism that religious ideas and practices were of central importance in Zimbabwe's *chimurenga*, by apparent contrast to the liberation struggles of Mozambique or Angola. David Lan (Lan 1985) and to a lesser extent myself (Ranger 1985) have emphasized the crucial contribution of spirit mediums. Lan again and Norma Kriger have shown the great increase in witchcraft accusations and the greater increase in executions of 'witches' which accompanied the war (Kriger 1985 and 1988).

But recent work does not only document a 'revival' of so-called 'traditional' religious ideas. I have myself argued (Ranger 1983) that guerrillas were as ready to work with Catholic or Anglican spokesmen for rural popular Christianity as with spirit mediums. Subsequent work seems at times to be arguing that *every* rural/ religious tradition was mobilized on the side of the guerrillas. Thus Hudson Magwa stresses that 'missionaries in general, the Catholics and Methodists in particular, supported the liberation struggle in Nuanetsi' and enjoyed 'cordial relations' with the guerrillas, going so far as to write of the churches' 'revolutionary stance' (Hudson Magwa 1987). In his recent book, Martinus Daneel writes that his research has shown:

> that the Independents' commitment to the liberation struggle was much stronger and more widespread than I had originally thought... Members and leading figures were - at least in the latter years of the war - fully involved in supporting the guerrilla fighters. From the accounts of numerous prophets of the spirit-type churches it is evident that they took part in the wave of witchcraft accusations which marked that period, that they 'prophesied' about many issues to the guerrillas to help them plan their offensives and that some of them were even required to move around with the fighters in the bush to assist the latter with their extra-sensory perception (Daneel 1987: 21-22).

And E. C. Mandivenga, dealing with the rural black Muslim communities in southern Zimbabwe writes that guerrillas visited the Chinyika Muslim Centre and

> instructed the *Imaam* to step up construction activities without further delay, adding that they had no quarrel with either this particular religion or its adherents. They were acutely aware that the liberation struggle had received much moral and material support from some Islamic states. In short, Muslims were unequivocally declared to be on the side of the patriotic guerrillas (Mandivenga 1983: 33).

Religion and the War

Sceptical readers might well begin to think that all this is the product of an oral tradition, which has hastened to claim a connection with the victorious side in the war - and it is indeed notable that all accounts so far of the war years have been based on the testimony of African civilians rather than that of the guerrillas.[1] But, in fact, what this accumulation of work about the war really effects is to show that some members of all religious traditions worked with the guerrillas and were favoured by them, but also that other members of all religious traditions were attacked.

Thus Magwa admits that in Nuanetsi 'some freedom fighters condemned missionaries' - singling out especially guerrillas who had assumed the *chimurenga* names of 'Captain Devil' and 'Soul Sadza' (Magwa 1987). Professor Ngwabi Bhebe, whose contribution to the Moyo and Hallencreutz collection of essays on *Church and State in Zimbabwe* is the fullest treatment of guerrilla-church interactions yet produced, takes as the central problem of his article the contrast between those Lutheran mission stations and schools which were sustained by guerrillas and peasants during the war and those which were threatened or destroyed by them (Bhebe 1988; see also Shiri 1985). Daneel records independent church martyrs at the hands of both the so-called Security Forces and guerrillas and speaks in a far from triumphalist mood:

> We have all paid a price in the liberation struggle which led to the independence of Zimbabwe. You cannot walk through the valley of shadows, with the agony of suffering and destruction marking your world for so long, and emerge unscathed. You cannot constantly walk the edges of your existence and survive without the experience of trauma and wonder (Daneel 1987: 15).

Once again, there is no distinction to be made between African Christianity and 'traditional' religion. Both Lan and I show that some spirit mediums were denounced and killed by guerrillas even as others became close allies (Ranger: 1982).

The impact of the war on Zimbabwe's religious traditions, then, is likely to turn out to be no simple matter of the triumph of some of them over others, but a much more complex business of how each of them experienced trauma and wonder. Nevertheless, despite (or perhaps because of) this, most of the recent scholarship has held the war to have been determinative and has treated the religious history of the post-independence years as a working out of the processes inaugurated by it. This is inevitably the focus of books like mine and David Lan's which carry the story up to 1980 and then look

---

[1]Sister Janice McLaughlin in her on-going research on Catholicism in the war is able to make use of the guerrilla intelligence reports which are stored at ZANU(PF) headquarters, and these may offer a very different perspective.

forward from there, both of us assuming that spirit mediums would go on playing an important role in independent Zimbabwe. It is also the focus of Norma Kriger, whose doctoral thesis argues that the war vastly exacerbated rural conflicts and that these would have no outlet after 1980 except in witchcraft accusations (Kriger 1985).

Others have assumed that the record of particular churches during the war would determine their relations with the new regime - an example of such an approach being Michael Lapsley's very critical examination of the Anglican record prior to 1980 (Lapsley 1986). Yet others argue that the war revealed the legitimacy of Christianity at the grass roots and the irrelevance of the central bureaucratic structures of the church, looking forward to networks of local lay activity in independent Zimbabwe (Linden 1980). After 1980, indeed, a radical Christian organization, Buriro/Esizeni, came into brief existence to argue precisely the case that

> outside of formal church programmes the people of Zimbabwe were reflecting critically on the meaning of their Christian faith in the context of the liberation war... The liberation war had changed congregations from unquestioning passive recipients of the word coming from authority, into challenging, analytical thinkers who recognize that degree of authority which is in themselves (see Ranger 1987b).

Finally, several authors have stressed the need for religious traditions to contribute to the healing process after the war. Gordon Chavunduka, President of the Zimbabwe National Association of Traditional Healers - and Professor of Sociology - writes:

> The end of the liberation war in Zimbabwe led to an increase in the work-load of many healers. A large number of religious and family rituals which could not be held during the war were held after the war. In the majority of cases traditional healers [amongst whom Chavunduka includes spirit mediums] are required at these rituals. They help to organize and preside at the ceremony (Chavunduka 1986: 37).

The stresses induced by the war called for Christian healing also. In 1979 and 1980 Zimbabwe's first black Catholic Archbishop assigned Brother Chisiri to work with distressed refugee women from the war-torn countryside:

> Chisiri liberated refugee women from their identity confusion
> caused by what had happened on the death of their husbands.
> Their husbands had been executed by guerrillas during the war;
> their bodies had been left unburied; neither the wives nor any
> other villagers had been allowed to mourn them. These women
> had been unable to release their grief; they felt separated from
> society and culture through their failure to give their husbands
> proper burial. Chisiri and his eight dedicated volunteer Catholic
> mothers moved into the refugee camps to find people 'who had
> lost hope, for whom life had become meaningless, people with
> big wounds that none could heal, but only God himself'. Chisiri
> began to try to work among these people, but it became intolera-
> ble to him to see the suffering of the afflicted. 'Every evening
> when I got back to my little camping room and tried to look back
> on the day or tried to say the Divine Office, which I love, I could
> see only the faces of mothers with tears in their eyes ... Trying to
> think was a nightmare' (see Ranger 1987b: 154-5).

Chisiri developed a method of healing based upon an enactment of
'traditional' rural community mourning, in which he and his volun-
teers joined, 'sitting down with them, crying and shouting and
howling, and after that talking with them about their husbands'.
Finally, when 'guilt, anger, sadness had been poured out..., the
women were then asked to forgive themselves for their thoughts of
despair and suicide. Everyone helped them formulate plans for the
future.'

Martinus Daneel, who 'through the years of the liberation of
Zimbabwe, lived and worked among the leaders and members of
the Shona Independent Churches' and together with them built
Fambidzano, the Conference of Independent Churches, writes that
'after independence many of us needed time to adapt, to change, to
emerge from the inner wilderness of alienation and hurt, to capture
a new vision for the tasks of everyday'. But he also goes on to urge
that the independent churches, experts in what he calls 'the quest
for belonging', are supremely qualified to create such a new everyday religion (Daneel 1987: 15).

Terence Ranger

Healing the Wounds

The aftermath of the war has called for a great outpouring of the religious imagination, for the development of myths and liturgies which can turn death and destruction into sources of strength and redemption. Every religious tradition has its martyrs to celebrate and invoke. Every district has its 'heroes' acres' in which are gathered together the scattered bones of the unburied war dead and which require sanctification (Ranger 1987a).

Bearing all this in mind, then, we can reasonably assert that the experience and memories of the liberation war constitute a crucial common framework for the practice of everyday Zimbabwean religion. Moreover, until recently, some parts of Zimbabwe remained in a state of war. Reports by African clergy from Matabeleland prior to the unity agreement remind us strongly of the experience of the churches during the 1970s elsewhere in Zimbabwe. 'It is now quiet again,' wrote one black priest in February 1987, 'after hundreds of' people were forced to walk long distances... The soldiers did this after the dissidents had killed about three people. This is the Fifth Brigade under a commander who used to call himself Jesus... Who is then on the people's side? Praise God. He is with us in the countryside.' In parts of eastern Zimbabwe, too, people are still being killed by mines laid in the 1970s and are now exposed to raids by the Mozambique National Resistance Movement (cf. e.g. Mutamba 1987).

In the refugee camps in eastern Zimbabwe, where Shona-speaking displaced persons seek to construct some sort of meaning in their constrained lives, there has been an outburst of local religious innovation. An inquiry by Christian Care found no signs of hierarchical religious affiliation - no Catholics, Methodists or Anglicans - but many Apostles, Witnesses and members of new sects, created in the camps themselves and already with their own elected Bishops and Prophets (de Wolf 1987). Christian Care also found many Mozambican diviners, mediums and witch-cleansers in the camps, exerting their own influence upon the everyday calculations of refugees. In Tongogara camp in Chipinge district, for example, a series of accidents and epidemics was explained by the anger of the unpropitiated ancestral spirit owners of the land on which the camp had been built. Refugees refused to build permanent huts there until these spirits had been propitiated: the Zimbabwean authorities replied that it was state land and that the state does not have spirit ancestors. Christian Care spent two years in research, finally establishing who were locally accepted as the spirit owners of the land; they then bought a sacrificial beast, cleansing ceremonies were performed and the huts were built. In these camps we are still in the everyday world of the war.

Nevertheless, it would certainly be mistaken and misleading to see everyday religion in contemporary Zimbabwe just as the working out of the transformations of the war. For one thing, many of the confident expectations of those who wrote during the war or just after it have been confounded. The bureaucratic hierarchies of the mission-descended churches have conspicuously *not* withered away. Indeed they have become more relevant than ever as government calls on the churches for assistance with education, health and rural development. It is a structure like Buriro/Esizeni which has faded away, and the Christian Council of Zimbabwe which has flourished.

Nor have war-time allegiances turned out to be decisive. It seemed the most plausible of assumptions that the United Methodist Church would be fatally disadvantaged after the war by the leadership of Bishop Abel Muzorewa, who had used the presses and the pulpits of the church to support the cause of the UANC and the Internal Settlement. Methodist radicals tried in vain after the war to overthrow Muzorewa and to replace him by a leader with better liberation credentials. Yet since Muzorewa has repudiated his political career and undertaken to act merely as a church leader there has been a rapid transformation in relations between Methodism and the state. The *Manica Post* of February 13th 1987 under the headline 'Muzorewa Praises the Government' described a virtual love-in between the Bishop and Edgar Tekere, then Chairman of ZANU(PF) in Manicaland. Muzorewa asserted that 'the United Methodist Church has been able to work freely in Manicaland to implement its development programme with the full support of both the government and the ruling party.' He thanked Tekere particularly for acting to evict 'squatters' from the church's land at Mutambara Mission - an ironic reversal of the expectations aroused by the war. For his part, Tekere said that 'he did not want to see any malcontents disturbing church business', promised to visit every Methodist church in the province to discuss development goals, and praised the UMC for its 'progressive' idea of a Methodist University of Manicaland.

Moreover, there is a real sense of the exceptional character of some of the religious innovations of the war and of the need to return to a peace-time everyday religion. On August 31st 1987, I had a long talk with the Reverend Ambrose Makuwaza, pastor of the Church of God in Chiduku Communal Land, Makoni District. I had talked with Makuwaza soon after the war and heard from him then of the traumas and wonders of the liberation struggle. Makuwaza's church is linked to an Afro-American prophetic illumination which sees blacks as the lost tribes of Israel and Christ as the fulfilment of the Mosaic Law. Before 1980, he was regarded as heretical by mission churches, independent churches and spirit mediums alike. Today, he presides over the Rusape Ministers Fraternal and leads the prayers of sanctification at the Rusape 'heroes' acre', where five thousand murdered guerrillas and *mujibas* lie jumbled together. His church has been recognized as a co-operative society by the Government and given Copper Island farm in Headlands - now re-named Bethel - to work collectively.

Makuwaza is very aware that he has entered a new era, which calls for new everyday preaching and practice. 'Like the Jews,' he told me, 'we Shona are a people who believe that it is a crime to shed innocent blood, which pollutes the land. In the liberation war we tried hard to learn how to kill. But now we can forget that again.' Preaching at the 'heroes' acre', Makuwaza deliberately broke away from the idea of the continued and active existence of the spirits of the dead. 'It is right to remember those who died,' he told the gathering. 'But the dead cannot hear you. The only Saints are those true believers who are alive.' For him the contemporary task of religion is to shape current Zimbabwean civil society. 'Mugabe is a very, very clever Prime Minister. This Marxist-Leninism is one thing we are not worried about. Judaism believes in sharing; so does Shona tradition. But you cannot make Africans materialist. That's impossible. Our socialism will *have* to be very different.'

Religion in Present Everyday Life

In a collection of essays on Zimbabwe's political economy, Ibbo Mandaza takes to task those romantic expatriate radicals who propagate 'the mythology that has developed around the issue of the *armed struggle* ' (Mandaza 1986: 4). Such persons argue that the armed struggle produced a truly popular revolutionary ideology and assess post-1980 Zimbabwe according to whether the government has been true to this revolutionary potential. Inevitably, they find that the revolution has been betrayed. Mandaza argues that it is absurd to see contemporary Zimbabwe only in the light of the liberation war, which was not in any case nearly as radicalizing as is often made out. Prospects for socialism in Zimbabwe have to be assessed on the basis of an analysis of society and economy as they have developed since the end of the war. The war was basically about freeing various and conflicting African interests to take action on their own behalf; since the war Zimbabwe's class balance has changed radically. There is no chapter about religion in Mandaza's book (and no index entry either), but we might sensibly take his message to heart when considering the modern religious history of Zimbabwe. The crucial general context in which Zimbabwe's religious traditions are now working out their everyday responses is not the war and its legacy, but Zimbabwe's developing society and economy.

Thus it is certainly possible to make a sort of crude preliminary class analysis of recent developments within Zimbabwean Christianity. If Makuwaza is out to spiritualize Zimbabwean collectivism, others are out to give spiritual sanction to accumulation. Press and television have been much scandalized by the development of the Jesus movement of Mudjigiwa Dzangare, for instance. I regret that I have no testimony from inside the movement, but to those outside it, the founder's business entrepreneurialism is as much a disproof of his claims as his crippled body:

> I am greatly surprised and confused by the man who claims himself to be the son of God. We have a good Government and a pure Jesus. We do not want confusion within the nation. Jesus died being a complete man... How can Jesus be crippled? How can Jesus marry three wives and run some business enterprises? Although there are prophesied activities to symbolize when Jesus is about to return, why necessarily upon you, rich crippled man? (Ncube 1987).

The press is equally hostile to fundamentalist movements of American and South African origin which attract large followings in Zimbabwe with their gospel of enterprise. In June 1987, one of my former Manchester students teaching in Zimbabwe wrote to describe his visit to such a body, the Rhemer Word of God Church in Harare:

> This is a South African transplant with big links with... the United States. It preaches 'Health, Wealth and Prosperity,' and seems to be a church of the rich seeking to make God in their own image. Through crude use of one or two psalms taken out of

context, the preacher argued that any Christian who was poor lacked faith, as God wants to bless everyone with riches. He likewise assured those assembled that God also wishes none to die of sickness. Much was made of the collection which was taken by blazered stewards. The worship was nice and charismatic so that all those assembled could lose themselves in it (Maxwell 1987).

The Zimbabwe Christian Council, representing interests and a theology somewhere between Makuwaza and the Rhemer Church, have called on the government to ban both the Jesus movement and the new fundamentalist sects.

I want to conclude this article by arguing that what is true for Zimbabwean Christianity - i.e. that it is engaged in everyday response to contemporary Zimbabwean society - is true also for socalled 'traditional' religion. Let us take the spirit mediums. Their future position seemed to be guaranteed by the war, from which many of them emerged with salaries from ZANU(PF), regularly consulted by the newly elected village committees of the party, and hailed in parliamentary debates as spokesmen for the ancestral spirits who had 'won the war for us'.

Since 1980 the government has sought to institutionalize its alliance with the mediums. Herbert Ushewokunze, then Minister of Health, made no secret of his regular consultations with the Nehanda medium. It was he who was largely responsible for the formation of the Zimbabwe National Traditional Healers Association, ZINATHA, in July 1980. The Certificate of Registration for ZINATHA bears photographs of Mbuya Nehanda and Sekuru Kagubi, spirit mediums executed in 1897, whom Chavunduka describes as 'healers who led the resistance to British colonialism'. The certificate describes ZINATHA as an organization 'for traditional medical practitioners including Spirit Mediums'. In short, ZINATHA defines the mediums primarily as healers and seeks to bring them into a bureaucratically structured national organization, with its own council to enforce proper practice.

But the continuation of the war-time alliance has proved much more difficult than government anticipated. Gordon Chavunduka told me in the summer of 1987 that senior spirit mediums resent being lumped together with herbalists and diviners; that they refuse to apply for ZINATHA membership; and that ZINATHA nevertheless sends them registration cards so as to 'get them on the list'. In

August 1987, four spirit mediums expressed their discontent with
ZINATHA;

> Your directive that any traditional healer... practising at places
> away from their homes must register such clinics with the
> Traditional Medical Council... is absolutely unnecessary and
> grossly unfair... We maintain as a matter of right that any tradi-
> tional healer is free to travel anywhere in the world... We would
> like to point out that we are guided in everything we do by our
> ancestral spirits. We are bound by tradition and practice to obey
> these spirits. Your directive conflicts with this tradition and prac-
> tice. This may be due to the fact that you and many of your
> committee-members are ordinary herbalists who acquired herbal
> knowledge through correspondence or conventional schooling...
> We see it as a very good thing that healers should visit other
> countries because that helps them to acquire experience and fresh
> knowledge which can be most useful to Zimbabwe as a whole
> (Mathanzima, Moyo, Moyo, Ngwenya 1987: 16).

This fascinating assertion that the spirit bloweth where it listeth
upholds 'traditional' mobility against modern bureaucratic localism!

In my view many of the other clashes between the policies of the
state and spirit mediums are not due either to the fact that mediums
have relapsed from war-time militancy into mere traditionalism. I
think the continuity really resides in the fact that both during the
war and today many mediums speak for the interests of the smaller
peasantry against the developing interventions of the state. Thus
there is a good deal of tension between mediums and the increasingly powerful conservationists. The four mediums quoted above
complain further that they are prosecuted by the Department of
Parks and Wild Life Management for possessing 'parts of certain
protected animals, snakes and birds', and there have been other
protestations by mediums against the growing authoritarianism of
the department. Often mediums complain that bureaucratic conservation overlooks and overrides their own spirit-legitimated rules for
environmental control. Writing in the *Newsletter of the Prehistory
Society of Zimbabwe* in October 1986, Josiah Moyo complains of the
problems of conserving 'monuments associated with traditional
spirits':

> Entry to them is highly restricted... Everything in them is highly
> secret. Nothing is supposed to be done or touched without first
> invoking the Mhondoro Spirit which may grant or refuse

permission. Indirectly this practice does curb vandalism by humans, but directly nourishes other destructive agents.

Moyo recognizes that 'force will only result in an unquenchable enmity' but in other instances local administrators have allowed the destruction of spirit groves - even while enforcing conservation rules (Moyo 1986: 3).

Press silence about the spirit mediums is occasionally broken to reveal other clashes with official policy. Thus mediums have been reported to have ordered so-called 'squatters' to move on to alienated land in Mashonaland North, so as to claim ancestral territories, and in other cases government has had mediums placed under temporary house arrest, while squatters have been forcibly removed from land. Mediums are reported to be opposing the government's emphasis under the five-year plan for the communal areas on 'villagization', i.e. movement of population into centralized settlements, which is widely unpopular with peasants in many parts of Zimbabwe. In these and other cases, I see the mediums as employing an appeal to tradition so as to represent patterns of peasant everyday life against the Zimbabwean state. In this instance, the government is more trapped in the memory of war-time alliances than the mediums are. Reluctant to denounce mediums as a whole as reactionary, but needing to distinguish between 'good' and 'bad' ones, Robert Mugabe got himself into a definitional tangle in early 1986, as he opened the first, and so far the only, district Culture House in Murewa:

> The Prime Minister denounced bogus spirit mediums... Some people were using the nation's belief in culture and tradition as a means to make easy money. 'What we want is the truth which is accepted by the people in the area.' He had heard of a person living in Highfield who claimed he was a spirit medium of the nation. This man had tea, bread and and butter for breakfast, drove a car and even claimed protection from law enforcement agents of the state. 'We don't want such a spirit medium who chooses to stay in the bright lights of the city and forsakes Murewa' (*Sunday Mail* , 26 February 1986).

Wanting to denounce some mediums for being too local and 'traditional', Mugabe ended up denouncing others for not being local and traditional enough.

Occasionally, one does indeed come across a report which sounds fully traditional. Thus on May 22nd 1987, the *Manica Post* reported that a 'Zimunya chieftainess' had been ordered to pay $90 defamatory damages for accusing one Milia Simango of causing the drought by witchcraft, whereas as the Presiding Officer insisted 'drought was an act of God'. The chieftainess 'said she was ordered by the spirit medium to deliver the message.' Those who have commented on witchcraft belief in Zimbabwe since 1980 have indeed seen it either as continuous from the war, or continuous in a deeper sense as a manifestation of immemorial superstition. Norma Kriger writes that 'the violence of the war is likely to be perpetuated, veiled as witchcraft and sorcery'; that the war 'had not solved local conflicts. Rather it had injected new divisions into an already divided society'; and that witchcraft accusation would continue to be 'an indicator of a deeply divided society' (Kriger 1988).

She illustrates her point with reference to the employment in Mutoko district in 1980 and 1981 of a Tanzanian witch-finder, Mataka, who claimed 'the authority of the healing spirit medium Nehoreka, ZANU(PF) and Comrade Mugabe'. Sean O'Neill, in a very able review of the history of witchcraft in Zimbabwe, urges that 'social dislocation was not the only negative result of the guerrilla war'; 'the war had devastated the rural health system', closing hospitals and clinics and causing a crisis of infant mortality which 'still registered as one of the main causes of witchcraft allegations'. Moreover, he writes, the war had undercut 'agricultural production and food resources' and witchcraft explanations were offered for local failures of crops (O'Neill 1986). Several authors show that the war-time equation between witches and 'sell-outs' continued after 1980 with supporters of Muzorewa's UANC being killed as witches.

On the other hand, the Zimbabwean press, self-consciously modernizing and progressive, has consistently interpreted witchcraft accusation as primitivism. The *Sunday Mail* rose to heights of denunciation in 1984, attacking ZINATHA as a cover for witch-hunting. On April 29th it condemned what it called the 'new reign of terror' by *n'angas*, asserting that in the rural areas, ZINATHA was more powerful than ZANU(PF). 'In fact it is assumed that independence has sent us back right into the heart of the fourteenth century with all its antediluvian and anachronistic practices. Today people gather for a witch-hunt as they gather for a political rally.' Earlier in April, the *Mail* wrote of 'this Old Gagoolish fantasy', and on December 23rd again insisted that 'there is no hope of material and moral progress in Zimbabwe if, in the moral age of science, people are encouraged to believe in, and remain shackled, by superstitious mystery, supernaturalism, necromancy, atavism, ventriloquism and other nonsensical beliefs.'

Conclusion

The problem with these two differing interpretations of the persistence of witchcraft belief and accusation is that they make no distinctions between its various forms, nor do they trace a periodization since 1980. It seems clear that many of the so-called 'witch-hunting' movements in the years immediately after the war were in fact witch-cleansing or witchcraft eradication movements. The *n'angas* and prophets who led them were well-known cleansers/eradicators from neighbouring countries, to whom people flocked to be cleansed of their own guilty fears or their neighbours' accusations. In short, such movements were part of the business of healing after the war rather than an expression of continued divisions. The Tanzanian Mataka in Mutoko was plainly a witch-cleanser or witchcraft eradicator rather than a witch-finder. So also was the Malawian Size Kapara Chikanga who attracted crowds of thousands in June 1981, many of whom had 'brought themselves forward to "prove" their innocence' (O'Neill 1986: 51).

Similarly, O'Neill in seeking to show continuity, cites cases and comments from 1981 and 1985-6 alike. And there is no doubt that witchcraft accusations are as numerous today as they were in 1981 and that witch-cleansers are also still active. On 21 January 1986, the *Herald* condemned the 'stone-age superstition' revealed by numerous reports of 'vicious witch-hunts'. Shortly afterwards Robert Mugabe, in his speech at the Murewa Culture House, condemned 'the practice of and belief in all socially divisive and retrogressive superstitions, including witchcraft and witch-hunting. The mushrooming of witch-hunting not only tarnished Zimbabwean culture, but it divided the people as well' (*Sunday Mail*, 26 February 1986).

Plainly, witchcraft belief, accusation, killing and also witch-cleansing and eradication are very much part of the everyday religious life of contemporary Zimbabwe. But it is time to ask harder questions about it than merely to assume that it represents a continuation either of war-time tensions or of immemorial superstition. Similar recrudescences of witchcraft belief are taking place in both Tanzania and Zambia at the present time, after all. It may be that there are things in common, not in the traditional culture of the three countries but in their contemporary political economy. In Tanzania, witch-cleansing has been very much a necessity for the formation of large *ujamaa* villages, which otherwise would founder on mutual suspicions. In Zimbabwe today it seems likely to be a feature of peasant response to villagization. Similarly, in so far as we can explain witchcraft accusations as indicators of social tension, it seems likely that the tension is no longer a matter of war-time divisions, or of failure of agricultural production. They seem much more likely to be a function now of the transformations of rural production since 1980 which have made some areas so much more prosperous than others, and some farmers in the favoured areas so much more favoured than others. Instead of constantly invoking the stone age, the Zimbabwean press might do well to explore the connection between the rapid social changes brought about by independence and the current vitality of the witchcraft idiom.

In my recent work I have focussed on district studies, and I am well aware of regional variation. No general explanation is likely to be persuasive either for what happened to religion during the war or what is happening to it now. Nevertheless, religious change in contemporary Zimbabwe, or an analysis of everyday religious experience, not only can, but must be set in a national - and supra-national regional - context.

References

Bhebe, Ngwabi (1988) 'The Evangelical Lutheran Church in Zimbabwe and the War of Liberation, 1975-1980' in: Carl Hallencreutz and Andrew Moyo (eds.) *Church and State in Zimbabwe*, Gweru.

Chavunduka, G. L. (1986) 'Zinatha: The Organization of Traditional Medicine in Zimbabwe' in: Murray Last and G. L. Chavunduka (eds.) *The Professionalization of African Medicine*, Manchester.

Daneel, Martinus (1987) *Quest for Belonging. Introduction to the Study of African Independent Churches*, Gweru.

de Wolf, Shirley (1987) Interview by Terence Ranger with Shirley de Wolf, Manicaland co-ordinator of Christian Care, 2 September.

Kriger, Norma (1985) 'Struggles for Independence: Rural Conflicts in Zimbabwe's War of Liberation', Ph. D. thesis, M. I. T., Cambridge, Mass.

Kriger, Norma (1988) 'The Zimbabwean War of Liberation: Struggles Within the Struggle' in: *Journal of Southern African Studies*, special issue on 'Culture and Consciousness'.

Lan, David (1985) *Guns and Rain. Guerrillas and Spirit Mediums in Zimbabwe*, London.

Lapsley, Michael (1986) *Neutrality or Co-option. The Anglican Church and the State from 1964 until the Independence of Zimbabwe*, Gweru.

Linden, Ian (1980) *The Catholic Church and the Struggle for Zimbabwe*, London.

Magwa, Hudson (1987) 'African Response to Missionary Activities in Nuanetsi (Mwenezi): A Case Study of the Activities of the Roman Catholics and Free Methodists, 1939-1982', B.A. thesis, University of Zimbabwe.

Mandaza, Ibbo (1986) 'Introduction' in: *Zimbabwe. The Political Economy of Transition, 1980-1986*, Dakar.

Mandivenga, E. C. (1983) *Islam in Zimbabwe*, Gweru.

Mathanzima, E., Moyo, G., Moyo, M. M. and Ngwenya, D. (1987) 'Open Letter to Dr. Chavunduka' in: *Prize Africa*, August.

Maxwell, David (1987) Letter to Terence Ranger, 7 June.

Mutamba, Shephard (1987) 'The Four Wars of Rushinga' in: *Parade*, September.

Moyo, Josiah (1986) 'Monuments Associated with Traditional Spirits' in: *The Newsletter of the Prehistory Society of Zimbabwe*.

Ncube, Mlabeni (1987) Article in: *Parade*, September.

O'Neill, Sean (1986) 'Witchcraft and Sorcery in Zimbabwe, 1890-1986', B.A. thesis, University of Manchester.

Ranger, Terence (1982) 'The Death of Chaminuka: Spirit Mediums, Nationalism and the Guerrilla War in Zimbabwe' in: *African Affairs*, vol. 81.

Ranger, Terence (1983) 'Holy Men and Rural Communities in Zimbabwe, 1970-1980' in: W. J. Sheils (ed.) *The Church and War. Studies in Church History*, vol. 20, Oxford.

Ranger, Terence (1985) *Peasant Consciousness and Guerrilla War in Zimbabwe and Mozambique. A Comparative Study*, London.

Ranger, Terence (1987a) 'Holy Places and Pilgrimages in Twentieth Century Zimbabwe' in: *Past and Present*, vol. 117.

Ranger, Terence (1987b) 'Religion, Development and African Christian Identity' in: K. H. Petersen (ed.) *Religion, Development and African Identity*, Uppsala.

Shiri, Jonas (1985) *My First Decade as Head of the ELCZ, 1975-1985*, Bulawayo.

Continuity and Change in the Constitutional Development of Zimbabwe

Welshman Ncube and Shephard Nzombe

Introduction

In our view, the term constitution has two integral aspects - a technical and a political one. In a technical sense, a constitution is a juridical act or document which legally regulates political and social relations. It delineates, structures, empowers and regulates the relationships between the different organs of state power in their inter-action with each other and with the individual citizen. In other words, the constitution regulates the foundations of the social and state system and the legal status of the individual within the state. In a political sense, as the basic law in any country, a constitution provides the formal basis for existing socio-economic and political institutions.

The technical definition of a constitution as a juridical document creating and governing the organs of state power does not tell us about the social and political character of constitutions. This is de-termined by their political function. On this latter aspect, most constitutional law scholars remain silent, and yet it is the political nature and complexion of a given society which determines the nature of the state organs that exist, what they comprise, and how they interact with each other and with the individual. The constitution is essentially a political document given juridical characteristics.

If there has been no political and social revolution, the change from one constitution to another does not necessarily create a new social order, since a constitution by its very nature does not create a new order - it merely registers in its norms changes that have been effected on the social and political arena. Thus, the adoption of a new constitution may only change the manner in which state organs relate among themselves in the regulation of the same social system.

The constitutions which Zimbabwe has had, with the exception of the Lancaster House one, can be historically classified as colonial bourgeois constitutions. They were bourgeois inasmuch as they regulated capitalist legal assumptions and concepts. They were colonial inasmuch as they were passed by a foreign legislature and enshrined the political and economic rule of a settler minority over the indigenous majority. The object of this article is to investigate the extent to which legal concepts and assumptions embodied in capitalist constitutional jurisprudence have been changed or continued during the years of Zimbabwe's independence. This will, of course, be tied up with an assessment of the extent to which the social system in itself has been changed, since, as we said earlier, the constitution simply registers changes in social and political practice. Finally, we shall attempt to look into possible future constitutional developments in Zimbabwe.

Colonial Constitutions

What was the nature of the social system in colonial Zimbabwe and what specific forms did it take? As already stated, colonial Zimbabwe, or Rhodesia as it was then called, was a capitalist society characterized by

(a) Private ownership of the major means of production (land, factories, mines etc.) by a minority white settler community in alliance with multinational corporations based in Britain and South Africa primarily.

(b) A division of labour based on race, with the majority of Africans condemned to unskilled and semi-skilled manual labour, and the Europeans performing and being paid on the basis of skilled labour.

(c) Discrimination based on race in favour of the Europeans in social, economic and political life.

(d) The use of force through the state and law in the suppression of all attempts by the African people to assert their right to self-determination and other democratic rights.

(e) The formulation of constitutions which enshrined the fundamental principles upon which the colonial state was based.

We shall dwell mainly on the structures and assumptions underlying constitution making and shall submit that the major aspiration underlying the constitutions of Rhodesia was to consolidate and develop colonial and capitalist rule. Therefore we find concepts and structures were deployed similar to those of the colonial master power, Great Britain.

The technical interaction of state organs was based, by and large, on British ideas of constitutionalism, summarized as follows by one of their leading proponents, Professor de Smith:

> ...constitutionalism is practised in a country where the government is genuinely accountable to an entity or organ distinct from itself, where elections are freely held on a wide franchise at frequent intervals, where political groups are free to organize in opposition to the government in office, and where there are effective legal guarantees of fundamental civil liberties enforced by an independent judiciary (de Smith 1981: 106).

Other constitutional concepts underpinning state organization contained in the British constitution and reproduced in Rhodesia included:

(a) The existence of a second parliamentary chamber, in Rhodesia termed the Senate.

(b) The establishment of so-called politically neutral zones, such as the judiciary, the attorney-general, the public service, the police and the armed forces as well as the electoral process as such with its delimitation of constituencies.

(c) The application of the bourgeois rule of law to the executive.

(d) Constitutional guarantees of individual civil liberties.

(e) The separation of the executive from the legislature and the judiciary and the establishment of a system of checks and balances.

The above features were to varying degrees contained in all previous constitutions, including the Lancaster House constitution.

The importance of these concepts lies not so much in their content as in their relationship with the social and political system in which they operated. For example, the same concepts were used more or less in their classical formulation in the colonial oppression of the majority of Zimbabweans. The existence of a second chamber does not do away with the injustices inherent in a particular social system. The purported shielding off from political control of certain state organs, if possible at all, does not ensure the realization of social justice for the people, and the application of the rule of law by the executive does not redress the social and economic imbalances inherent in society. This was acknowledged by the International Commission of Justice in the declaration from its 1959 Congress at Delhi, where it is recognized that the rule of law is a dynamic concept

> which should be employed not only to safeguard and advance civil and political rights of the individual in a free society, but also to establish social, economic, educational and cultural conditions under which his legitimate aspiration and dignity may be realized (quoted in Gutto 1982: 349).

The constitutional guarantees of individual rights merely contained, and still contain, what can be termed the 'first generation' of human rights, namely civil and political rights as they were declared during the anti-feudal revolutions of the eighteenth century, and as they are contained in the European Convention of Human Rights from 1950. The 'second generation' of rights, i.e. rights of a social, economic and cultural nature, as described in the United Nations charter, are only referred to scantily, if at all. The 'third generation' of rights, namely the rights to development, peace, social identity and a clean environment, generally referred to as human and peoples' rights, have been getting no attention whatsoever. As far as the majority of people in Zimbabwe are concerned, they only managed to get 'first generation' rights with the coming into being of the Lancaster House constitution, but even these rights, without being complemented by the second and third generations of rights, would be meaningless and incomplete.

The existence of checks and balances in the state apparatus is merely a way of dividing labour between the different state organs and is designed to make the state operate more efficiently. It does not result in a more just state being created, on the contrary, it may produce a ruthlessly efficient undemocratic state.

The above constitutional concepts can be found in literally all the constitutions before Lancaster House. They were used as part of the constitutional machinery for the oppression of the majority of our people. After Lancaster House, the glaring racial connotations given to these concepts were removed, and the concepts themselves continued, albeit in a changed political environment, but serving and presiding over essentially the same social and political system. The form may have been changed, but the essence remains the same.

The point we are making is that it is misleading to try to analyse constitutional categories without looking at the social and economic system over which the state is presiding, since the categories are in the end derived from that system and help to reproduce it within the context of constitutional legality. Their importance should not be underestimated, however, but neither should it be overstated. It must be seen within the overall context of the motive forces behind the development of society. Only in the sense that the form has changed, and the essence remained the same, can we say that there has been change as well as continuity in the constitutional development of Zimbabwe.

We shall now proceed to analyse in greater detail the specific forms of change which have occurred after the passing of the Lancaster House constitution. We shall also look into some possible changes which might occur in consequence of the 1987 unity agreement between ZANU(PF) and PF-ZAPU.

The Lancaster House Constitution

On April 18, 1980 Zimbabwe became an independent sovereign state after a prolonged and bitter armed struggle. The constitution under which the country became independent became known as the Lancaster House Independence Constitution - agreed to and signed by the Rhodesians, the Patriotic Front alliance and the British government. Until now, Zimbabwe has been ruled under this constitution, except for certain major changes which have been effected after 1987. Before we discuss and analyse these changes, it is essential to set out in brief the major political and legal features of the original Lancaster House Constitution in order to determine the relationship between continuity and change in the constitutional developments of the post-independence period.

In broad terms the Lancaster House constitution can be described as based on a Westminster model which incorporated the basic and general principles of the British constitution. The Lancaster House constitution established a parliamentary system of government based on the British experience. The executive authority of the state was notionally vested in a titular head of state commonly known as a non-executive president (see section 64 (1) of the Lancaster House constitution prior to its 1987 amendment). In practice, the president was merely a ceremonial head of state who had no real executive powers. Real executive power was vested in the prime minister and the cabinet which he appointed and dismissed at will. It was upon the advice of the prime minister and his cabinet that the president performed virtually all his functions (section 66 (1)).

The prime minister and the cabinet were responsible to parliament which was legally the most powerful of the three organs of state power created by the Lancaster House constitution. However, the constitution itself was superior to parliament in the sense that parliament could not pass any laws that were contrary to the constitution, the constitution being the supreme law of Zimbabwe (section 89).

The idea of a ceremonial titular head of state was borrowed directly from the British constitution, under which the monarch is the ceremonial or titular head of state, whereas the prime minister is the head of government possessed of real political power and therefore of real executive authority. The monarch acts mainly on the advice of the prime minister. This British system of a titular head of state who acts on the advice of the prime minister must be understood within the context and confines of British constitutional system.

The relationship between the monarch and the government in the British constitutional system was born out of a British history of social and political struggles. Unlike in France and other European countries, the British monarch, who represented feudal despotism, was not totally defeated, rejected, destroyed and vanquished by the new emerging class of capitalists which fought for and introduced bourgeois parliamentary democracy. The modern position of the British monarch was born out of compromises made between the new rulers - the capitalists - and the monarch who had before held all political power and was the law maker, the executive and judiciary.

The system of a titular head of state controlled by an elected government, which has meaning only within the historical context of the development of the British constitution, was imposed on the

Patriotic Front alliance at the Lancaster House constitutional conference by the British, represented by Lord Carrington, and the Muzorewa-Smith alliance.

The Patriotic Front alliance made it clear that it preferred a constitutional system which established an executive presidency, and not one that adopted the British non-executive head of state arrangement. Without a historical context and, therefore, without specific meaning and relevance to Zimbabwe, the British model of a non-executive head of state presented itself, in a historical sense, as an anachronism which was bound to be jettisoned for better or for worse. We shall return to the subject of the presidency a little later when discussing the constitutional changes which have later been made to the Lancaster House constitution.

The Lancaster House constitution was written out and agreed to in the wake of a bitter war of national liberation, in which the white settlers fought primarily to preserve capitalism and white control of the state, the economy and all political and social processes in the country. The settlers' vision of the future of Zimbabwe (or Rhodesia, rather) was one in which the white man was to be the dominant economic, political and social figure in society for all time. The black man was there to be ruled for ever - ruled under a capitalist system which preserved the white man's racially determined economic, social and political privileges. Accordingly, in their fight against democracy, the Rhodesians were 'mobilized around primitive, crude and uniformed anti-communist and racist rhetoric' (Ncube and Nzombe 1987: 12).

The Rhodesians went to the Lancaster House constitutional conference to preserve in legal form their racially determined economic, political and social privileges. However, the most important thing the Rhodesians, together with their imperialist allies, desired was the constitutional registration and recognition of the sanctity of private property.

It was through the constitutional entrenchment of private property and capitalist property relations that Rhodesians and their allies hoped to perpetuate their dominance in Zimbabwe. This entrenchment they won through the provisions of section 16 of the constitution. Section 16, by outlawing the compulsory acquisition of property by the state, guaranteed that the socio-economic structures of Rhodesia would remain intact in Zimbabwe.

For the entrenchment of private property and capitalism to be complete, there had to be a mechanism by which the independence government would be prevented from changing the constitutional provisions which entrenched the protection of private property. The mechanism chosen by the Rhodesians and their allies was to set aside twenty white seats in the House of Assembly and ten white seats in the Senate (sections 38 (1) (b) and 33 (1) (b)). It was stipulated further that the provisions entrenching private property and capitalist property relations together with other fundamental rights could not be repealed or amended within ten years from independence without a one hundred per cent affirmative vote in the House of Assembly (section 52 (4) (a) together with section 52 (3) (b) (i)). Nor could the reserved white seats be abolished within a period of seven years from the date of independence without a one hundred per cent affirmative vote in the House of Assembly (section 52 (3) (b) (i) with section 52 (5)).

The net effect of these constitutional provisions was that if the entrenchment of private property was to be removed within the first seven years of independence, the white MPs representing the interests of capital in the hands of multinational corporations and Rhodesians would have had to vote for such a removal. In addition, if their seats were to be abolished before the expiration of seven years from independence the white MPs would have had to agree to that abolition themselves.

Consequently, the practical implications of all this were that the reserved white seats were a mechanism designed to prevent the abrogation of the economic and political interests of Rhodesian whites which were entrenched in the Declaration of Rights. The calculation of the think-tanks of imperialism and capitalism was that by 1987 or 1990, very few of the revolutionaries of the nationalist movement would be committed and willing to abolish the entrenchment of private property on the scientific assumption that by that time they would have been co-opted into the capitalist system. Their scientific reasoning was that capitalism and capitalist institutions require capitalists to manage them, and a revolutionary Marxist-Leninist-oriented party, taking power at independence, would need to move quickly and decisively to smash capitalism and its institutions, failing which the government would gradually be impelled by the system to be on the side of capital.

The question which must be answered is whether or not the constitutional changes that have since been effected to the Lancaster House constitution have served to overturn or perpetuate the economic and political domination of the state by capital and by the forces which controlled capital at the time of independence.

The effective protection of private property and other essentially bourgeois fundamental rights depend on the existence of a seemingly non-partisan and neutral judiciary to uphold the basic tenets and provisions of the Lancaster House constitution. Thus the judiciary had to be one of the 'politically neutral' zones, 'impartially and dispassionately' upholding the rule of law. However, upholding the rule of law meant the preservation of the status quo under which the bourgeoisie dominated and controlled all the economic, social, political and legal processes in the country. The rule of law in Zimbabwe had to mean that laws which favoured the ruling classes as against the workers and peasants were rigorously enforced.

To accomplish this, the Lancaster House constitution provided for a seemingly politically neutral judiciary appointed by the government acting on the advice of the Judicial Service Commission (section 8 (4)). This body was inevitably dominated by former Rhodesian judges who shared the same values with respect to the rule of law and wanted it to operate in favour of the propertied classes.

The judges appointed after 1980 were to be independent and free of all political control. They had to be lawyers of several years standing (section 82), and once in office, they could not be removed except after an elaborate process controlled by the judges themselves (sections 86 and 87). Their renumeration was secure inasmuch as their salaries were to be paid from the consolidated Revenue Fund and could not be reduced during their term of office (section 88). All these were constitutional safeguards designed to protect the security of tenure of judges so that they would act independently from executive control, as it was thought the executive would not be in favour of the continuation of the rule of law under bourgeois conditions of domination. The judiciary was to be the ultimate protector of private property in accordance with the constitution. A quick survey of property-related cases decided in the post-independence period reveals that the judiciary has effectively upheld the sanctity of bourgeois property.[1]

---

[1]See e.g. *Hewlett vs. Minister of Finance and Another* 1982 (1) SA 490 (ZSC), *Minister of Home Affairs vs. Bickle and Others* SC 145-83 and *Rensford vs. The Commissioner of Police* SC 3-84.

Post-Independence Constitutional Changes

The abolition of separate and reserved white representation which became possible after 18th April, 1987, was effected through the Constitution of Zimbabwe Amendment Act, No. 6 of 1987. This act abolished the reserved white seats in both the House of Assembly and the Senate. They were replaced by open seats to be filled through an election process that involved the remaining eighty members of the House of Assembly and the remaining thirty senators sitting as an electoral college to elect members to fill the twenty seats in the House of Assembly. The ten seats in the Senate were to be filled through the new complete House of Assembly sitting as an electoral college to elect the new senators.

What is significant, however, is whether the abolition of the reserved white seats has brought about substantial changes in the constitutional structures and powers established at Lancaster House. Also whether the abolition has altered the political and economic direction of the state, since the reserved seats had been intended to safeguard capitalist and white dominance of the economic and political processes in the country.

At independence, whites dominated the organs of state power, they controlled the entire national economy - all the powerful commercial, mining, farming, banking and industrial sectors. They enjoyed luxurious lifestyles to the exclusion of blacks. They dominated the professional, technical, medical, educational, administrative and managerial fields in both the public and private sectors.

As the post-independence years dragged on, the whites lost their control of the organs of state power as well as of other public institutions such as parastatals. However, their control of the national economy increased, and they continue to dominate the farming, industrial, commercial and mining sectors. Indeed all but about twelve (or six per cent) of the two hundred top executives in Zimbabwe's leading companies are white. As a result, to this day, the former white settlers enjoy luxurious lifestyles that would certainly be the envy of any group of defeated former colonizers.

Dominance of the economy gives to whites a substantial and immeasurable, albeit subtle, influence on government policies, and those who control the economy ultimately control the state. Over the years, the white community has come to realize how unimportant direct political power is and hence when the abolition of the white seats took place hardly any whites complained. Indeed, most of them welcomed the abolition in the hope that it would remove attention from the white community so that they could be left in peace to dominate the country's economic processes.

Thus, while the abrogation of reserved white seats may have marked a formal and symbolic burial of the direct political sway the white population had enjoyed in Rhodesia, the fact is that the whites no longer needed those reserved seats to protect their interests. Their economic empire continued and indeed continues securely under a majority black-dominated government.

To conclude this part of the argument, we ought to state that the abolition of the reserved white seats represent a substantial change in the form and substance of the constitution as a juridical document, as there is no longer any direct continuity with the racial juridical assumptions of the drafters of the Lancaster House constitution. However, the economic, social and political assumptions of the Lancaster House constitution, which the white seats were calculated to preserve and protect, remain intact, and in this sense, there is a clear continuity in the political, economic and social basis upon which the Lancaster House constitution was premised. The foundations of the Lancaster House constitution as representing a specific political system remain unaffected by the abolition of the white seats.

The Constitution of Zimbabwe Amendment Act, No. 7 of 1987 abolishes the non-executive titular and ceremonial office of president and replaces it with an executive presidency. The executive presidency combines the powers formerly vested in the non-executive president with those formerly vested in the prime minister. Consequently the executive president becomes the head of state, head of government and commander-in-chief of the defence forces (section 27 (1)).

All executive authority of Zimbabwe is vested in the president and such executive authority may be exercised by him directly or through the cabinet or the vice-president (section 31 H (1). The president shall exercise his executive authority, except where otherwise provided, on the advice of his cabinet which he has sole responsibility for appointing and firing (section 31 H (5) with sections 31 D (1) (a) and 31 E (1)). The president acts without cabinet advice and on his own discretion with respect to the dissolution of parliament and the appointment and removal of the vice-president or any minister.

The president has the power to declare war or make peace, and to proclaim and terminate martial law without reference to parliament (section 31 H (4). However, in so doing he must act on the advice of his cabinet. It must be noted that the cabinet, holding office at the unfettered pleasure of the president, cannot in reality act as a check or restraint on the excesses of a president. The president may declare a state of emergency at any time, provided that it shall lapse at the expiration of fourteen days after its declaration, if it has not been approved by the House of Assembly within that time (section 31 J (1) and (2)).

The president holds office for a period of six years whereupon there shall be elections for the office of president. The president can be removed from office by the House of Assembly before the expiration of his term if he has acted in wilful violation of the constitution, if he is incapable of performing his functions by reason of physical or mental incapability, or is he has committed gross misconduct (section 29 (3)).

The House of Assembly has the power to pass a vote of no confidence in the president (section 31 F (1). Normally, if a vote of no confidence has been passed on a government that government must resign. Curiously and strangely, in the Zimbabwean constitution, a vote of no confidence in the president gives him three options, to dissolve parliament, to dismiss his cabinet or to resign his office (section 31 F (3)).

This is a strange constitutional provision, for it gives the president unusual constitutional options which makes of parliament a kind of 'toothless bulldog'. While it has the legal power to pass a vote of no confidence in the president, the president can bypass the vote of no confidence by either dismissing his cabinet or dissolving parliament itself. This renders the constitutional safeguard against executive excess and arbitrariness nugatory.

The assumption underlying this provision is that once the president has dissolved parliament, he should call a general election. However, a president determined on maintaining his power can, after dissolving parliament, proceed to declare martial law and still claim rightly that he is ruling in accordance with the constitution.

From the above presentation of the powers of the office of president as embodied in the constitution it is clear that the presidency is a very powerful office. The constitution undoubtedly overturns the usual balance of power between the various organs of state power within bourgeois constitutions.

For our present purposes, the crucial issue is not that the presidency has accumulated a lot of constitutional power, but in whose interest that power will be exercised - whether it will be exercised in the interest of the bourgeoisie and their allies, or not. This question can only be answered with the passage of time.

The introduction of the executive presidency clearly marks a fundamental departure from the juridical assumptions of a Westminster-type constitutional model. It shifts the balance of power in favour of the executive at the expense of the legislature. However, it is the actual exercise of the presidential executive powers which will determine whether this will involve continuity or change of the economic, political and social assumptions of the Lancaster House constitution. In other words, whether the social structure and property relations assumed and registered by the Lancaster House constitution will continue or change will depend on how and in whose interests the executive powers of the office of president are exercised.

Future Constitutional Changes

A certain change in our constitution after 1990 is the abolishment of the second house of parliament - the Senate. The president and the government have already indicated that they will take measures after 1990 to abolish the Senate and create a uni-cameral parliament. In our opinion, this is an expedient thing to do, it cuts down on the red tape in legislation making, and it reduces the burden on the Treasury. We cannot, however, attribute much political weight to the initiative. In any case, the Senate did not have the same historical origin, significance and role as that of the House of Lords in Britain.

Another likely change after 1990 is the legalization of a one-party state. The unity agreement between ZANU(PF) and PF-ZAPU makes it now seem politically less controversial and suspicious. There appears to be a high degree of consensus within both parties around the need for a *de jure* one-party state.

We are not in favour of or against a one-party state as such. What we think is important, however, is the nature of the party. Is it a party which expresses the aspirations of the majority of the people? Or is it an undemocratic structure expressing and furthering merely the interests of a minority section of the population, i.e. the capitalists and their hangers-on? If it is the former, then a one-party state is a legalization of democratic rule by the people and for the people. If it is the latter, then one-party rule means legalizing an undemocratic system which will perpetually exploit and oppress the people, until there is a revolution or a coup which may not necessarily meet the aspirations of the people.

Another consideration is how the one-party state comes into being. Is it at the behest of the people, or is it at the behest of the leadership alone? We believe that if a one-party state should come into being in Zimbabwe, it has to be by popular demand and as an expression of the aspirations of the masses. This is the standard by which we shall judge the one-party state if it becomes a reality in Zimbabwe.

References

de Smith, S. A. (1981) *Constitutional and Administrative Law (4th edition)*, London.

Gutto, S. B. O. (1982) 'Kenya's Petit Bourgeois State, the Public and the Rule/Misrule of Law' in: *International Journal of Sociology of Law*, vol. 10.

Ncube, Welshman and Nzombe, Shephard (1987) 'The Making of Constitutions: The Lancaster House Constitution and the Interests It Registers and Protects' in: *Journal of Social Change and Development*, no. 18.

Part Three

The Culture and Politics of Popular Participation

Structures of Meaning and Structures of Interest: Peasants and Planners in North-Western Zambia[1]

Kate Crehan

Thus, all real and integral understanding is actively responsive, and constitutes nothing other than the initial preparatory stage of a response (in whatever form it may be actualized). And the speaker himself is oriented precisely toward such an actively responsive understanding. He does not expect passive understanding that, so to speak, only duplicates his own idea in someone else's mind. Rather, he expects response, agreement, sympathy, objection, execution, and so forth... any speaker is himself a respondent to a greater or lesser degree. He is not, after all, the first speaker, the one who disturbs the external silence of the universe. And he presupposes not only the existence of the language system he is using, but also the existence of preceding utterances - his own and others' - with which his given utterance enters into one kind of relation or another... (Bakhtin 1986: 69)

Introduction

This article began with a trip I made in the summer of 1986 to North-Western Zambia together with a group of students from Berlin, all of whom were carrying out short research projects in the

---

[1] This article is based largely on research carried out while I was helping to supervise a group of students from the Free University, West Berlin. My co-supervisor was Achim von Oppen, who has been very generous in sharing data and ideas with me. In the course of writing this article I benefitted from numerous discussions with him. I should also like to thank the participants in seminars at the African Studies Centre, University of Cambridge, St. Antony's College, Oxford University, and the Centre for Southern African Studies, University of York, where earlier versions of this article were presented. But of course none of these participants, nor Mr. Von Oppen, can be held responsible for the final article.

region. The area in which we were to work, Zambezi, falls within
the area of an Integrated Rural Development Project (IRDP) which
also covers the Kabompo, Zambezi and Chizela districts. This particular IRDP is jointly funded by West Germany (through the
German Agency of Technical Co-operation, GTZ) and Zambia, and
locally the project and its workers are often referred to simply as
'the Germans'. The students were to be based in Dipilata, a group of
villages about twenty-eight kilometres from Zambezi, and for all of
them this was their first such research trip. All were German
speakers with varying levels of competence in English, working
through interpreters with similarly varying English language skills
in a region with a long history of ethnic tension, where the
particular language you choose to speak inevitably has certain
political overtones.

And not only were there the different languages in the sense of
Lunda, Luvale, German and English, there were also the very different sets of assumptions carried around by the various participants in this particular encounter. Sociology of development students, local bureaucrats, expatriate planners, and the various
groups of peasants[2] involved do not always use the same basic
concepts to structure and make sense of the reality in which they
live. They may, for instance, have quite different assumptions about
the meaning and function of 'development' and 'development projects'. So that in the case of these German students, even when the
interpretation between English and Luvale, for instance, seemed to
be working and there appeared to be mutual comprehension, there
was always the question of just what communication was in fact
taking place.

But the rather extreme example of these German students is only
a heightened version of what happens in human communication in
general. No communication, whether between individuals or
groups, is in reality the simple transmitting of a message by a
speaker to a listener who merely receives it as it was transmitted. It
is not that listeners either understand correctly or misunderstand,
rather they are involved in an active process of interpreting what
they hear; shaping the meaning according to how they perceive the
context, their relationship to the speaker, their understanding of the
type of discourse to which it belongs, their assumptions about the
'realities' to which the utterance they have heard alludes, and so on.

[2] Throughout the article the term peasant is used simply as a useful shorthand for
small-scale agricultural producer.

Whether or not a listener responds explicitly to what he or she has heard, becoming in turn the speaker, there is always in some sense a response, even if this is only in the listener's head. Any communication, and this applies whether we are concerned with speech itself, something written, or any other expressive act, is always just one moment in a continuing and multi-layered dialogue. And this dialogue is not only between those directly addressing each other at that moment, but also between all those other speakers and utterances that have shaped the beliefs, ideas and forms of language of those addressing one another (Bakhtin 1981; 1986).

In the course of this never-ending dialogue, different meanings struggle with one another, certain meanings - for however long or short a time - managing to achieve a greater or lesser degree of hegemony, while others are denied or suppressed. Crucially, it is not that people speaking different languages, or having different world-views - and ultimately every individual has to some extent his or her own unique set of beliefs and ideas - simply fail to understand each other in some neutral way which could be solved, at least in theory, by better interpretation, more explanation, or better brokers. At the heart of this unceasing dialogue, of which individual utterances and communications are no more than moments, is a struggle over meaning in which individuals and groups, representing different interests, struggle for their understanding of a given situation to be accepted as 'correct', 'morally right', the only one possible in 'the real world', or in some other way superior to competing interpretations. At its most successful and hegemonic a particular way of seeing things can prevent other ways of seeing things even being thought.

But how do the various contending meanings themselves come into being? In part, they too can be seen as emerging out of the same dialogue; but they are also a product of the specific conditions, including the basic material conditions, within which particular groups and individuals live. We all, in however mediated and indirect a way, test ideas, and not only against other ideas but against our experience, and it is here that the realities within which we live tend to exert a shaping force on our view of the world and to push themselves up into the hegemony of received wisdom. Those groups which share certain sets of conditions, such as a particular location in relation to economic structures, will tend to produce some kind of shared interpretation of those conditions, although the prevailing hegemony may make this very difficult for some subordinate groups. Each group will then, to the extent that it can, be likely in some form or another to struggle for its own interpretation of its conditions of existence.

Travelling through North-Western Province with my polyglot group, I became increasingly interested in the struggles over meaning in which we were both witnessing and participating; and in particular in the struggles over various meanings generated within the context of a development project or having to do more generally with that large and slippery concept 'development'. For instance, since our group, with the exception of myself and assorted interpreters, were all Germans and were driving around in a car hired from the GTZ, which had on its doors in large letters, IRDP, it was generally assumed, not surprisingly, that we were in some way connected with the project. We continually tried to explain that these were only student projects and that we had no official links with IRDP, nor any say in its decisions, but our protests were greeted with some scepticism.

There is, for example, an IRDP programme that provides marketing and other support services for local bee-keepers, and one of the students, Horst, had chosen bee-keeping as his topic. In general, the bee-keepers are very anxious to obtain access to the IRDP's marketing services, but due to all the usual problems, particularly with transport, there are many areas the marketing tours hardly touch, and even elsewhere the services tend to be rather sporadic. As a result, Horst never had any difficulty in finding bee-keepers to interview, often he did not even have to make appointments since word would spread that he was in a particular area and soon local bee-keepers would turn up, demanding to be interviewed. Despite Horst's careful explanations of his student status, in local eyes he was one of 'the Germans', and as such someone who might be able to put pressure on the bee-keeping division of the IRDP to provide more services; and this undoubtedly had an effect on the way the bee-keepers explained their situation in this specific context.

Inevitably, our whole research trip was firmly embedded in local power struggles, and especially in those over the IRDP and its resources. What I have tried to do in this article is to look at how certain different meanings, all of which have to do in some way with concepts of 'development', are struggled over by those with different interests. The key term around which the article circles, is one that belongs very much to the world of development planners, and that is the term 'self-reliance'. I look first at the creation of the IRDP and the importance its architects attributed to 'self-reliance', and the meaning this concept had for them. I then turn to what the planners liked to term the 'target group', and look briefly at how certain groups of peasants responded to the project's main agricultural programme. On the basis of this response, I try to deduce the kinds of meaning the peasants themselves attributed to the project. Struggles over meaning can take many different forms and a particular interpretation of the significance of a development project, for instance, is not necessarily articulated in any clear way, but may be implicit in people's actions even if those individuals themselves might well find it difficult to put their interpretation into words.

The third and longest section of the article is devoted to a single case study, a man, whom I shall refer to as JS, who belongs to the small minority of better-off peasants, those who are in a position to accumulate, the actual or potential entrepreneurs. I decided to use this case-study approach partly because JS was both articulate - or perhaps more accurately was able to operate not only in English, but also with a kind of discourse with which I too am familiar, so naturally he sounded articulate to me - and at the same time his biography and attitudes seem to me generally representative of what might be termed the aspiring entrepreneur. Such 'emergent' farmers were explicitly excluded from the IRDP's target group since this was defined as small-scale producers. Men like JS, however, as we shall see, see themselves as part of the development vanguard and as entitled therefore to various government services, and theirs is a crucial voice in the development dialogue.

But I also chose to include one long case study because I wanted to let at least one of the actors in this development dialogue speak for himself, and since I made a long tape-recorded interview with JS in English, this is possible in his case in a way that it is unfortunately not for the other groups of peasants with whom I am concerned. At the end of the article, I touch very briefly on a very different group of peasants, those at the bottom of the heap, those, often women, with few resources of any kind and all of whose energies are absorbed by the day-to-day struggle for survival. Many other categories of peasants could be identified; my aim is not to be exhaustive, but within the confines of a short article to show the kind of struggles over meaning that take place within the context of what we might call the 'development enterprise'.

A Poverty-Oriented Project and a Poor Province

The Kabompo/Zambezi IRDP was set up in the late 1970s and its general goal was defined as:

> the improvement of the living conditions of the majority of the rural population by mobilizing their productive potential. This includes an increase of their cash income as well as an improvement of their subsistence level (Rauch 1983: 1).

Central to the programme was the LIMA project, which aimed at promoting market production by small-scale producers by providing them with a package comprising seeds and fertilizer, given if necessary on credit, instructions as to how these inputs were to be used, and a cash-on-delivery marketing service. The inputs were given in the form of a standardized package based on units of 0.25 hectare (one *lima*),[3] the maximum sized plot that could be cultivated by any individual LIMA participant being four *lima*. Since the project was part of an *integrated* development programme the original idea was that, as far as possible, already existing Zambian institutions and services should be used, the foreign money and the foreign experts being intended to have a co-ordinating and supportive role.

North-Western Province itself is one of Zambia's poorest and most disadvantaged provinces and the area covered by the IRDP includes some of the poorest and least 'developed' regions within the province itself. Poorly served in the way of roads and other basic infrastructure, remote from the urban and industrial centres of the Copperbelt, North-Western Province has never contributed significantly to the nation's food market. In 1976, for instance, it contributed just 0.48 per cent of official crop sales (Stilz 1981: 34). It was precisely North-Western's poverty and 'backwardness', however, that attracted the German sponsors of the IRDP; not only was it comfortably outside any of the 'spheres of influence' established by competing aid donors, it also seemed a highly appropriate location for a development project focussed on the alleviation of poverty and aimed at the mass of small-scale producers rather than any progressive élite.

The two planners who were sent by the GTZ to carry out a feasibility study, and who were later closely involved in the project's

---

[3] LIMA is used to refer to the project itself, while *lima* refers to a unit of measurement equal to 0.25 hectare.

implementation, were both academics who had been active in the critique of development movement in West Germany and wanted to try in practice how far a development project could overcome the 'marginalization' of rural producers. Both were firmly committed to a programme geared around the needs of small-scale producers, and the concept of 'self-reliance' was, and remained central to their thinking. 'One of the three key elements in the small-scale producers' approach is increased self-reliance of small-scale producers' is how one of them put it in a 1983 long-term strategy report (Rauch 1983: 10). What was meant by 'self-reliance' here was above all a lack of dependence on what was seen as the inherently unreliable services of the state. 'Self-reliance' is, indeed, one of those stirring terms that it is difficult to be against, but like a number of other such terms, unless its specific meaning in a specific context is carefully defined, it remains a little vague, its meaning depending on where you are standing. What might seem like sturdy 'self-reliance' to one person, might to those who are being urged to be 'self-reliant' look more like the abandonment of perfectly legitimate claims for certain goods and services, so that however carefully and sensitively the need for 'self-reliance' is explained to them, they are likely to insist on their own interpretation and their own meaning.

Both German planners were very well aware that what they were engaged in was at one level a political struggle; their 'target group' - and this was a project that explicitly adopted a 'target group orientation' approach - included not only the peasants of the region, but the Zambian Government itself. As they saw it, part of their role was to bring about certain changes in the government's thinking on 'development'. They hoped, as it were, to represent the cause of the small-scale producer. Once again an aim that it is difficult to quarrel with, but just what are the needs of the small-scale producer and who defines them - the small-scale producers themselves or the planning experts? And what are the forces that prevent these needs being met? Also, very importantly, does the small-scale producer constitute a single category, or are there not, in fact, a number of conflicting interests so that the improvement of one person's living conditions may well entail the worsening of those of someone else?

In part, the stress these particular planners laid on 'self-reliance' can be seen as a response to the criticism that development aid merely creates a class of dependent clients. In the same strategy report from which I have already quoted, for instance, the following statement appears as a self-criticism of the project as it had been operating up to 1983: 'Among participants the feeling is far spread to be a dependent supplier of the government or of the Germans' (ibid: 15). The stress on 'self-reliance' is repeated in a recent booklet on regional rural development published by GTZ, the organization responsible for setting up the Kabompo/Zambezi IRDP, which defines the goal of such development as follows:

> Above all, it is the intention of Regional Rural Development to put the poorer sections of the population of a region in a position largely to improve their living conditions on their own (BWZ/GTZ 1984: 26).

At one level a thoroughly laudable statement, even if it begs the question of how 'the poorer sections of the population' are defined, and who is responsible for this definition, but what does it actually mean and what are its implications? The answer to that question depends on what are seen as the causes of the present poor living conditions. If we see these as essentially to do with certain deficiencies, a lack of knowledge about 'modern', more 'productive' agricultural techniques, a lack of management skills, lack of capital or whatever, then it is plausible that a properly designed aid project should be able to supply some of these deficiencies. What is needed is some careful study to identify the constraints, and a well thought-out project, efficiently managed and sensitively implemented to include 'the disadvantaged rural population groups as active participants in the process of change and national growth' (ibid: 18). Once, however, we begin to see the way people live as one moment in a continual historical process, and the structures in which they are embedded as outcomes at that moment - outcomes possibly already beginning to change - of struggles between contending interests; once that is, we take history seriously, then this goal I have quoted starts to look rather ambitious. Putting the poorer sections of the population of a region in a position largely to improve their living conditions on their own would then involve confronting the often very powerful forces responsible for the reproduction of those conditions.

The planners' fear of creating dependent clients would seem to have had little resonance for most villagers in Zambezi, since in village eyes a crucial dimension of any such 'development aid' tends to be its ability to mobilize crucial political resources. The experience of producers in a peripheral area like North-Western Province is that access to the inputs and credit necessary for 'improved farming', and above all for access to the market, is not something that can be taken for granted, but depends on the manipulation of political relationships whether at the local or national level.

One of the assumptions underlying the planners' stress on 'self-reliance' is the notion of the 'self-reliant' individual market producer who interacts directly with the market. But this is also to assume that producers can take the existence and reasonably orderly functioning of the market for granted. When, as in Zambezi, producers cannot rely on access to a market, they tend to be very aware of the need to create a supporting armature of relationships between people which can sustain the exchange of things. Significantly, some of the LIMA farmers, particularly those in the more remote areas, bought the inputs for LIMA on credit - not because they lacked the cash, but because they saw this as a way of ensuring that the marketing lorries would actually turn up after the harvest to collect their produce. The notion of the individual 'self-reliant' market producer interacting directly with the market contradicts in fact much of local peoples' historical and current experiences of the wider market beyond the village.

The Fragile Market

The peasants whose living conditions the IRDP aimed to improve practise an agriculture based on cassava; contrary to what the IRDP planners initially supposed, however, these people were very far from being 'subsistence producers' who needed to be carefully introduced to the strange and novel phenomenon of the market. The Luvale, Lunda and Chokwe around the upper Zambezi have, in fact, been connected to the world market longer than most other peoples in what is now Zambia - trading slaves, food for slave caravans, beeswax and wild rubber via Angolan middlemen (v. Oppen 1988). During the colonial period, there was an extensive trade with Western Province with large quantities of cassava being shipped down the Zambezi to be exchanged for fish and cattle. For various reasons, such as the inability of cassava to compete with the low - because increasingly subsidized - prices of maize after independence, and the ban on moving cattle north from Western Province, this trade dried up in the years after independence. The idea of selling to the market, therefore, was nothing new to the small-scale producers for whom the LIMA project was intended; in fact they saw the project as a way of regaining their former access to the market which they had only lost relatively recently.

An inherently fragile and unreliable market is one of the basic realities that peasants in areas like Kabompo and Zambezi have always lived with, and they have always known that access to almost any market beyond the immediate village community depends on various extra-economic relations. The way that access to the national market in the more remote areas can often depend as much on the managing of political relationships as on the manipulation of market forces is illustrated by the case of one Zambezi farmer, whom I shall call TS.

TS was a farmer on the west bank of the Zambezi, one of the most remote and inaccessible areas - not only of Zambezi District, but of Zambia as a whole. It is an area with few roads, and those that there are need four-wheel drive throughout the year to negotiate the heavy sand. Certain areas of the flood plain, however, are very suitable for rice cultivation, and TS, on the recommendation of the local UNIP ward, received a loan from the state Agricultural Finance Company (AFC) to grow rice, which is not an established crop in the area, in the 1984/85 season. As a result of AFC's problems in assessing the credit-worthiness of loan applicants, the village level party organizations, the wards and the branches, have been urged by UNIP nationally to take on this task and to recommend suitable farmers. A role which in any case fits easily into their general brief to promote local agriculture and productivity.

TS succeeded in producing about fifty bags of rice, but the problem of how to market them remained. The only possible buyer was the North-Western Co-operative Union (NWCU), the local state-run organization responsible for marketing and input supply, but they had only two four-wheel-drive lorries supplied to them by IRDP explicitly and exclusively for the collection of LIMA crops, which TS's rice was not. But TS was not deterred. Supported by the local ward chairman, a particularly active and dynamic man, he set off for Zambezi Township where he appealed directly to the District Governor for help. The governor then 'suggested' to the NWCU representatives in Zambezi that they send one of the IRDP lorries to fetch TS's rice, a suggestion it was difficult for them to refuse, and the lorry was duly sent to make the two-day trip and pick up the fifty bags of rice, much to the subsequent anger of the IRDP officials when they finally found out long after the rice was safely in Zambezi.

In order to ensure their access to the national market, and indeed to state services in general, peasants in the more remote areas often have to resort to similar, if not so direct, political leverage as TS. A frequent theme when UNIP politicians of all levels hold meetings in the rural areas is the rural producers' duty to 'feed the nation', but as far as the producers are concerned if they have an obligation to 'feed the nation' then they also have a right to the marketing services, supplies of inputs and so on that they need. Producers and the state are seen as bound together in a relationship of mutual obligation. The planners' concept of 'self-reliance', therefore, does not merely belong to a *different* world-view to that of most villagers, but is based on a conception of the relationship between the producer, the market and the state that both challenges the producers' own experience of how these things work, and would demolish a central legitimizing underpinning for peasant claims on the state. Such a notion also contradicts the central stress in village ideology on the web of reciprocal obligations in which kin members are enfolded; the manipulation of such obligations playing a crucial role in ensuring access to the means of production, labour and the social product.

No matter how 'self-reliant' individuals are, if they want to sell produce, they are dependent on a pre-existing market, but there is considerable debate between the different parties as to the respective responsibility of the state, the local community and the individual producer as regards the facilitation of access to the market; and over the question of who should bear the risk involved in production for the market. Particularly, since the risks that are part of the new systems of cultivation, such as LIMA, which necessitate investment in inputs such as seeds and fertilizer that can only be recouped by the sale of what is produced, are often new risks. The history of the region shows that a readiness to take advantage of potential markets is not lacking, but at the same time, partly perhaps because of earlier government promises and a rhetoric that stresses the important role the farmers have to play in 'feeding the nation', local peasants are very conscious of certain rights they have *vis-à-vis* the state. They are reluctant, therefore, to accept the planners' notion of 'self-reliance' - not because they do not understand it, but because it would seem to involve both a renunciation of certain claims on the state, and to ignore the farmers' *de facto* dependence on state services.

The Response to LIMA

But although local peasants may reject much of the planners' concept of 'self-reliance', the LIMA scheme has, since its beginnings in 1979, succeeded in attracting considerable numbers of small-scale producers. In 1987 there were approximately 5,500 LIMA participants, which means that over thirteen per cent of the men and women over the age of fifteen, and living in the rural areas covered by the scheme, were involved (unpublished IRDP Progress Report). Compared to many such agricultural projects the LIMA scheme has also managed to attract a fairly high proportion of women; between 1979 and 1983 twenty-four per cent of all LIMA members were women (v. Oppen et al. 1983). Of course, even twenty-four per cent still means that LIMA is heavily weighted towards men, but nevertheless less so than many other such programmes.

The way the majority of LIMA farmers have made use of the scheme, however, suggests that there is some divergence between the way LIMA is seen by many local producers, and the aims of those who designed the original LIMA package. The latter were not the German architects of the Kabompo/Zambezi IRDP, but researchers at the Mount Makulu research station in Lusaka, and it was largely for political reasons that the package was adopted by the IRDP planners despite a number of reservations on their part. The designers of the LIMA package saw the LIMA scheme as being a way of, among other things, helping the small-scale producer advance up 'the farming ladder' towards commercial farming (McPhillips 1984: 4). But in 1983, sixty-two per cent of LIMA farmers were cultivating two or less *lima* of LIMA crops, that is, 0.5 hectare or less. For these small-scale producers LIMA is not normally a step on the way to specialization in market production, but rather a way of earning a small, but often vital, cash income, all of which is spent on such necessary items as clothes and children's school fees rather than being available for any kind of productive investment.

For both men and women, participation in LIMA involves new and different risks from those of ordinary village cultivation. Unlike the latter, it entails an initial investment for seeds and fertilizer, and even though these can be obtained on credit, should the crop fail completely, which is always a possibility particularly with the new high yielding, but more demanding varieties grown under the LIMA scheme, the producer is then left with a debt which must be repaid. The point is not that producing for the market is something new, the buying and selling of various crops has indeed been a part of village life for a very long period, but the surpluses that were sold previously, especially those that were sold by women, were produced in the course of a cultivation geared to home consumption rather than sale. The production of crops for the market was not something separate, about which decisions had to be made in advance, and it did not involve investment that could only be recouped through the sales of produce. It was rather that certain surpluses might be produced in the course of normal cultivation, which could then be used to generate some much-needed cash, exchanged by women for various of the highly valued foodstuffs produced by men, such as meat or fish. Or, through the giving of gifts, particularly to other women, 'invested' in the creation of the social networks that constitute such an important form of security in times of hardship or scarcity.

Ironically, the design of the LIMA project has in some ways acted to discourage certain kinds of 'self-reliance' and has created new dependencies. For instance, in the preliminary discussions that the IRDP experts held with peasants, many of the latter said that what they wanted was a project based on normal village staples - cassava, sorghum, millet, non-hybrid maize, and other well-established village crops such as beans and groundnuts. These are all crops that villagers are very familiar with, and essentially what they seemed to have hoped for was a restoration of the old marketing opportunities that had been lost after independence. For various reasons, however, almost from the start, the LIMA scheme was primarily concerned first with hybrid, then later composite maize, the growing of which meant new unfamiliar techniques, and new input costs for the special seed and the essential fertilizer. The only places where these inputs can be bought are the local NWCU depots, where supplies often arrive late, causing serious problems - particularly since the new varieties of maize must be planted and receive fertilizer within rather strict time limits if they are to perform well.

Also as regards the sale of LIMA crops, producers are completely dependent on NWCU, which is the monopoly buyer of all LIMA crops and in many areas is the only accessible market for agricultural produce other than the village community itself, within which only very small amounts can be sold. The maintenance of the crucial network of NWCU buying depots is as much a political as an economic question.

In reality, in order to be 'self-reliant' producers, local producers have to maintain a continual political pressure at all levels of the local UNIP hierarchy. One of the practical consequences of this is a demand, articulated in all public forums, that the government honour its obligations to producers. The emphasis is on a powerful and binding relationship of mutual obligation between state and producer, but the idiom is one that can sound very dependent in Western ears. For instance, in a meeting to introduce two foreign consultants to one village the headman said to the experts: 'We are your sons and daughters, you are developing us.' But such appeasing-sounding statements are part of the normal rhetoric of village debate, and are often the way *claims*, not appeals for aid and support are put forward.

Where the IRDP planners' rhetoric of 'self-reliant development' does have a certain resonance, however, is among the tiny group of better-off peasants, the actual or potential entrepreneurs; those in fact who were explicitly excluded by the project's small-scale orientation. And it is to this group that my case study belongs. My focus here is on the way the individual I have selected, JS, is located - both in relation to the wider market beyond the village and within the local village community; and I have tried to explore some of the ideas that JS uses to explain the realities within which he lives. Clearly these were explanations given to a foreigner in a very specific context, but I think that it is none the less legitimate to take certain elements of these accounts, and particularly some of the unstated underlying assumptions behind the explicit statements, as also being a part at least of the stock of explanations that JS gives to himself.

The Farmer

The small group of larger producers to whom JS[4] belongs often refer to themselves, and are referred to by extension workers and the like, as 'farmers', a category that is sharply distinguished in local thinking from that of 'villager'. The local ward chairman, for instance, described his father in the following terms:

> My father was by then just a villager, you know he is a farmer now, he is a peasant or small-scale farmer, but during those years

---

[4] My account of JS is based on a long tape-recorded interview (Dipilata October 1986) and a number of other conversations with him on which I have made notes, but which were not tape-recorded. All the quotations from JS are taken from my interview with him.

he was just an ordinary villager (interview, Dipilata 26 October 1986).

The number of 'farmers' in this area is very small, in 1977, for instance, prior to the LIMA project probably somewhere between three per cent to five per cent of households in the Kabompo District were regularly marketing crops to the National Agricultural Marketing Board (NAMBoard), or had received credits from AFC.

In the course of my interview with JS, I asked him what he thought were the main differences between him and other local people who practise the more typical small-scale village production.

JS: This LIMA programme has come here to teach us so that we can become advanced. Tomorrow, we shall be commercial farmers, but they [i.e. most other villagers] only stick to LIMA that's all. They don't want to step from LIMA to five hectares, ten hectares, they only want to stick to the LIMA programme. Now this is the difference, because with me, if God is still keeping me, I will have about forty or fifty hectares... [In] this area we didn't know farming, our farming was only cultivating cassava.

KC: And that's not farming?

JS: That's not farming definitely... Farming, you have to produce something, and then the surplus - you have to supply it to other people, other districts, that's farming, but this peasant farming we are doing here, from the hoe to the mouth, no.

JS repeatedly stressed the importance of continual expansion:

JS: Each year you have to increase, because this again is what people are forgetting, because farming needs for you each year to make an addition of new cleared land... With me, I have now seven hectares of cleared land, now this year I've managed again an additional half ha... I'll be increasing the number up to ten or fifteen hectares. That's how it should be done.

For JS therefore, what distinguishes 'farming' from 'hoe to mouth' cultivation is primarily the production of a marketable surplus and continual expansion, and his biography illustrates the kind of initial accumulation that is an essential precondition for 'farming' as it is defined by JS.

JS was born in Dipilata in 1945 and went to school there, reaching Standard Six. After this, he worked briefly for one of the main traders in Zambezi Township, moving to the Copperbelt in 1963 where he had a number of jobs including, for some years, that of manager of a bus depot. In 1976, he experienced a sudden and powerful religious conversion, becoming a member of the Christian Mission in Many Lands (CMML) which has continued to provide a central focus for his life. Due in part to his conversion, he told me, he began to think about going home, and with the idea of settling down and starting farming, he attended a year's course at Kalalushi Farm Training Centre. Although only being paid K6 a month pocket money, JS managed to save K3 a month which he used to buy eggs from the college which he then resold in town. He also traded in charcoal, and by the end of the year he had managed to accumulate something like K40, and with this he returned to Dipilata.

But he still lacked sufficient capital to start the kind of farming he had in mind. At this point, a successful relative stepped in with a gift of K160, and with the K200 he now had, he began to trade in fish. After accumulating another K100 in this way, he started trading in cattle, going across the Zambezi to the west bank to buy animals and then selling them to the butcheries in Zambezi. Once his funds were sufficient for him to buy several animals at a time, he began taking them for sale to the Copperbelt where prices are higher. By means of this trading, JS very rapidly acquired enough capital to establish a small shop in Dipilata which he ran for about two years from 1978 to 1980, but after various troubles with the shop, including a burglary, he went back to his original intention to begin farming. Two factors which may have had some effect in delaying his decision until four years after his return home are, firstly, that he only married in 1979, and a wife would seem to be a prerequisite for any man who wants to farm, and secondly, that the prices paid to agricultural producers in the late seventies did not provide much incentive for a move into market production. His decision to begin farming was almost certainly also prompted by the LIMA project which was first implemented in the 1979/80 season.

In 1980, JS also began clearing a large site several kilometres outside the village to which he and his family moved. Recent legislation allows individuals to acquire private title to land, but only after going through a long and complicated process involving the local chief, the District Council and officials in Lusaka. JS is at present attempting to acquire title to an area of eighty-five hectares on his present site, although, not unexpectedly, he is encountering a certain amount of suspicion and hostility from local people. His original idea was to concentrate on growing vegetables such as cabbage and tomatoes, and he bought a diesel pump for irrigation; once again, however, the problem is the lack of a reliable market. Small quantities of vegetables can be sold on the market in Zambezi Township, but demand is limited since, even for most wage earners, vegetables are an expensive luxury. Although the school and the hospital are ready to buy relatively large amounts, the problem here is their slowness to settle their bills. JS has therefore tried a number of different crops, although relying principally on maize, and is always ready to experiment with something new. In the 1985/86 season, for instance, he had grown soya beans, a new crop in the area, but at the time of the fieldwork was still struggling to get his money out of the state agency to which he had sold his crop of beans.

For one year, JS participated in the LIMA scheme, but he is now farming on too big a scale, and when he needs credit he goes either to AFC or Barclays Bank. In order for him to cultivate on the scale he does, he needs to hire a certain amount of labour. At the moment, he only hires pieceworkers during labour peaks, but he hopes to employ one or more permanent workers in the future. A couple of years ago he became involved with a local Dutch volunteer's scheme to set up a Young Farmers' Club, offering them some of his land, partly in the hopes that the club might supply him with suitably trained workers - something that was very far from the aims of the Dutch volunteer. Access to additional labour is, in fact, an important precondition for any farming entrepreneur such as JS. At present in Dipilata, much of this labour is provided by Angolan refugees, a large number of whom have fled across the border to escape the UNITA/MPLA conflict. Since these refugees are usually Luvale speakers, they find it relatively easy to become assimilated into local communities, among which there are many families who themselves have Angolan ancestry. Many of these refugees are prepared to work for the low wages which, given the low productivity of their labour, are all those like JS are in a position to offer, while they are establishing an agricultural base for themselves. Many of those employed are women, JS like other employers expressing a preference for employing women who are reckoned to be harder working and less 'troublesome' than men. Even in the absence of refugees, there are usually a certain number of people, sometimes unmarried men, but above all women without an adequate cassava base, prepared to take on piecework. Complaints about pieceworkers are common among the bigger farmers, and problems with 'troublesome' pieceworkers is often one of the reasons why the larger farmers are so anxious for tractors and mechanization generally.

JS's predominantly market-oriented farming activities depend heavily on the separate farming activities of his wife, who in addition to working as a nurse at the near-by missionary clinic, has her own cassava fields which provide the family's basic staple. JS described the division of responsibility between himself and his wife in the following terms:

> She's doing with this cassava, because that is our staple food... She's helping in living, and I am doing the future planning. If we shall have a good house, the education of our children, we have to do it with other resources. I don't think we can educate our children with cassava, cassava is only for consumption, that's all, so she's doing our consumption... for our future, for dressing, for education of our children, for sickness and so forth, it's myself who's looking after that.

Having provided a sketch of JS, I want now to draw out what I see as certain key themes in the way JS expresses the relationship of 'farmers' like himself both to fellow villagers and to the state.

The views of 'progressive farmers' like JS are often close to those of certain development experts. As I have already mentioned, the designers of the original LIMA package saw LIMA as helping the small-scale producer advance up 'the farming ladder'. A similar sentiment was expressed by JS:

> ...this LIMA programme, it has come here to teach us so that we can become advanced. Tomorrow we shall be commercial farmers

Those villagers who do not advance up the farming ladder are criticized by JS - 'they only stick to LIMA, that's all, they don't want to step from LIMA to five hectares, ten hectares.' As JS sees it, a good deal of the responsibility for this failure lies with the extension service:

> Our extension workers are not teaching our people... this LIMA programme which started in something like 1983, up to date the same people who started on that LIMA programme are still doing it, because they are not being taught how they should expand

their fields, so that in the near future they shall become halfway peasant farmers, halfway commercial farmers.

In explaining the lack of 'farmers' in North-Western Province generally, JS continually stressed to me the need for education in farming, that one of the basic problems is the ignorance of ordinary villagers, and that this is why something like the LIMA project is necessary. It is interesting, however, that for JS the ignorance of villagers refers not to any lack of knowledge about 'modern' farming methods, but to their failure to appreciate the importance of continual expansion. It is their ignorance on precisely this point, in fact, which has led to sometimes difficult relations between JS and his less 'progressive' neighbours. Both his attempt to secure title to what is by local standards a huge area, and his involvement with the Young Farmers' Club have met with suspicion and a lot of bad feeling. When he offered land for the Young Farmers' Club, some people went to the chief and complained that, in JS's words, 'this young man is starting now to give the land to the white people... he is trying to sell the land to those white people'. Things got so bad that finally the governor came and held a meeting to explain the scheme - or at least that is how JS remembers the incident. As yet, JS has only cleared a small part of the eighty-five hectares to which he is trying to gain title, and he is very conscious of what people are thinking about him, that he is

> just getting the land from them, because they don't know farming, how it is, because with them, when I said I will have this piece of land they thought, farming, you have to clear all that eighty-five hectares at one spot. This is when they will recognize you, 'this one is a farmer.' When you have only got seven hectares, ten hectares, the other land is remaining, they say 'he is only wasting the land, what is he doing with the land?' Because they don't know what farming means, because you have to shift from this place to this area, you have to use one area, another area will be used by my children. But with them, they want all the land to be cleared at one spot, and that is when they can recognize that this is farming. Why? Because they have got no idea of farming.

For JS the concept of 'development' seems to provide him with some kind of self-legitimation that enables him to withstand the local hostility - something that calls for particular strength in his case, because in the part of Dipilata in which he lives, he is by far the largest farmer and clearly feels himself to be very much alone.

> If you are only alone in the area... you have to face problems, because you will now be the subject of talking every time, because they don't know what you are doing. They will say he is only doing it for his personal showing off, but they don't know he is doing it for the development of the nation.

Something else that has helped JS distance himself to some extent from the claims of his relatives, and inevitably a lot of his neighbours are also relatives, is his religion, but although his religion may provide him with some legitimation, it cannot totally silence the aggrieved voices of those relatives.

> Well, with relatives it's a problem, because in the first instance they thought it's a lie, they thought that you are escaping from their problems, because when they see somebody and he says 'I'm a Christian,' in their thinking they say, 'Ah no, he's doing it deliberately, he wants only not to be attending to our problems, that is why he wants to become a Christian.'

And when I asked JS whether he felt a greater sense of obligation towards his relatives or his fellow Christians, he said, 'My relatives, if they are Christians, well I can assist them, but if they are not Christians, really my heart is with my fellow Christians.'

For someone like JS, the network of kinship obligations is often at odds with entrepreneurial ambition, particularly since claims by kin have a marked tendency to expand in direct relation to the success of the entrepreneur. But at the same time, JS seems far from any bourgeois concept of the sturdy, self-reliant individual whose only relationship is with the market. He seems rather to be attempting to construct some kind of new community for himself, whether this be his fellow church members, other entrepreneurs, or a more restricted kinship.

As regards the relationship between farmers and the state, JS's attitude reflects a realistic assessment of the *de facto* dependence on state services of rural market producers such as himself; and in this context JS provides another explanation for the lack of farmers in North-Western Province.

> The market is NAMBoard, but if the government tried to introduce effective markets where people can be selling their crops in

time... I think these people [in NWP] can be well advanced in farming, because I can remember our friends on the Copperbelt, where the market is very easy, transport is very easy, they are doing okay, but with us here, especially us in North-Western Province, the market is a problem, transport is a problem, payment is a problem. So even if myself I say I shall become a commercial farmer, it's a cheat. Sure I will fail, because these are the problems.

JS is quite clear about what he sees as the state's responsibility, as he explained when I asked him what he thought about the slogan that is heard everywhere in Zambia now, 'Go back to the land'.

For 'Go back to the land' to be effective, the power should be from our top people there [Lusaka]; they have to assist us in the problems we are facing here

In JS's eyes, there are certain necessary preconditions for any kind of 'self-reliance' on the part of farmers in North-Western Province, and these have to be provided either by the state or by foreign donor agencies.

We have to get markets within this area, the foreign agencies they have to help us with ways and means of trying to bring in some markets, some organizations which will buy our crops here, then we shall be very thankful, we shall be depending on ourselves, but today we are still depending on the Copperbelt, because we have got no transport, no markets, we have got no proper communication with the people who need these things.

If, both for farmers like JS and for those in a position to take advantage of schemes like LIMA, the maintenance of a series of claims on the state is crucial, for those at the bottom of the village heap, those whose energies are taken up with simple day-to-day survival, it is the network of claims on those within the village community that is crucial. Exactly those claims, in fact, from which someone like JS is trying to distance himself. Although there is not the space here to look at the kind of meanings for which this category of poorest villagers struggle, it is important that this group is not excluded, and in the final short section of the article I want to say something very briefly about how they fit into the development dialogue.

'Self-Reliance' and Survival Strategies

The poorest group of villagers includes most female-headed house-holds, the old, those who because of sickness are unable to engage in the normal productive activities for a prolonged period, and those living in households with an unfavourable ratio of non-productive members, such as the very young or the very old, to productive members. These are the people who find it difficult to satisfy basic subsistence needs without help from others, either in the form of labour or gifts of food, money and suchlike. At different stages of their life, most villagers risk falling into this category, and the building up of a network of claims that can be called on in times of need could almost be described as a 'basic need' of village life.

The poorest group of villagers are those who tend to have the least direct contact with state institutions and officials, and to be least involved in making specific claims on such bodies. Indeed their experience of the state is rather in the form of various repressive measures, such as when local party officials periodically try to restrict women's beer-brewing activities or place prohibitions on hunting. At the same time, however, the state is a powerful hidden presence that is responsible for shaping many of the basic realities of their lives. All villagers, for example, need certain industrially produced goods, such as hoe-blades, water containers, blankets, soap and so on, and the prices and availability of these depend very much on national economic policies such as price control and the value of the *kwacha*. But here the state confronts them as an impersonal force quite outside their control; their explicit strategies are concerned more with merely avoiding the more obvious repressive manifestations of the state, but above all with the manipulation of relationships within the village community. Women in general - the economic situation of women having an inherent precariousness due to their dependence on the men to whom they are attached - tend to struggle to maintain the old norms of kinship obligation, often against those like JS who would like to limit them.

One dimension of what is happening here, as new possibilities of accumulation become available for individuals such as JS, is that there is a transformation of an older pattern, whereby surpluses were primarily invested in the building up of networks of dependents, into the newer pattern, whereby money earned from the sale of surpluses can be saved in Zambezi Post Office or even Barclays Bank and used directly for investment in economic enterprises. Even if such savings are not used directly as capital for some business enterprise, they can provide the necessary security for an individual to take on the risks involved in entrepreneurial activities, to risk investing, for instance, in the new seeds, fertilizer and additional labour required by what JS terms 'proper farming'. Similarly, such individual accumulation makes it less necessary to build up through the distribution of surplus a network of potential claims for support, which can be called on in times of hardship.

Conclusion

I began this article by talking about struggles over meaning, and in the article I have tried to show how concepts stemming from the experience of one group, such as the IRDP's planners' notion of 'self-reliance', can come up against ideas held by their 'target group' which have grown out of very different experiences, and that are not only different, but fundamentally opposed and conflicting. In such conflicts, it is common for the different parties to claim that the problem is a lack of understanding, or ignorance. For instance, some of the IRDP experts most sympathetic to the 'plight of the peasants' see peasants who refuse to accept their, the planners', version of 'self-reliance' as simply failing to understand the practical realities of a project like LIMA. They feel that what is needed is for the planners to sit down with the villagers and explain things to them, whereupon since the planners' view is so eminently sensible, the peasants will understand and accept it. For JS, too, it is 'ignorance' that is responsible for the hostility and suspicion of his neighbours, and what they need is to have the facts of modern farming - above all the necessity of continual expansion - explained to them by the extension workers.

But explaining such conflicts of meaning as the result of some kind of failure of communication is to ignore the complex web of power relations in which they are embedded. In the context of debates about 'development', and particularly if we are genuinely interested in people being able to improve their living conditions *themselves*, it is vital that we examine just what is going on when the different actors talk to each other, whatever form this dialogue may take. And ultimately part of what is going on always has to do, in however mediated a form, with some kind of struggle between material interests.

References

BWZ/GTZ (Bundesministerium für wirtschaftliche Zusammenarbeit/Deutsche Gesellschaft für technische Zusammenarbeit) (1984) *Regional Rural Development: Guiding Principles*, Eschborn.

Bakhtin, M. (1981) *The Dialogic Imagination: Four Essays*, ed. by M Holquist (ed.), Austin, Texas.

Bakhtin, M. (1984) *Problems of Dostoevsky's Poetics*, Manchester.

Bakhtin, M. (1986) *Speech Genres and Other Late Essays*, Austin, Texas.

McPhilips, J. K. (1984) 'The LIMA: a Zambian Approach to Better Fertilizer Use by Small-Scale Farmers', Lusaka (unpublished ms.).

v. Oppen, A. (1988) 'Alles nur "Maniokfresser"? "Informelle" dörfliche Warenproduktion in einer periferen Region Zambias', in: E. W. Schamp (ed.) *Der 'Informelle Sektor'*, Göttingen.

v. Oppen, H. J. *et al.* (1983) 'Intergrated Rural Development Programme NWP: LIMA Target Group Survey Final Report, Kabompo' (unpublished IRDP report).

Rauch, T. (1983) 'Integrated Rural Development North-Western Province: Long-Term Strategy', Eschborn (unpublished ms.).

Stilz, D. (1981) *LIMA Marketing and Credit in North-Western Province: Assessment and Proposals for Integration into the Cooperative System*, Eschborn.

Local Cultures and Development in Zimbabwe: The Case of Matabeleland

Luke Mhlaba

Isizwe singalahla amadlozi aso silandele amasiko lemikhuba yezinye izizwe sizagcina siyisigqili sezinye izizwe.[1]

Introduction

For most countries which have been subjected to colonial rule - and this is the case with the majority of African states - the liberation struggle is conceived in two phases. Firstly, a struggle for national political liberation is waged to dislodge the colonial authority and replace it with an indigenous government. Secondly, every government of an independent African state has to face the reality of economic backwardness characterized on the one hand by the underdevelopment of productive forces and on the other by the huge income gap between the poor - who constitute in nearly all cases the vast majority of the population - and the handful of well-to-do. Basically, two solutions have so far been tried in the bid to remedy the economic problems: in some cases, Marxist or neo-Marxist formulae have been prescribed and - whether in reality or only purportedly - put into play; in others, attempts have been made to inject some development stimulus into the economies of the countries concerned while preserving the capitalist character and relational networks of those economies.

While it is difficult to speak of any success, whether Marxist or capitalist, among all these experiments, definite failures can easily

---

1 'Once a nation abandons its own traditions and follows the cultures of other nations, it renders itself vulnerable to domination by other nations and loses the power to defend itself.' This saying is attributed to the Zulu king, Tshaka, in the play *Silubhekise Ngaphi* ('Where are we going to?'), by N. C. G. Mathema.

be confirmed. The influence of Western technology and values, if it did produce a 'cultural shock' among the Africans, did not, however, 'internalize' itself within the African space. It did not so take root among African societies as to be articulated by them as a voluntary, spontaneous and authentic foundation for socio-economic organization and development. And yet these 'Western' phenomena, some principles of which can be regarded as universal to all humanity, need not have been so impossible - whether for Africans or for that matter any other peoples - to assimilate.

Just as resistance or revolutionary cultures had to take root in the Zimbabwean society for the liberation struggle to succeed, it is vital for a development-oriented culture to internalize itself for socio-economic progress to take place. Socio-economic progress must in this sense be understood as progress which is mass-based and over which the people themselves have control, as opposed to élitist 'progress' which is imposed and manipulated from above and tends by nature to be exploitative of the people. What, then, are the obstacles to the emergence of a mass-based development culture in Zimbabwe? The fundamental problem appears to lie in the cultural alienation of the people, which consists in the imposition of arbitrarily defined institutions of socio-political organization, values and, even more importantly, ineffective means of communication between the masses and the élite. Cultural alienation renders difficult - even impossible - the effective mobilization of the masses for national development. Cultural alienation will have the same pervasive results on national development whether or not the political élite considers itself to be genuinely nationalist or simply fulfils a neo-colonial role. It is, of course, a formidable weapon at the service of neo-colonialism. As Cheikh Anta Diop observes: 'The use of cultural alienation as an instrument of domination is as old as the world; it has been used each time one people conquered another' (Diop 1954:14).

Tibor Mende, for his part, distinguishes countries such as Japan, the Soviet Union and China whose industrialization efforts succeeded: they were never colonized by Western countries and their socio-cultural heritage was never subjected to the same pressures as African cultures suffered under colonialism (Mende 1972: 201). In the colonized countries, however, the European industrial system was transplanted on to a completely different cultural environment. In all the cases, a small minority was integrated into the foreign system, adopting the alien life-styles and ways of thought; the masses, on the other hand, remained outside this foreign system. In the majority of cases, the lack of co-operation or resistance by the masses gradually turned into apathy (ibid.).

As Zimbabwe has consistently emphasized mass-based development and self-reliance since independence, it is obvious that these objectives cannot be achieved as long as mass apathy exists. And yet, according to Zwelibanzi Mzilethi, provincial administrator for Matabeleland North, lack of economic progress in Matabeleland is due to lack of initiative or, put differently, apathy (Anon. 1987). Indeed, there is almost a consensus that Matabeleland's economic development has been, to say the least, disappointing. Drought and dissident activity are no doubt valid reasons for this lack of progress, but since they are not by nature permanent phenomena, and because they are not necessarily superior to the human will, they do not provide the ultimate or comprehensive explanation of the problem. The cultural factor is ultimately a more important consideration as it might determine the willingness of, and the amount of effort exerted by, the people towards achieving some progress against the obstacles they face.

Culture as a determinant of development is probably the most important factor not only in Matabeleland but also in the other Zimbabwean provinces, and indeed in the country as a whole. The choice of Matabeleland for study is convenient in that, firstly, it helps once again to bring to the fore a problem that has confronted this part of Zimbabwe since independence, i.e. economic stagnation; secondly, it recognizes the essentially bi-cultural (more precisely, perhaps, bi-lingual) character of the Zimbabwean nation.[2] Following the experience of popular mobilization which characterized the liberation war during which a culture of resistance and revolution established itself, one of the questions that arise is whether there has been the necessary relay from this spirit of resistance and war, to one of reconstruction and socio-economic progress at the grassroots level. In search of an answer to this question, we may look at texts (literature), popular theatre, music and, last but not least, the media, all of which represent the instruments and the means for the 'articulation, communication and manipulation of experience' (Frederiksen and Kaarsholm 1986). Through such a study, it should be possible to assess the interplay between development goals and

---

[2] In this paper, I place special emphasis on language as the embodiment of a people's culture. Without negating or minimizing the vital role of English as a means of communication, one none the less has to concede the primordial position of Shona and Ndebele in the day-to-day lives of ordinary Zimbabweans.

aspirations on the one hand, and culture on the other, which Bodil Frederiksen and Preben Kaarsholm describe as 'the level at which the circumstances, events, and conflicts of everyday life, of private, political and economic existence are given form, appropriated by consciousness and made available for social dialogue' (ibid.).

Political Disunity, Culture and Development in Matabeleland

The period between 1980 and 1987 was, apart from interludes of mutual tolerance, characterized by bitter political animosity between the ZANU(PF) and PF-ZAPU parties, a situation which, judged from the division of electoral votes and certain events involving political violence, boiled down to an inter-ethnic conflict - in essence pitting Matabeleland against the Shona-speaking parts of the country. No politician dared admit the ethnic dimension of the conflict, but presumably they dared not ignore it either in their search for a solution.

During this uneasy period, the political situation weighed on cultural activities and forms of expression. Overall, certain development themes were highlighted by literature, theatre and music, sometimes boldly and at other times somewhat timidly. The media, mostly, walked the tightrope of trying to balance conflicting interests; some sections, however, saw only one side of the coin.

No Ndebele author has so far had any success with writing novels in English, and - except for Barbara Nkala (neé Makhalisa) hardly any have ventured in this direction despite the fact that English is Zimbabwe's official language. And, apart from brief summaries of Ndebele-language novels by Krog, no English translations of Ndebele works exist to date (cf. Krog 1966). This does not mean, however, that Ndebele literature is not developing. On the contrary, new publications have come on to the literary scene which reflect a wider thematic scope and which merit better than the criticism of being either 'crudely sensational or sanctimonious' and always 'apolitical' levelled at earlier works (Nelson *et al.* 1975:131).

Popular theatre, which began sprouting in Bulawayo particularly from 1986, is gradually establishing itself at the centre of entertainment activity as well as securing a prominent place in the culture pages of the local press, thus breaking a long-held monopoly of the Bulawayo Theatre Club which during the colonial era served mainly whites. Since 1986, more than twenty theatre groups have been formed in Bulawayo alone. Independence has also seen the arrival of a new breed of musicians whose lyrics strike a chord of harmony both at the local and national levels.

Self-reliance, national unity, mass education and health are among the developmental themes echoed by Ndebele artistic works. They are themes which occupy a central position in the government's national development programme. Impressed by the development of popular theatre in recent years, the authorities have had recourse to this form of popular communication in order to explain their objectives and mobilize the masses. Thus 1986 saw the formation, under the auspices of the Bulawayo City Council, of Iluba Elimnyama Theatre Co-operative, whose performances have always drawn capacity audiences - rarely below 300 - in the community halls of the high-density suburbs. The group has so far been commissioned by the ministries of health, agriculture and education to write and perform plays which convey messages considered essential to the development objectives set by the government.

In the new theatre, development itself is seen as depending on a number of factors for its success: there has to be national harmony and stability, which invariably implies social justice in the treatment of individuals, classes and the different national peoples.

The most comprehensive example is Cain Mathema's play, *Silubhekise Ngaphi*, which has been recommended by the education authorities for all secondary-school levels. Mathema's analysis of Zimbabwe's problems is similar to that of the political leadership in that it follows Marxist-Leninist theory. But he comes out unambiguously and vigorously in favour of not only purely economic rights for all citizens of Zimbabwe, but also of the recognition of the cultural rights of the different peoples that form the Zimbabwean nation. He asserts, through the hero in his play, the equal rights of the Shona, Ndebele, Manyika, etc. to a 'national' language. His principal argument consists in a denial of any supposedly intrinsic superiority of the culture or civilization of imperialist nations. In brief, the message to Zimbabweans is - 'until you can rediscover your cultural identity, until you can have confidence in your own capabilities, which have been proved for certain historical epochs, you will always be dominated.' Cultural emancipation is thus seen as one of the preconditions for meaningful development.

This search for an identity can also be seen in the historical play, *ULobhengula kaMzilikazi kaMatshobana: Isilwane Esimnyama sakoMabindela* ('Lobhengula, son of Mzilikazi of Matshobana'), written by the late G. N. S. Khumalo. Whereas Mathema's book, through the wider scope of issues discussed, is intended for a bigger audience - the entire nation - Khumalo, in dealing specially with Lobhengula's reign, attempts to refute the colonial presentation of the ama-Ndebele king as a barbarous dictator. He attempts to unmask the ulterior motives behind the denigration of Lobhengula, i.e. that Ndebele-Shona animosities were a simple pretext used by British settlers to colonize Zimbabwe. A striking demonstration of this lies in Khumalo's interpretation of the *inkethabetshabi* census held by Lobhengula at what is now known as Nketa Hill in Bulawayo. Whereas it has so far been presented as an act of discrimination by Lobhengula against the different groups of the Ndebele nation (the abeZansi, abeNhla and abeTshabi), Khumalo stresses that this census was considered as necessary by the king for the purpose of redistributing chieftainship posts, most of which had hitherto been held by the original group, the abeZansi. We can find support for this argument in the earlier novel by the late Mayford Sibanda, *UMbiko kaMadlenya* (Mbiko, son of Madlenya), and in other sources relating to Mzilikazi which show that the Zansi group increasingly became a minority as the nation grew through the assimilation of other groups, and that it became necessary to redistribute leadership posts by allocating more to the new groups (cf. Saunders 1979:31-44). Thus even in the historical accounts, there is an acceptance of the fact that national unity and progress lies, ultimately, in being open to other groups and in the search for a harmonious integration.

The linguistic-cultural pluralism which forms the reality of present-day Zimbabwean societies can also be seen in the names of characters in some Ndebele novels. This pluralism is never featured as an element or characteristic of division within the nation. Ndebele, Shona and English names are used for characters in most novels - the works by Mthandazo Ndema Ngwenya, Macrey Tshuma and Cont Mhlanga are only a few examples. The roles of these characters and their relationship with the heroes in these works are also significant. In Cont Mhlanga's *Ngakade Ngisazi* ('Had I only known'), the Shona-speaking character, although not active throughout the story, is the business manager of Linda Malunga, the hero of the story, who plays the role of an ex-combatant turned into a private detective, which demonstrates the existence of mutual trust between the two personalities.

It is worth noting that many Ndebele artists often perform in more than one language in order to take account of the linguistic diversity of their audiences. Thus Solomon Skhuza will sing in

Kalanga, Venda, Ndebele, etc. while different theatrical groups often use more than one language for the same play. Some Ndebele novels contain a few lines of English or Shona. The tone of the language is important as well: the amicable exchange greetings between Linda Malunga and his Shona neighbour (the old man says: 'Makadii mwanangu?' - 'How are you, my son?' - to which Malunga replies, rather in slang, 'Ndiyoyo' - 'Not bad'), can be contrasted with the use in colonial novels of *silapalapa* - an English corruption of Ndebele which almost invariably appears, as Julie Frederikse notes, in the imperative form and signifies a master-servant relationship (cf. Frederikse 1982).

One of the greatest problems facing post-war Zimbabwe has been the rehabilitation of more than 30,000 former freedom fighters and their reintegration into the mainstream of society. Cont Mhlanga's story in *Ngakade Ngisazi* presents a singular success in this field, because the principal character, Linda Malunga, and his work-mate are both ex-combatants. Unwilling to stay in the police force, they decide to use the investigative skills acquired as part of their training during the war, to set up their own investigation service. Hardly any case brought to them goes unsolved. Even more serious is the problem of disabled ex-combatants whose reintegration into society calls for greater and more specialized efforts. The theatre group Tose Sonke tries to highlight the problems of disabled people in general, whose numbers were increased by the war victims.

A theme which is prone to raise controversy each time it is evoked, but which presents an obstacle to progress, is corruption. It is little wonder that Cont Mhlanga's play, *Workshop Negative*, despite being popularly received during its tour in 1986 throughout the country, caused a storm in some circles within the government. But it was certainly not a groundless criticism, given the some scandals of fraud, theft and embezzlement involving holders of public office which of necessity hampered the nation's development efforts. This play can be likened to other critical works such as those by Dambudzo Marechera (*Mindblast*) and Gonzo Musengezi (*The Honourable MP*), which have highlighted the potential of cultural activities as a forum for public criticism of power. This criticism is vital for democracy - particularly if the media are are seen not to be adequately fulfilling their function.

Luke Mhlaba

The Media: Balancing Elite and Popular Cultures

The media have a central role in the communication of development objectives set by government and local authorities as well as in providing a forum for popular debate. According to Geof Nyarota, the former editor of the *Chronicle* newspaper, the press would be failing in its duty if it neither disseminated information on government policies nor sensitized the government to the views and feelings of the masses on various national issues (Nyarota 1986).

However, the media operate under certain pressures and constraints and often have to balance off different and conflicting interests. Both the broadcasting media and the newspapers depend, as was the case before independence, on advertising revenue. Secondly, the principal media in Zimbabwe are essentially controlled by the government and their criticism of government is therefore limited to the extent of the patronage exercised by the government.[3] Thirdly, newspapers have to attain a minimum level of credibility among the potential readership - the masses - so as to maintain relatively high circulation figures which in normal circumstances would instil confidence in advertisers. In some cases, however, advertisers might withdraw their support for any particular section of the media if they disagree with its editorial policies.[4] In the case of Matabeleland, for the greater part of the first seven years of independence, the situation was rendered even more delicate by the rivalry between ZANU(PF) and PF-ZAPU, which presented the risk of the media in Matabeleland being seen, rightly or wrongly, as a political instrument of ZANU(PF). The likelihood of such criticisms, and their veracity or otherwise, could be assessed and verified by an empirical analysis of the attitudes expressed by Mass Media Trust-controlled broadcasting and newspaper services, which on all controversies and issues pitted the government and the ruling party on the one side against ZAPU-dominated local authorities and PF-ZAPU itself on the other.

Regarding the attitude of the media towards the role and place of local or mass-based cultures, there has been probably a greater

---

[3] See for example Zaffiro 1986:127. The writer argues that one of the objectives of the Zimbabwe Broadcasting Corporation is to motivate potential opposition (to the ruling party) to comply or withdraw from the political scene and to mask basic conflicts and public opposition to changes.

[4] See ibid. Despite increasing its circulation by more than two-thirds between 1980 and 1985, the *Chronicle* saw its cumulative advertising average decline from an annual total of 25468 to 19171 columns.

change in the newspapers than in the broadcasting services, although the conception of the media as an instrument at the service of political power remains the same as under the colonial administration. The rule that he who pays the piper calls the tune applies, and it may be argued that a government is entitled to such an attitude. But a situation like this seems less acceptable in a country where the government-controlled media have a virtual monopoly, that is to say, where no other media exist so as to preserve the pluralism of the sources of information.

Television, by its nature, still serves an élite audience. American, sometimes British, films and serials occupy most of the broadcasting time and are largely backed by advertising from the business sector. Occasionally, local productions such as Felix Moyo's *Umbaxambili* ('The fork', 1980) and M. N. Ngwenya's *UTshaka kaSenzangakhona* ('Tshaka, the Zulu king', 1982) - both produced under the auspices of the Mthwakazi Actors' and Writers' Association - have also been shown, together with Safirio Madzikatire's *Mhuri yavaMukadota* ('the Mukadota Family') comedy series, which is in Shona. But the authorities have always indicated that it costs much more to produce plays locally than to hire foreign ones. It is little wonder therefore that sometimes some seven-year-olds can recite the whole cast of characters in *Dallas* and yet fail to name a single Bulawayo theatre artist or actor. Since 1986, Television Two, which was originally established as an *ad hoc* station to cover the Non-Aligned Movement summit in Harare, has been maintained as an educational and political channel on which national development questions are discussed. However, it only transmits in Harare and is yet to reach the other cities.

Radio is without doubt the most important form of media services because of its adaptability to plurilingual coverage and its capacity to reach all parts of the country and therefore the greatest possible audience. Various changes were made at independence in the form and organization of the radio services, but these changes were not substantive, except for the addition of the educational channel, Radio Four. Radio One, which broadcasts principally in English, can still be likened to Radio Rhodesia of the colonial days: urban-centred, catering essentially for a white audience and a limited black urban élite; Radio Two is the reorganized African Service, with Shona and Ndebele programmes being fused while, for a few years in the 1970s, a separate Ndebele station, Radio Mthwakazi, was operating. Radio Two is the real mass station and also allocates time for broadcasts in minority languages such as Chewa, Kalanga, etc. It caters for the working class in the urban areas and for the rural dwellers.

Radio Three is a mixed-bag type of music station, catering mainly for a youthful audience and broadcasting only in English. There is an attempt to distribute evenly the airtime allocated to Western music on the one hand and local and South African black music on the other.

Radio One, despite its smaller audience compared with Radio Two, still holds greater prestige while the latter has a somewhat marginal place. For example, rarely are government ministers interviewed, nor do they make major policy announcements or speeches on Radio Two unless such interviews or speeches are being beamed simultaneously on all four channels. Radio One on the other hand is the more usual choice for an interview or policy speech.

Since 1980, newspapers have made a big thrust into the rural areas and this has boosted their circulation. For example, the *Chronicle* increased its circulation from 39,000 copies a day in 1980 to 70,000 in 1986. The *Sunday News*, for its part, doubled its circulation to more than 65,000 for the same period (Nyarota 1986).

This was a result of the move away from the urban-centred editorial policies of the pre-independence era, and it stemmed from a realization of the fact that the majority of the people live in rural areas. According to Geof Nyarota, some urban readers had complained about the increased coverage of developments in rural areas, but 'as the papers now circulate in rural areas, it is only fair that rural readers identify themselves with the papers by reading about themselves' (ibid.). The strategy of the *Chronicle* has therefore been to continue increasing its circulation in the hope that this will attract even those advertisers who disagree with its editorial policy. Since 1984, the *Chronicle* has widened its coverage of cultural activities by including reports, critiques and features on local music and theatre.

The greatest omission of Bulawayo newspapers, however, is their failure to carry regular literary reviews. Such a service appears necessary given the increasing volume of locally produced literary works. The task for the newspapers would consist essentially in reviewing works published in the vernacular languages and thus making them available for a wider readership - unless the newspapers, being published in English themselves, are not well-disposed towards literature written in the vernaculars.

In this connection, the absence of a full-fledged Ndebele-language newspaper constitutes a huge gap in the media services. A short-lived experiment was carried out by the launching of *Umthunywa* ('The Messenger') as a counterpart to *Kwayedza* ('Sunrise' - Harare-based and in Shona) in 1985. *Umthunywa* as a separate newspaper was subsequently discontinued on grounds of financial non-viability. But given the political climate in which it had been established, coupled with the fact that it was discontinued so quickly while there were still grounds to think that it could sustain itself on the market, doubts persist as to whether it was given a fair chance. The name *Umthunywa* has been retained for a two-page Ndebele-language production in the centre spread of *Kwayedza*, and this can hardly be expected to draw the attention of, let alone satisfy, Ndebele readers.

In discussing the question of local cultures, the media and development by looking at literature, theatre, music and the press, one observes the reality of a nation trying to rid itself of the clutches of cultural alienation, a nation in search of a language - language being not only the vehicle for the articulation of culture but also the incarnation of culture - and of institutions that will best articulate and harmonize its cultural realities, given the fact that cultural liberation is a precondition for any meaningful development.

Cultural Renaissance: Idealism or Necessity?

Is cultural alienation, its traumatic psychological consequences and socio-political *mimétisme* inevitable? Is every thought of a cultural renaissance in Africa a simple pipe-dream or a necessity? Among those opposed to a culturally Afro-centric approach to solving Africa's development problems are the 'modernizing scientific cosmopolites' (Diop 1954:15). For them, it is a waste of time to search into the darkness and the debris of the African past for an African civilization. In this increasingly modern and unified world, we have to forget the chaotic and barbaric past and instead join the rest of the world which is advancing at the speed of the electron. According to this same school of thought, it is impossible to have a language of culture other than that imposed by colonialism (ibid.). This attitude masks the fact that even those who have accepted this cultural subjugation have not been spared a stagnation which has kept them far behind the metropolises. Secondly, it is characterized by a summary rejection of all that emanates from Africa and by a refusal to even consider possible African solutions to concrete African problems. Thirdly, this attitude ignores the fact that for their part, metropolitan countries - regardless of their political or philosophical inclinations - make a real effort to preserve the national cultures which are the foundations for *their* development.

Some intellectuals, even sections of those purporting to be Marxists, may regard as reactionary or chauvinistic any attempt to re-establish an authentic cultural identity as a pivotal force in the national development process. They ignore the fact that for a people to have some control over its present existence and its destiny, it has to know its past and especially establish some continuity with the best values of its history. As Lenin put it in 1920: 'The proletarian culture does not suddenly spring up ready-made from nowhere, it is not an invention of people who call themselves specialists in that field... Proletarian culture must arise as the sum total of knowledge elaborated by humanity' (quoted in Diop 1954: 19). If we consider a cultural renaissance, i.e. a rejection of political and social *mimétisme* and its replacement by institutions and values grounded in the African experience, which are more conducive to a development based on self-reliance, we must logically reject the present Jacobin structure of the African state, characterized as it is by heavy centralization. In the second place, it is an urgent task to adopt language policies which recognize the value of African languages as the principal media of communication and as vehicles for the articulation of national cultures.

As long as political animosity existed between the principal political parties, ZANU (PF) and PF-ZAPU, this was often advanced together with drought and dissident activity as the main explanation for economic stagnation and insufficient mass mobilization in Matabeleland. Little has so far been done to show how political and administrative institutions, alien and hardly adapted to the cultural diversity of the Zimbabwean nation, contributed to polarization and hampered national unity.

It must be noted that despite their quarrels of yesteryear, both ZANU (PF) and PF-ZAPU subscribe to the same fundamental principles and the same philosophy of development. They have been in constant agreement on the adoption of Marxism-Leninism as a national ideology as well as on the establishment of a one-party state. They are equally committed to the present unitarism of the Zimbabwean state, the only talk of federalism having been unsuccessfully raised by Chief Kayisa Ndiweni (cf. Sithole 1986: 80 and Hitchens 1980). While the theoretical framework of the new state differs from the colonial one because of its ideological thrust, it is vital that it be inspired by Zimbabwean particularities, whether cultural or otherwise, which will permit a better mobilization of the masses than previously.

The one-party system may be regarded as being closer to the traditional African system, but, when coupled with the heavily centralized nature of the present African state, it can be a source of conflict and oppression. Once the balance of forces in this equation tilts in favour of the central state, the outcome is indifference at the local levels. This indifference deprives the state of the energies of the populations affected which, if properly mobilized and integrated into the state system, could propel its development initiatives.

Zimbabwe has recognized certain fundamental elements of the African heritage, such as collective work and management of land resources as well as grassroots-based political organization. These appear in the government's policies of self-reliance, collectivization through the establishment of co-operatives, and the transfer of responsibilities to various local levels through village development committees and ward development committees. Local government has seen major reforms with the introduction of governorships at the provincial level, which in fact enhances the decision-making powers of the provinces. However, it must be pointed out that the provincial governors, just like the provincial and district administrators, are the principal executives in the local administrative bodies concerned. They exercise this authority as representatives of the central government which appoints them. At the provincial level, no elected authority exists; at the district level, the elected district council has to play second fiddle to the state-appointed official in the decision-making process.

The reform of the local government system therefore remains limited in scope: it is dominated less by decentralization than by deconcentration. Once officials of central government are seen as being imposed on local authorities and dominating the decision-making process at the expense of locally-elected leaders, hostility could be engendered towards the state officials. Sometimes, hostility may not manifest itself directly, but there may be apathy on the part of the local population towards the programmes proposed by the officials concerned. On the other hand, decentralization places a real responsibility on locally designated leaders, who know they are answerable to the local population. The local people, for their part, know that they have the right to demand an account from the people they have elected and can always sanction their leaders by voting them out of office. It is only by means of this electoral weapon and the possibility of dialogue and answerability that mutual enthusiasm to achieve development objectives is sustained. Matabeland has known an unhappy experience during the first seven years of independence. Government, suspecting the collaboration of district councillors loyal to ZAPU with dissidents, sometimes suspended or arrested them. Other councillors fled their districts in fear for their security. In some cases, as in 1987 in Matabeleland North, suspended district officials were replaced by government-appointed functionaries.

No doubt, locally elected authorities would tend to be more conscious of preserving the aesthetic values and tastes of their people in the architecture and design of public works, as well as of preserving the historical and cultural heritages of the people in the naming of public places and respecting the particularities and identities of the people that are reflected in historical monuments or landmarks. It would be easier to mobilize people in favour of a development which recognizes and respects their cultural identity, just as it would be easier to mobilize them in their own language.

Conclusion

According to Zimbabwe's former Minister of Education, Dzingai Mutumbuka, the majority of students who fail the ordinary-level examinations do so not because they are incapable of understanding the subject matter, but because they have not sufficiently mastered the English language (Mutumbuka 1987). This situation is of course not peculiar to Zimbabwe. Ngugi wa Thiong'o observes: 'The present language situation in Kenya means that over ninety per cent of Kenyans (mostly peasants) are completely excluded from participation in national debates conducted in the written word' (quoted in Frederiksen and Madelung 1985: 46).

Those completely opposed to the official recognition of African languages on an equal footing with English in Zimbabwe may argue that with the introduction of universal education up to the fourth year of secondary school, the next Zimbabwean generation will be fluent in English, and it is therefore cumbersome and unnecessary to impose on them a bilingualism or a trilingualism. Such a conclusion ignores the reality that language is both a way of thought and a way of being, that only a small percentage of even the present educated élite have so mastered and internalized this way of thought and of being as to claim it for their own; further, that many students still leave school after four years of secondary education with a knowledge of English quite inferior to that of their mother language.

Guy Héraud makes the following observation about nations on whom a foreign language is imposed: 'Rare are subjects who manage to master an imported language of culture, to speak it without an accent. Such subjects are therefore deprived of the precious property which almost every human being receives from society almost without effort: a national mother language' (Héraud 1963: 43).

Of course, it is necessary to carry out thorough research so as to assess the likely implications of whatever language policy is adopted. K. C. Mkanganwi has suggested a set of criteria to be applied and issues to be investigated. It seems possible, without prejudging the likely results of any such research, to make some suggestions as follows:

1. Shona, Ndebele and English could be recognized, country-wide, as official languages on an equal footing.

2. In a decentralized or regionalized state, Shona and Ndebele could be declared as official regional languages, with English being officially recognized in the two regions.

3. The public service should adopt new regulations requiring in the near future all new civil service recruits to have knowledge of at least two of the three languages, and in the long term, for subsequent recruitments, a knowledge of all three (cf. Mkanganwi 1981).

According to Héraud, it would be more reasonable to reserve bilingualism for an élite while the rest of the population concentrated on mastering one language (Héraud 1963: 44). If this solution were to be applied in Zimbabwe, English should be taught as a second language to those who choose and have the flair for it. For the rest of the population, Shona and Ndebele should be made available. In reality, this would probably change little the numbers of people who manage to learn English. It is unlikely that those who would have chosen or been able to learn English under the present system would be prejudiced by its being presented optionally and not compulsorily. On the other hand, the majority of those who for some reason or other have not been able to learn it under the present system would still have an officially recognized language.

Some critics may argue that it is unrealistic to recognize African languages as they have been by-passed or rendered obsolete by scientific advancement. This type of argument maintains that the vernacular languages are completely deficient in technical and scientific vocabulary. While the argument does raise an existing problem, it grossly exaggerates this deficiency and attempts, in reality, to deny the existence of African languages. Neither does it take account of the fact that no one language, not even the most widely spoken in the world, is in itself adequate and self-contained. Many officially recognized national languages have undergone considerable mutation and continue to expand and to adapt themselves to scientific discoveries. In so doing, they invariably borrow, but in their own way, from other languages. Nothing prohibits African languages from evolving in the same way; in fact, few can assert that present-day Ndebele is the same as it was spoken by the Khumalo clan. It is only by accepting that science and knowledge are the monopolies of particular cultures and languages that we can categorically dismiss African languages as being incapable of being used as media of communication and instruction in the modern world. But, historical factors put aside, nothing confirms such a monopoly by any culture or language.

References

Anon. (1987) 'Mat. North Hit by Lack of Initiative' in: *Sunday News* (Bulawayo), 27 September.

Diop, C. A. (1954) *Nations, nègres et culture: de l'antiquité nègre-égyptienne aux problèmes culturels de l'Afrique noire d'aujour'hui*, Paris.

Frederiksen, Bodil Folke and Madelung, Marianne (eds.) (1985) *Imperialism Comes to Africa*, Herning.

Frederiksen, Bodil Folke and Kaarsholm, Preben (1986) 'The Transition from Resistance to Establishment Culture in Zimbabwe, 1965-1985', paper presented to conference on Culture and Consciousness in Southern Africa, Manchester.

Frederikse, Julie (1982) *None But Ourselves. Masses vs. Media in the Struggle for Zimbabwe*, Johannesburg.

Héraud, Guy (1963) *L'Europe des Ethnies*, Nice.

Hitchens, Christopher (1980) *Minority Group Rights Report*, no. 9, London.

Krog, E. W. (ed.) (1966) *African Literature in Rhodesia*, Gwelo.

Marechera, Dambudzo (1984) *Mindblast*, Harare.

Mathema, N. C. G. (1985) *Silubhekise Ngaphi*, Harare.

Mende, Tibor (1972) *De l'aide à la recolonisation* , Paris.

Mhlanga, Cont (1982) *Ngakade Ngisazi*, Harare.

Mkanganwi, K. C. (1981) 'Zimbabwe, Sociolinguistically Speaking: An Open Letter to all "Planners" ' in: *Sociolinguistics Newsletter*, vol. 12, no. 2.

Musengezi, H. G. (1984) *The Honourable M.P.*, Gweru.

Nelson, Harold D. *et al.* (1975) *Area Handbook for Southern Rhodesia*, Washington D C.

Saunders, Christopher (ed.) (1979) *Black Leaders in Southern African History*, London.

Sibanda, Mayford (1981) *UMbiko kaMadlenya*, Gweru.

Sithole, Masipula (1986) 'The General Election 1979-1985' in: Ibbo Mandaza (ed.) *Zimbabwe: The Political Economy of Transition*, Dakar.

Zaffiro, James J. (1986) 'Political Legitimacy and Broadcasting: The Case of Zimbabwe' in: *International Journal for Mass Communication Studies*, vol. 37, no. 3.

City Life and City Texts: Popular Knowledge and Articulation in the Slums of Nairobi

Bodil Folke Frederiksen

Introduction

The cultural dimension of development research is receiving growing attention. Researchers are being urged to see, listen, understand and even feel in order to grasp the situation and development priorities of Third World populations. Development strategies and projects fostered in the international aid community are being questioned and sometimes discredited, and meanwhile new catchwords like 'sustainable development' or 'participation' have come in to oil the wheels of the aid machine, making sure that this colossus, made up of delicately balanced structures of personal and organizational networks, representing vital economic and political interests, can go on functioning.

In a recent article, Michael Edwards calls for 'participatory research', challenges researchers to use indigenous resources and the hitherto untapped reserves of popular knowledge in order to identify, understand and act upon local development needs:

> People act on issues about which they have strong feelings, so 'all education and development projects should start by identifying the issues which local people speak about with excitement, hope, fear, anxiety or anger' (Edwards 1989: 121).

In a similar manner, Thomas Metzger in his examination of Neo-Confucian values, *Escape from Predicament*, suggests that a key to understanding cultural practices is a knowledge of a group of people's 'points of concern' - 'what they worry about... what their shared points of uncertainty and concern are' (Metzger 1977: 14). He sees a dominant cultural system as a 'grammar' which enables members of a community to enter into dialogue and disagree, but to do so on the basis of a shared understanding of rules and traditions informing the discourse.[1]

How does the researcher learn the rules of this grammar - get access to the popular knowledge debated in local communities, but feeding on the grander issues placed on the agenda by the dynamics of social change in the wider society? Sociological analyses are capable of providing data on both objective and subjective structures in a social situation. Sociological examinations of the subjective dimension, like those of anthropology, base themselves on qualitative interviews and participant observation. Anthropology is furthermore equipped to interpret symbolic systems and articulations.

But in the final analysis, an outsider, sociologist or anthropologist, structures or constructs the reality which is being examined. Researchers base their priorities on their own notions of importance and relevance, and the data used for generalizations are coloured by this selection process.

Fictional literature written by persons closely involved in the process of social change constitutes a different kind of data, dealing with the subjective dimension of social situations. This type of text is of course also the product of priorities and selection, but based on values held by the author, presumably reflecting or at least discussing those of the community he writes about (though this is open to discussion). Analysis and interpretation of this type of text may enter into dialogue with, and perhaps supplement, insights obtained from sociological and ethnographical material. In order to try out this notion, I wish briefly to outline some characteristics of the literary text as I see them, and to discuss passages from a Kenyan novel, *The Slums* by Thomas Akare, as an expression of popular knowledge.

In this 'defence of poetry', I wish to postulate some traits of literature which are of interest for the use I propose to make of literary texts: as sources for gaining insight into a social situation.[2] Works of literature are symbolic structures, ordered according to the priorities of the author, distilling out of wide areas of concern focal

---

[1] Presumably Metzger's concept of 'grammar' harks back to 'focal concerns', a key notion in Clarke, Hall and Jefferson 1975: 53.

[2] My characterization of literature owes much to discussions with Preben Kaarsholm.

points which are being defined, redefined and argued about by shifting 'voices' in the text. Outside the text, in 'reality', these voices can be identified as belonging to various social and subcultural groupings, available for sociological and anthropological approaches if they want to be so. Literary texts are ambiguous. Elements in the text only give away their meaning when they are seen in relation to other textual elements. Which makes the role of the analyst central; a realization of this centrality is evidenced in the institution of literary criticism which throws the occasional lack of concern over the interpretation of sociological and ethnographic texts into relief.[3]

Literature is both universal and local. This is a classic claim for literature. For the purposes of this article, it may be taken to mean that literary texts overcome the limits of the parochial by articulating, in the voices or discourses of local communities, such interpretations of wider social tendencies as are of significance locally, and thus lead to changing forms of social practice. And finally, a characteristic of literature which is of great practical importance: literary texts exist as material objects in space and time, permanent and public - data for everyone to consult.

False Muslims of the Slums

The Slums is a novel of big city life. It belongs to a sub-genre of urban novels which has emerged in Africa since the 1960s, giving voice to the concerns of the huge groups of the rural population who for various reasons have migrated more or less permanently to the cities. Urbanization is a universal social tendency of urgent local importance. As a theme, it figures prominently in new African literature. Big cities and novels belong together. That has been the case in Europe, and it is the case in Africa. From Balzac through Dickens to modernism, a central theme has been the development of the individual in relation, not to society in general, but to the potentialities and limitations set by the social structure of urban life.

In Kenya, most towns were bastions of the settler culture and economy. Nairobi serviced the needs of the agricultural and industrial sectors, run by settlers and foreign companies, and it was the

---

[3] In fact, the discussion within the 'new anthropology' inspired by Clifford Geertz among others stresses the fictive or constructed nature of the ethnographic text. See e.g. Clifford and Marcus 1986.

seat of the externally imposed colonial regime. The cities were meant to be foreign territories for Africans, who were brought in to work only and had to carry passes and work permits. Social relations between Europeans and Africans were strictly hierarchical, based as they were on violence and extreme inequality.

In reality, however, a great variety of African communities and subcultures proliferated in the cities. Their social and cultural norms and organization were influenced by the locality of their places of origin, but also by their common experience of the social forces which had made them migrants: forced removals, money taxes, expressions of a rural differentiation speeded up by colonialism and leading to a breakdown of family and kinship structures. Groups of married men with insufficient money income, young men without enough land, women without husbands found themselves thrown together, most often on the outskirts of the white cities, 'liberated' from customary ties, although most kept up close links with 'home'.

The neighbourhoods in which the Africans settled were sometimes ethnically and linguistically homogenous, like the huge Kaloleni Estate in Nairobi, which was inhabited mainly by Luo who had come from Western Kenya to work on the railway. But often competing claims for identity formation, such as religion, work situation or gender, brought disorder into customary allegiances and made for modes of settlement which were not unsystematic, but reflected mobility and shifting patterns of identification. These choices happened, of course, in a very circumscribed social situation in the colonial period. Provision, particularly for families, was inadequate, and illegal wattle, cardboard and tin slum settlements were constantly threatened with extinction or actually bulldozed away, if they did not go up in flames or were not drowned in rain and mud.

In Kenya, the emergency of the 1950s constitutes a break in Nairobi's development towards becoming an African city. Operation Anvil sent 1,000,000 Kikuyu, Embu and Meru out of the city, and for long periods remaining Africans were harassed, infiltrated and supervised. In this situation the cultural richness and variety of city life was a strength: many Kikuyu changed their names and became associated with one of Nairobi's Muslim communities, which were central in the formation of an African urban culture in Kenya. Others carried on with secret organization and oath taking, using urban or urban-rural networks which were not easily detected by the colonial authorities, because of the density, mobility and fluidity of urban life.

The Slums, which was published in 1981, echoes with pre- and post-independence Nairobi history. It is the story of a group of young unemployed people, led by Eddy and Hussein, and their endeavours to do more than just survive in the city: to create meaningful lives. The structure of the novel is picaresque. We follow Eddy and his gang in their wanderings through Nairobi and in their attempts to make sense of their lives and the city by the help of the various groupings and milieus they encounter. By entering into discussion with and reflecting on the 'points of concern' articulated in the subcultural communities, Eddy reaches out to find a broader meaning to his own life and some way of handling his own most pressing concerns: unemployment, crime, sexuality and political oppression.

Two types of organization are of particular significance to Eddy and Hussein. One is the Muslim community centred in Pumwani. The other is a more loosely organized group of unemployed youth - peers in the manner in which they scrape an existence, in their cultural choices and preferences, and in their powerlessness.

Hussein and his mother and sister were 'reborn' as Muslims during the emergency of the 1950s, after the detention and removal of his father. They lived near Pumwani, were Kikuyu and therefore conspicuous in the context of the Mau Mau revolt. So the mother and the children left their old identities behind and re-emerged as non-ethnic Muslims: 'Njeri, the mother, changed her name to Mamu. Asha for Wangoi and Hussein for Mwangi' (Akare 1981: 57).

Eddy calls them 'false Muslims'. They do not observe Ramadhan, but use Islam as a veil inside which they create a private space. Their cultural choice is raised as a problem and debated in the novel: it is an expression of expediency rather than of belief and values, and history is being invoked in the search for depth and meaning:

> 'But who is really interested in fasting?' asked Susy. 'As for me, I can't.' 'And who is fasting in the Slums here?' asked Wangare. 'You Muslims,' said Dan, who had joined us. 'To hell with religion,' said Burma. 'The true Muslims are no longer in the Slums.' 'Which ones?' asked Susy. 'The ones who used to dance chakacha. Those were the real ones,' said Dan (Akare 1981: 123).

Susy is what the novel, loosely, terms a Swahili, and discussions about women in the Muslim culture of the city particularly, arouse

emotion, but also the need to understand, define, set up borders between the acceptable and the unacceptable:

> 'But you women of this place, who will marry you?' asked
> Burma. 'Our days are gone,' said Susy. *'Mna taabu sana nyinyi
> wanawake wa Majengo. Afadhali mtaa huu ubomolewe.* You have
> troubles, you women. They better demolish this place,' said
> Burma (Akare 1981: 123).

The attraction of Islamization as a social and cultural strategy, particularly for single women, has been described and analysed by
many social scientists interested in urban culture (Burja 1975; Obbo
1980; White 1983). In Kampala, where Christine Obbo made her investigations, the form of Islamization was Nubianization. The
Nubian city culture, like its Swahili counterpart, was open and
flexible:

> Individuals who for one reason or another find themselves alien-
> ated from the rural areas can seek refuge in a small group that
> increases its members by an open door policy. The implications
> are that ethnic identity can be acquired, that symbols are vital for
> recognition, and that people can learn and unlearn ethnic social-
> ization (Obbo 1980: 109).

A statement by a 'Nubian' women, which is quoted by Obbo, gives
the impression that although becoming a member of the Nubian
community is not difficult, it is still a cultural choice of some
importance:

> At the time I was contemplating moving to another neighbour-
> hood, I became friends with an elderly Nubi woman... Through a
> lengthy process I became a Nubi. I changed my name from Faith
> to Fatuma. The rest was easy. The Nubi woman became my
> 'mother' and instructed me in Nubi ways and I became con-
> verted. Although my jobs have not changed, I am a much re-
> spected woman (ibid.).

Nubianization is a kind of rebirth.

Hussein's sister Wangoi/Asha like Faith/Fatuma was a prostitute. Or rather, that was *one* of her identities. Practical Islam in
Nairobi and Kampala is a culturally coded discourse, which in its
interplay between general doctrine and socially dependent practical

interpretation is full and flexible enough to contain a woman's ambivalent position as a prostitute and yet respectable.

The City Speaks

It is probably more difficult to trace and identify youth subcultures in the African cities than Muslim cultures. They do not have the same visible institutional expressions in the urban landscape, or the same formalized doctrines. Youth culture is furtive, oppositional and changeable, held together by symbols and ideals which are often incomprehensible to outsiders - and meant to be so: argot, naming, demarcation of territory, style.

For the approach to the study of youth culture which arose at the Centre for Contemporary Cultural Studies in Birmingham in the 1970s, the key to the formation of youth subcultures was the attempt to magically or symbolically solve social problems which could not be solved in real life. The analysis of subcultures was a kind of detective work in which indices pointing towards the values which held a group together were to be collected from the group's behaviour, particularly its symbolic preferences and likings in matters of style and language. Methods taken from anthropology and textual analysis were then used to extract and interpret elements of cultures, which could be characterized in the context of the history, economy and ecology of a local community (Clarke, Hall and Jefferson 1976).

This is not the place to discuss in depth how far it is possible to get with these kinds of procedure when the analysis feeds on parking boys in Nairobi or *tsotsis* in Soweto rather than 'mods' or 'skinheads' in Newcastle. But some indices, referring to a youth subcultural grouping which appears in *The Slums*, can be put forward.

In the late 1960s, David Parkin, a social anthropologist with a special interest in language, worked in Kaloleni Estate in central Nairobi which was mainly inhabited by Luo. His interest was the adaptation of Luo culture to the urban surroundings and its modification of the urban social relations. He identified and discussed two groups of young men, all Luo and almost all unemployed (Parkin 1978).

The two groupings called themselves *wazuri* and *wakori*, Swahili for the good ones and the bad ones. The good boys were organized in youth welfare societies, named after popular football teams - Benfica, Black Santos, etc. The bad boys were organized in gangs with names resounding with a different kind of militancy - Biafra, Korea, Black Power, Henchmen. According to Parkin the significant difference between the two groupings was not so much their activities, which overlapped, nor their social status or level of education, but their hopes and aspirations. The bad boys had no plans of making good and behaved accordingly. They did not want to speak English although they were quite capable of it, because the use of English might signal a wish to get on and imply a recognition of the importance of education.[4]

They named themselves *wakori* to create space. The naming is a condensed, symbolic utterance, sending out signals to the local community. It is ambiguous, even paradoxical. One message is, 'we are bad according to conventional standards of good and bad', the other is something like, 'if you accept us as we are, we won't bother you - we will be good'. In the vein of the Birmingham approach, the naming is part of a strategy which attempts 'magically' to solve insoluble problems. It is as expressive as the symbolic utterance of the young 'skinhead' who dresses up every day in complete miner's gear, ready for non-existent work.

An example from *The Slums* may illustrate a similar process of creating local meaning by naming, thus offering possibilities of cultural identification for Eddy and his mates. In his wanderings, Eddy comes across graffiti, inscribed on a church wall in Sophia, near Pumwani and his home. The text has him spellbound:

> Viet Nam, very shiny because the paint was still wet, followed by El Fatah, Black September, Ku Klux Klan, Black Panthers, Black Power, Fu Manchu, Black Sunday, Dracula, The Suicide Commando, CIA, FBI, Peace-Makers, Harlem, Black Ghettos... (Akare 1981: 6).

The inscription is so important for him that he calls on his most city-wise friend, Masoppo, to discuss its interpretation. Masoppo can fill in the kind of universal knowledge which Eddy is uncertain about, and from the fact of the episode appearing with such weight in the text (near the beginning and for several pages), we know that it has great local significance. The inscription itself, in its context, contains indices about the subculture to which Eddy belongs, or aspires to belong, so what more precisely does it mean?

---

[4] Phil Bonner makes a similar observation about *tsotsis* in South Africa, based on Coplan 1985; cf. Bonner 1986.

The text is written on a wall - it is a writing on the wall: a warning. But a writing on a wall also means that the city speaks, or that the city is a text which can be read. It is difficult to understand - the city is difficult to understand. Eddy finds the text on a church, but in a Muslim neighbourhood, near a mosque: belief systems and cultural identifications are in a flux. The neighbourhood is called Sophia, a reference to the now extinct culturally flourishing and ethnically mixed Sophiatown in South Africa - an expression of an ideal. The cultural utterance of the inscription itself is highly complex. It certainly connotes militancy, solidarity and resistance - Viet Nam, Black Power, Harlem - but also marginality. The objective lack of power is dreamed away in grandiose fantasies of crime and subversion: Ku Klux Klan, Black September, Dracula.

The episode illustrates the way local knowledge reaches out and becomes significance - building blocks for more generalized utterances about the meaning of the city, as we find in this prose poem, addressed to the slum:

> It is the mother of Nairobi. And that is true, though some call it a two-shilling city because of these two-shilling women, others Majengo, Pumwani, Matopeni because of the mud buildings with brown rusted roofs, or Mairungi city or Miraa because of the drug; a place where the Old Man during his times was a tough nut with his friends, among them the bald headed Kaggo, in Sophia Town. Yes. That is the Slums (Akare 1981: 139).

Conclusion

In conclusion, I wish to return to the postulate of literature being a reservoir of popular knowledge, potentially useful to development researchers and practitioners. In a very general way, different literary sub-genres can point to a developing society's areas of concern: the novel of urban life, the novel of political intrigue, the novel of village life, the novel of education, the novel of sex and crime, the novel of resistance, to mention just some genres which have become prominent. More specifically, these broad areas are being debated in local communities, informed by 'codes' or 'grammars' which are socially and culturally determined, and at the same time made understandable to the reader.

Finally, the very complexity of the literary text, resounding with historical and cultural knowledge, makes the researcher more acutely aware of the complexities of the 'real' social situation to which the literary text refers. Meaning and significance is not something given. It is at the centre of the cultural dimension of development research; it feeds on popular knowledge, and it is always the product of interpretation - by the people involved in the cultural situation and by the researcher.

References

Akare, Thomas (1981) *The Slums*, London.

Bonner, P.L. (1986) 'Family, Crime and Political Consciousness in the East Rand 1939-1955', paper presented to conference on Culture and Consciousness in Southern Africa, Manchester.

Burja, Janet (1974) 'Pumwani: Language Usage in an Urban Muslim Community' in: Whiteley (ed.) 1974.

Clarke, T., Hall, S. and Jefferson, T. (1976) *Resistance through Rituals*, Birmingham.

Clifford, James and Marcus, George (eds.) (1986) *Writing Culture. The Poetics of Ethnography*, London.

Cooper, Fred (ed.) (1983) *The Struggle for the City*, Beverly Hills.

Coplan, David B. (1985) *In Township Tonight. South Africa's Black City Music and Theatre*, London.

Edwards, Michael (1989) 'The Irrelevance of Development Studies' in: *Third World Quarterly*, vol. 11, no. 1.

Hope, A., Timmel, S. and Hodzi, C. (1984) *Training for Transformation: A Handbook for Community Workers*, Gweru.

Metzger, Thomas A. (1977) *Escape from Predicament*, New York.

Obbo, Christine (1980) *African Women. Their Struggle for Economic Independence*, London.

Parkin, David (1978) *The Cultural Definition of Political Response. Lineal Destiny among the Luo*, London.

White, Luise (1983) 'A Colonial State and an African Petty Bourgeoisie: Prostitution, Property and Class Struggle in Nairobi , 1936-40' in: Cooper (ed.) 1983.

Whiteley, W.H. (ed.) (1974) *Language in Kenya*, Nairobi.

Basotho Miners, Oral History and Workers' Strategies

Jeff Guy and Motlatsi Thabane

Introduction

This article was written in response to the view that, firstly, the concept of a 'working-class culture' presupposes formal working-class organizations based on a conscious awareness of the objective conditions which give rise to, and constitute, a working class under industrial capitalism. And, secondly, that in most of the Third World, where workers are subordinated to non-class forces such as ethnicity, religion and traditionalism, it is misleading to use the concept 'working class'. The article presents an opposing point of view. Using material gathered in a series of interviews with men from the Kingdom of Lesotho who had spent a great part of their lives working in the mines of the Republic of South Africa as migrant labourers, it argues that if one insists on identifying a working-class culture with working-class awareness of itself as exploited free labour within the capitalist system, then one will be forced to dismiss a substantial portion of the lived experience of labour spent in struggle against exploitation under capitalism. What is necessary is to contextualize their specific class experience without losing the broader theoretical perspective.

In the case of the Basotho workers whose evidence we have collected, the dominating feature of the testimonies was the existence of a sense of Basotho ethnicity. This ethnic culture was used to organize and to protect the workers in a largely rightless and dangerous environment. At the same time, however, ethnicity was exploited by the state to divide the workers and to control them. Thus ethnic consciousness was an ambivalent weapon in the hands of the workers, but the evidence also shows that it has been a powerful element in the culture of the African working class in South Africa.

In the context of discussions on élite and non-élite cultures, it is clear that the evidence collected from Basotho mineworkers reveals features which can be applied generally to non-élite cultures: an ethnic rather than national consciousness; traditional religion rather than Christianity; both subservience and unruliness and violence rather than an assertion of individual rights or the use of legal forms for the defence of these rights. What is needed is an approach which can include the specific conditions of this particular group while at the same time not excluding more overall theoretical insights and a broader context.

Similarly, on the question of the meaning of 'strategy', we have to try to find a middle path. To apply the concept only to the self-conscious, stable institutions of organized labour, which in their different ways confront organized capital, is too restricting. On the other hand, strategy should not be allowed to apply to all aspects of activity on the part of the working class. In one sense, it is possible to see every action taken by a worker as a 'strategy' - given that the social context is to a large degree defined by capitalism. The problem with the term is not unlike that of 'resistance' in that it is so broad that it can disappear in the minutiae of everyday life.

Thus too narrow a definition restricts the idea of the 'worker' and ties the strategies adopted to those dealing with working conditions, the wage, and revolution. Too broad a definition loses such indispensable concepts as production and class and their capacity for analysis and comparison, and moves history away from the crucial ideas of labour, conflict and capital and much too far towards the narrowly personal and psychological.

The article attempts to deal with these problems of definition and conceptionalization - not so much by defining them beforehand as by providing a context and looking at aspects of lives as process.

Basotho Migrant Workers

The workers who form the subject of this paper were migrant labourers and dependent to a large degree, although not entirely, on the wage. They made up a significant part of the huge migrant work-force which has built the gold mining industry of South Africa, and with it the most powerful regional economy in Africa. The South African mining industry has dominated the political economy of Southern Africa and has been built upon a large African work-force drawn to a significant degree, until the 1970s, from beyond South Africa's borders. It is a formally unskilled work-force, working on contract, whose members return to their place of origin between contracts.

Lesotho is a politically independent state completely surrounded by South Africa. It was annexed by the British in 1868 and regained its independence in 1966. For a century, its people have played a major role in the industrialization of Southern Africa. At the end of the Second World War, about a quarter of a million men were working on the South African mines - perhaps one-fifth of the total population of Lesotho.

Lesotho has always been seen as home by the majority of workers, and the family land and livestock have far greater value than any price they might raise on the market. However rural production is dependent upon the wages earned by the migrant workers. Consequently, despite the strong social attraction created by this rural base which families continued to farm, under traditional forms of land tenure, chiefly rule and customary law, the significant presence in other words of pre-capitalist forces of one kind or another, these men should be considered 'workers'.

Labour migrancy, together with organizational co-operation between the mining houses, made it possible for mining capital to keep African wages low. Moreover, it was a controlled work-force, the mine workers being housed and fed in large, strictly controlled compounds attached to each mine. Work was racially defined. Most African miners were kept by law in unskilled positions with limited movement into supervisory roles. White miners supervised and managed the African labour force. The mines are deep and the ore-body narrow. Working conditions are therefore uncomfortable and dangerous.

The context, then, in which this article has to be read is that of an extremely repressive working environment: of badly-paid labour, harsh working conditions, and the continual threat of racial violence where workers' rights were minimal. Living conditions were regimented, and controlled, in huge single-sex compounds. Those workers who lived in towns escaped some of these aspects, but their lives were generally deprived and insecure. The article concerns the attempts which were made to ameliorate such conditions - attempts which, we would argue, can be seen as a strategy.

We use the word 'strategy' to mean not just resistance to these repressive conditions, but attempts which indicate that workers have projected their predicament into the future as a means of gaining some control over it. We have been selective in the topics presented here and try to isolate aspects which seem from the testimony collected to have a wider significance, concentrating on the social rather than the intensely personal.

Ethnicity as Strategy

In the workers' life histories there is one overwhelming 'strategy'. It is based on the sense of ethnic commonalty - of being a Mosotho amongst other Basotho, and the need to guard and draw on this for support and protection - of being a worker amongst other workers from the same background, with a shared history and language. Of coming from a country which resisted the attacks of the Boers, and which had not been incorporated into the Union of South Africa. Of coming from a British colony, and therefore with a history very different from that of black South Africans.

This sense of being a Mosotho is to be found at all points in the workers' lives. It exists in the initial decision to take a contract often with advice from an experienced relative and using his contacts on the mines. It is to be found in the planning of the shared journey to the recruiting station, on the train and in the vast, controlled, single-sex compounds where workers were housed according to ethnic groups. It is also to be found in those districts in the townships and slums which became Basotho enclaves, and in the urban gangs of Basotho who guarded the community from similar ethnically defined groups and against attacks by criminals or the police.

It is, however, hard to document in the sense that it is something of such obvious significance that it is assumed and not articulated. But in the personal histories we collected, it is to be found most urgently and dramatically in the cry of the isolated individual suddenly in danger as he calls out for help: 'Banna ba heso!' - 'My countrymen!'[1]

This sense of ethnic identity and the ethnic support it could mobilize in times of need in a hostile and dangerous environment provided the basis for the most important strategies developed by Basotho (and other workers from different backgrounds) during this period in South African mining history. However, we must stress from the outset that we do not consider this sense of ethnicity to be an objective manifestation of links with a clearly-defined

---

[1] Oral History Project of the National University of Lesotho (OHP), informant 11, (pseud. Rantoa). Born 1922. First contract 1937. For a discussion of such appeals to 'my countrymen', see Guy and Thabane 1987: 448.

ethnic past. It is also, to an important degree, an 'invented' tradition with a dynamic, socially created content. Secondly, this content has been created not only by the people themselves as a strategy in a changing and threatening world but also by those who seek to control them - specifically by the South African state and the mining industry, and its benefactors and beneficiaries.

Thus, the nineteenth century conquest of the peoples of Southern Africa reinforced the divisions between them as a pre-requisite for effective rule. The attack on rural agricultural self-sufficiency and the resultant creation of the South African work-force was associated with policies based on ethnic compartmentalization and racial segregation, in which perceived ethnic differences were stressed and ethnic rivalry encouraged. One strategy of mine management was to divide the work-force and the compounds under the control of *induna* in a system which was supposed to imitate 'traditional' and 'tribal' political structures. This was capped by the policy of apartheid which promoted ethnic difference to the rank of state ideology.

Alternative strategies were present - the broad-based nationalism of the African National Congress, the call for political equality of the liberals, and the call to class of the trade unionists and communists. At certain times these alternative ideologies have been influential. But ethnic identity has remained a powerful force coming to the fore time and again during crisis and struggle. And the men whose life histories form the basis of this article fall back on their sense of local identity, shared histories and experience as protection in the struggle of their working lives.

In an earlier article, we have considered the identification of ethnicity with specific work skills - in this case the widespread belief that Basotho mine workers had unchallengeable skills as manual rock loaders. This was especially true in the organized rock loading process during a particularly dangerous stage in mining - shaft sinking (Guy and Thabane 1988). Shaft sinking was associated with the mines and the compounds - the 'classic' Basotho worker environment.

But it has to be remembered that for much of their history - and especially in the three decades before and after the Second World War - many Basotho workers took a contract on the mines as a way of entering South Africa. Once the contract was completed, they left the mine to find work in industry, exchanging the discipline and deprivation of the mine compound for the freer and more varied life in the African townships or locations which had sprung up near the places of work.

The townships, with their shacks, shebeens and squalor, were places of poverty and violence, but offered a degree of freedom and contrast to the regimented violence of the compounds. A feature of the township was criminal violence and the urban gang. There were the juvenile bands of *tsotsis* on the look-out for the lone worker with his pay packet as well as the more organized criminal gangs like the Berliners or the Gestapo. There were also ethnic outfits - and the best known of these was the gang of urban-dwelling Basotho called Ma-Rashea, the Russians.

The Russians seem to have originated in the 1930s in the Basotho enclave to the west of Johannesburg in the township of Newclare. It was a gang made up specifically of men from Basutoland. They were identified by their black trousers, white shoes, covered by the 'traditional' Basotho blanket in the folds of which they hid their weapons - in particular the *melamu* - the fighting stick. Their declared intention was to provide safety and security for Basotho in the working-class areas. To do this, they sought out the *tsotsis* and the ethnically organized gangs and attempted to destroy them. By the 1940s and 1950s, these inter-gang struggles had gained a momentum of their own, and there were epic clashes as members of one gang travelled across the Witwatersrand to confront their enemies or to defend their own territories.

Our knowledge of the Russians comes from an informant who was a member, and whom we have called Rantoa (OHP 11). From his evidence it is clear that the Ma-Rashea was a Basotho gang, an urban gang and a gang of workers, and that its origins lay in the need for protection in a lawless environment. But Rantoa's evidence goes further than this. It enables us to see that the function of the violence was not just to protect and to plunder. Participation in the gang and in gang warfare took on a wider social role in the deprived environment of the townships. The intellectual demands in the planning of the fight, the physical demands in its execution, the celebration of victory, the outwitting of the police - all provided stimulation and excitement for the participants. Indeed, Rantoa made it clear that the Russians spent much of their time fighting amongst themselves, and they were divided into two factions which reflected two regions in Lesotho whose rivalry had its foundations in factions surrounding the king in pre-conquest days.

Once again, Basotho ethnicity was expressed as a form of worker strategy. In this case, a strategy primarily for physical protection, but also one which had the effect of enlivening the sterile, deprived environment of the urban slum. It was a deeply contradictory strategy. The violence necessary for self defence could also be turned upon the members themselves. More than this - in the South African situation, it was and is obviously a serious miscalculation to define the enemy as another African ethnic group. Both then and now, the Russians have been unable to discriminate effectively between their friends and their enemies. Thus, in the 1950s, it is clear that the Russians were being used by the most reactionary elements to break boycotts, used strong-arm tactics against other Africans to raise funds, and, it was believed at the time, were perhaps even assisting the state in the destruction of other African communities.

Individualist Strategies

The security and the advantages to be gained by staying within the ethnically defined group and accepting the limitations of communal responsibility in return for certain monetary benefits and privileges provided the general framework of the strategy adopted by the miners who were interviewed. None the less, there were some men whose strategy included attempts, if not to leave the ethnically defined group, then at least to find the means to become dominant within it and move up the organizational structure to positions of responsibility - as team leader, foreman or 'boss boy' underground, or as *induna* or tribal representative in the compound. Moreover, in the case of some informants, promotion was obtained not just by convincing management that they had the abilities needed to take positions of responsibility - it was also necessary to obtain supernatural assistance from traditional doctors and their medicines.

The visit to the traditional doctor for medicine to assist in work on the mines seems to have been widespread. It could take place to ensure safety during the contract, or to assist in gaining the favour of white supervisors in the hope of getting fair treatment and possibly promotion.

Rantoa describes his visit to a famous doctor in some detail. In 1937, at the age of fifteen and before taking his first contract, he consulted a woman doctor with a reputation for being especially skilled in safeguarding miners. Payment was three pounds, a portion on delivery and the balance on completion of the contract. Rantoa told her of his wish for promotion. She gave him two different types of medicine, one of which was mixed with water and applied when washing and the other taken orally. She also gave him a warning:

> My countryman, there at Motselekatse [the labour centre in Johannesburg] - when you get there, you remove your clothes. You are searched in every article in your clothes, and the medicines are thrown away there. But if you are clever you can pass with them (OHP 11: 15).

Experienced miners taught Rantoa how to hide these medicines by crushing them inside his shoes against the toe-cap so that they remained in place when the shoes were searched.

On arrival at the mine, Rantoa immediately discovered the harshness of mine labour and began his plans for less onerous work. He decided that he should become a 'piccanin' - the personal servant of a white miner underground. The next day, Rantoa woke early and went to the washhouse to apply one of the medicines. He then went to the mine supervisor's office, placed the other medicine in his mouth and approached a white supervisor directly in his office asking for work. To the amazement of the other senior black workers (Shangaans from Mozambique, who accused him of bribery) he was made piccanin to a ventilation engineer.

> It was then that I saw for the first time that traditional medicines are important things, my man. Yes truly a person who says they do not work [does not know]. I have tried them at different places. I can tell you the history of them and they work (OHP 11: 20).

Traditional medicine was not used just for promotion - it was also used to ensure general well-being and to provide safety in the dangerous working conditions. One of our informants experienced a terrifying accident during shaft sinking which, although he escaped injury, killed men at the bottom of the shaft, including his cousin. However, the conclusion he drew from this experience was the opposite of Rantoa's - it persuaded him that traditional medicine was not effective. Consequently, he turned to another form of supernatural assistance, Christianity.

> We worked under such terror. I learnt faith when I was there. It was there that I learnt that faith - that I had to pray because

traditional medicines did not work. It was at the shaft that I became certain of this...[2]

An important use to which magic was put by workers was to gain the favour of white supervisors. One informant spoke of the part it played in the rivalry between miners as they tried to gain the favour of white overseers and discredit their rivals,

> ...they use medicine. It is a matter of medicine. They do not speak with their mouths, instead they speak with these medicines. They eat medicines in such a way that a European is disgusted just by looking at you and then wants to fight you. Now, if you have not protected yourself, you suddenly realize that even though he once trusted you, this European now cannot even look at you...
> These people work with things [medicines] that are dug from the ground. They are very dangerous.[3]

The desire for promotion and the benefits it brought clearly conflicted with the desire to belong to a wider social group. A number of our informants expressed a disinclination to accept positions of responsibility despite the increase in earnings:

> No, I did not want to be a foreman. I hate pushing a person. A foreman has no compassion. He does not appreciate that people are not equal in strength. That is, he pushes each and every one in the same way. When he sees that one is strong, he thinks that the other one is deliberately shirking at work. Now, this shows a lack of understanding because people are not equal in strength...
> (OHP 9: 51)

And as the implications of individual strategies came into conflict with the desire for commonalty they created severe social tension - which could manifest itself in the use of witchcraft. Another informant explicitly linked his refusal to assume responsibility with a fear of the magic that could be used against him as a result: 'I do

---

[2] OHP, informant 15. Interviewed Ha Mofoka, August 1984. Born 1927. First contract 1948. Cf. Guy and Thabane 1988: 268.

[3] OHP, informant 9: 40. Interviewed Alwynskop, Quting, April 1983. Born 1914. First contract 1934.

not like being a foreman. There is a lot of witchcraft there. These foremen bewitch each other. They bewitch each other'.[4]

It seems likely that the tension surrounding the African supervisor in the mines was a result, in part, of the fact that promotion in some ways contradicted the major premise upon which Basotho mining strategy was based - the support to be gained from being a member of a larger ethnically-defined group. Thus while medicine helped to gain promotion it also broke the communal ties of ethnically organized labour, thereby exposing the promoted individual to danger both from rivals and from the consequences of exercising discipline over erstwhile comrades.

One of our informants gave a detailed account of this. He had gained the position of senior *induna* - a man responsible for order amongst a group of miners in a compound on the Free State mines in 1956. He took his job seriously and was proud of the way he resolved conflicts between management and labour in a manner, as he saw it, which served the interests of both sides. He acted strongly against white miners who abused or assaulted African workers, and did what he could to end work stoppages and indiscipline on the part of the black miners. 'I knew how to talk to people... especially Basotho, because I am Mosotho'.[5]

His account of his downfall through magic has an epic quality. The actors are the major figures on the mine. It was his very reliability and efficiency as senior *induna* which brought him to the attention of the general manager of the mine, thereby incurring the resentment of the white compound manager.

Jealous of our informant's access to the general manager, the compound manager corrupted his best friend. He sent him to Lesotho to obtain medicine from a traditional doctor. A number of attempts were made to trick our informant into taking the medicine, and eventually he was persuaded to smoke a treated cigarette. He collapsed, but before being taken to hospital managed to make contact with a Zulu doctor and to work a counter-medicine. He hovered at death's door until his own medicine worked - the man who had given him the bewitched cigarette was killed in a car accident.

Our informant recovered his health but never his position on the mine - this had been destroyed by the jealousy of a white rival, the

---

[4] OHP, informant 13: 4. Interviewed Thaba-Tseka, April 1984. Chronology confused. Birth ?1918. First contract ?1928. *Induna*.

[5] OHP, informant 8: 18. Interviewed Ha Leshoele, April 1983. Born 1909. First contract 1925. Served in North Africa and Italy during the Second World War.

duplicity of a black friend, and their use of traditional medicine. This association of medicine and magic with promotion and status, and with failure and disgrace, seems to be a consequence, in part, of the inherent tension in the process of leaving the wider, ethnically defined group in the search for better working conditions, and also with the insecurity and isolation that promotion and responsibility imply (OHP 8: 19-25).

Violence and Strikes

Most of our informants had experienced some form of communal violence on the mines. The threat of violence was always there, and had to be avoided by management. At the same time, they did not see violence towards the authorities as a strategy in any consciously planned sense. It took place against a specific grievance or to end a particular abuse, and with the realization that such action was likely to provoke greater violence in return from management or the state.

A complicating feature of the accounts of violence, as in the one that follows, is the tendency for them to assume an ethnic character. It also reveals that the word 'strike' was used very broadly and could stand for any form of generalized violence against the mine.

Yes, I think it was in 1936... a compound was burnt, people went on strike... right at the compound, right there where I was. I did not know the reason because I was still young. I did not know what the older ones were fighting for... I suddenly realized that there was a fight there, because when people go on strike, they beat the cooks [laughter] – that is the first thing they do when they are on strike. The cooks, they give us so little food there at the kitchen, and we therefore start at the kitchen, and they spill all the food, and we eat the meat there, and - they start fighting with the Shangaans. It was such a big fight, and the Basotho beat the Shangaans. And we threw so many stones - we used coal as well, because we had no fighting sticks. One Shangaan, he was beaten up by a man who still lives here. He was passing by our change house, and he beat him, and he fell down. As it turned out, he was finished. There was such a big fight. It did not have an owner [ringleader], and it was confined [to the compound]. When the people fight, the compound police run to the outside, and they close the door so no one can get out, and they kill one another there in the compound. And then they called in the police from the town... The Shangaans can fight even though they are ignorant. They know how to fight, but they got beaten. We beat them so that they should know. I do not know how many died, perhaps it was four, but I don't know. And those soldiers came... They were armed with guns and they were terrifying. They were the ones who wear dresses, the Scotch. We thought, 'They are going to shoot us with those guns.' Those guns were fitted with bayonets at the front there... if he pierces you with it, it will come out the other side. And then they talked to us and the trouble came to an end (OHP 9: 20-1).

None of our informants had planned a strike. As in the case above the word 'strike' easily blended into generalized violence with strong ethnic overtones rather than representing an organized worker's strategy for defined objectives. The term 'worker's organization' was usually identified by our informants with a 'burial society' - that is an organization which collected funds to pay for, in the case of a fatal accident, the return of the body home for burial (cf. e.g. OHP 9: 24-5).

There were of course strikes during the period when these men were at work - including the historic 1946 mineworkers' strike. One of our informants was involved in what seems to have been the 1946 strike, but was a somewhat reluctant participant with little awareness of the issues involved (OHP 7).

None had much faith in strikes as a workers' strategy. One believed that they were usually planned by the ambitious and the self-seekers. They were generally aware of the very serious consequences - of the vulnerability of the worker at the hands of management which could starve them out, leave them stranded underground without air or water, or, as some knew to their cost, call in the army.

Ai, strikes are things that are just caused by people with their own plans, because they go on strike for money, sometimes they go on strike for a very minor things, or just to fight, because people sometimes just quarrel like that.[6]

Others disagreed with striking as a means of dealing with dissatisfaction and felt that negotiation with management was better, in the

---

[6] OHP, informant 2: 24-5. Interviewed Maseru. Born 1918.

hope that 'that they smear us with some jam and throw a little money our way'.[7]

Good Boys and Bad Boys

Some of our informants were convinced that co-operation and conciliation were in fact the best strategies. They had taken contracts to earn money, and there was no point in jeopardizing that all-important goal by forcing a confrontation with management. The best strategy was to recognize the existing distribution of power and authority, and work hard to ensure maximum earnings.

But co-operation could move a stage further and pass over into collaboration with management. One informant stated that the whites liked him because they found him 'straight'. He was proud of the fact that, when Xhosa workers met to discuss how to organize work stoppages as a means of bringing about the dismissal of a white overseer, he and his Sotho workmates exposed their plan. Then the meeting would break up, and

> they would all disperse like that, and the European would laugh... that was my life - immediately they tried to get a meeting together, I would destroy it (OHP 9: 13-4).

Another informant gave a full account of the advantages of co-operating with white management. He spoke of how, when he got older, his white supervisor tried to ease his work load:

> He wanted me to be a foreman. I refused. 'Ao,' he said, 'If you do not want to be a foreman now, I will put you at the top of the mine here. Your job will be just to sit at the top of the mine here, and you should write these tickets of these people, as they go down to the mine. Your job will be just to write out their tickets.' Truly, I had really worked. The white man just refused to let me go on working. He said, 'You have been working here for too long. You have been my man for a long time. We have worked together. We've been to many places together. I don't want you to have to do hard work any more.' He wanted to make me a foreman. He said, 'What don't you like about being a foreman?' I said, 'I do not like being a foreman. There is a lot of witchcraft. These foremen bewitch each other there. They bewitch each

---

[7] OHP, informant 1: 70. Interviewed November 1982. Born 1919.

other. Now I am happy with this job you have given me. It is enough.' And he just kept on writing a lot of money for me. It was high. I was getting two tens and five units of pounds. That was my job. I was getting more than the foremen [laughter]. The winchboy used to get two tens. The foremen got two tens and two units... and as for me I was getting two tens and five units. I was higher than them. I was 'good boy' [laughter]. Yes, I worked there, truly (OHP 13: 4-5).

Against the 'good boy' we can set the 'bad boy'. We collected little evidence of theft or sabotage as a strategy against mine management. There are suggestions of the way in which records of work could be falsified in order to receive higher pay (OHP 4), and one informant took his revenge on an aggressive and violent white supervisor on the railways by quietly re-arranging the document-ation of the goods carriages - sending the carriages to a destination thousands of kilometres from where they were supposed to go.[8]

But there are also examples of sustained rebelliousness and of the determination to defend one's position if threatened - with violence if necessary. Moreover, this could gain advantages. An informant saw himself as such a man, a fighter, someone who 'ever since I was born, I have never run away from another man'.[9] He fought the older boys when herding, he fought to guard the homes of his rela-tives when they were away on the mines. He stood up for himself physically when mistreated at work in South Africa.

As a result, his life story also includes some horrific accounts of the inside of the colonial gaol, its mortuary and the gallows. But his account of his life is filled with spirit and vigour. He captures with ironic humour the predicament of the African mineworker. If you are passive or docile, the white man exploits you - extending the work hours and tampering with your work record to reduce your wages:

The point about Europeans is that when he realizes that he has little to worry about from you, then he comes and eats your money if he has seen that you are sleepy.

---

[8] OHP, informant 3: 17. Interviewed Mokhokhong 1982. Born 1913. First Contract 1934.

[9] OHP, informant 4: 38. Interviewed Tsieng, January 1983. Chronology still obscure.

However,

> when he sees that you are clever, then he says, 'Motho enoa o
> ruta choe lebelo' - 'this person teaches an ostrich how to run'.
> Then you should know that they have understood you, and that
> they will not want anything to do with you. You are evil, they do
> not like that kind of thing. Europeans want you to talk like this:
> You should say,
> 'Yes, old boss'... [and he will say,] 'Good boy.' Yes, indeed, you
> are 'good boy' when you do not cause problems. But if you are
> like... if he sees you are like this - jumpy like this, no, then you are
> evil. [He'll shout,] 'Bloody hothead, you are no good [laughter],
> you do not become tame, eh? It is a monkey, this thing, it does
> not become tame' (OHP 4: 51).

And the predicament is repeated: be passive, and you will be exploited; stand up for yourself, and you are assaulted or dismissed.
But the latter course was not only the brave and honourable one, it
could also succeed. It could, in fact, be a successful strategy to
counteract exploitation by white management. Thus he told more
than once the story of how, when he was working on a diamond
mine, the white supervisor attempted to extend the gang's working
time without pay. His account vividly recreates the verbal violence
of this sort of confrontation. Unable to get a satisfactory explanation
for this extension of working hours, our informant threw down his
shovel, picked up his coat, and walked off the job. His workmates -
who were Xhosa, and, in contrast to the attitude of most of our
informants, admired by him for their spirit - warned of what was
going to happen. Our informant, however, replied: 'No, a white
man cannot do harmful things to me - not when I am surrounded
by so many stones.'

> The other workers followed me off the job. When we were about
> to go through the gate, the white man arrived, we bumped into
> him, and he opened the gate, and he said immediately, 'Hey,
> Mosotho, where are you going?' 'I am going to the compound.'
> 'Ai, fuck off, man, who told you it is time up? Fuck off! Fuck off!
> Go - go and work!' I said, 'Ayikhona' - 'Never.' He - he rolled up
> his sleeves, he rolled up his sleeves, like he was used to. I hung
> up my jacket. I stood and looked at him. I held my lamp prop-
> erly. He said, 'Do you want to fight, Mosotho?' I said, 'If you
> want to fight, I also want to fight.'

He said, 'What's the matter? What did you say?' And then he said, 'Hey, boss boy! Come here!' The boss boy came running, and he said 'Mosotho, what's the matter, man?' I said, 'You, I don't want even to see you come near me.' Then this white man turned, went to the other side, and then went away... You know, from that day on, the compound became all right. Immediately at seven, the whistle blew. And the compound was all right. It is like it is always said – the compound isn't necessarily put right by a lot of people. It can be put right by just one person. And that was the way it was (OHP 4: 44ff.).

The most sustained example of rebelliousness came in Rantoa's evidence and in the account of his life as a member of the Basotho gang, the Russians. Indeed, Rantoa's testimony is especially interesting because it is structured around one central theme - and that theme is the strategy he developed in order to survive in a harsh and dangerous world.

A Worker's Strategy

Rantoa was born in 1922, herded his father's stock, and took his first contract on the gold mines in 1937. In 1942, he left the mines for industry and the Basotho district in Newclare. He was imprisoned for assault and then murder, released in 1947, and joined the Russians - playing an active part in their defence of their areas and the attacks on their enemies before returning home to Lesotho in 1959. When he was out of prison and fighting for the Russians, Rantoa depended upon wage labour. At times of unemployment, he joined a gang and robbed trains - but this was an activity resorted to only in times of great difficulty. His life in Johannesburg was founded on wage labour, and it was while he was employed as a worker that he fought as a member of the Russians.

Rantoa is important to our argument not only as an articulate informant on the Russians. His oral testimony is exceptional and varied. The range of his experiences is vast - as a miner, a worker in industry, or on the run from the police. He has been assaulted by the police and has killed men in fights. He has suffered whipping in gaols and has experienced digging and dealing in illicit diamonds. At the same time, he has retained a great interest in Basotho tradition and culture.

From Rantoa's evidence, it is clear that he believes himself to be a man of talent and intelligence, because only a man of ability could have survived what he has experienced in the towns and gaols of South Africa. These are not the abilities perhaps that a formally educated person would recognize. He is, in fact, illiterate - or as he put it, 'I leave my letters at the post office now, knowing they are mine, because I did not study.' His lack of formal education, however, does not affect him because, 'What I have, is a natural sense that God gave me, and gifts - as for them they are many' (Guy and Thabane 1987: 441).

His gifts include what can be called a finely developed strategic sense, and this underlies his whole testimony. It is not stated overtly and directly, but is present in his descriptions of the conflicts which made up his life. In a previous article, we summarized it as follows:

> His philosophy is not an abstract one, but emerges from concrete situations. He sees life as a struggle, a fight, in which one must always be consolidating one's forces, undermining the opposition, and developing a strategy which avoids the obvious frontal attack and strikes where it is not expected. To succeed in life one has to be continually wary, calculating, and prepared to attack when necessary (ibid.).

For Rantoa, life is a struggle for which one has to have a well-developed sense of strategy. It is

> a battle which makes the correct assessment of the opposing forces imperative, requires one to develop strategies of skill and daring, and makes it essential to ensure that when one delivers the final blow, it is a telling one (ibid.: 445).

This philosophy is expressed in the three great interests of his life - all to do with different expressions of conflict and the development of successful strategy. Lawyers fascinate Rantoa, and their methods epitomize his ideas of a successful strategy: the correct assessment of the situation, of your own strength and your enemy's weakness; the aggression used to intimidate the opponent into making an error. Again, this is not just an abstract interest. Lawyers were an essential part of Russian life. They kept the members out of gaol, and much of the gang's time was spent in extorting money to be used for lawyers' fees. Another great interest in Rantoa's life is football. For him, it is not only a game of strength and skill, but one of strategy. Moreover, it can be compared directly with the other activity which absorbed so much of his time - fighting.

> A fight is like football. The strength of a football team is at the quarter, at the flanks. Now, in a fight, if your flanks are weak and they slacken because of the pressure from the other side, those that remain in the fight will be hit from behind and can no longer concentrate on their front because of the people who attack them from both sides. Now, because of this, the strength of the fight is at the sides. That is where I used to like it. If it was football, I would be called Two, at the quarter. Yes, I liked fighting from the sides (ibid.: 441).

In situations where life is so reduced that physical survival is the dominant element, strategy is virtually an end in itself. Rantoa prides himself on the fact that he has survived the most difficult situations. He believes he has survived because he has used his inherent gifts effectively, assessed the forces ranged against him shrewdly, and shown skill in the way he has dealt with them. He is in fact proud of his talents in devising an effective strategy.

It is a deeply ambiguous strategy. It can lead to a vital and exciting life but one which is also dark and violent. There is bravery without principle, planning and strategy without long-term goals or ideals. It is little wonder, for example, that Rantoa dismisses workers' organizations - 'A lawyer is much better than a union - I have been there and I know.'

Nevertheless, it seems to us legitimate to consider such a response a form of 'workers' strategy'. The context created the imperatives. A worker's life was dangerous and restricted. Gang activity of this kind provided protection and stimulation by drawing on the idioms of rural, peasant life and putting them into practice in the urban ghettos. It was visually encapsulated in the image the Russian consciously projected when he stared with menace at the world from under the felt hat pulled low over one eye, wearing his traditional blanket over black trousers and white shoes, and holding his fighting stick.

Conclusion

The ambiguity continues to the present day. We have not interviewed Basotho members of the National Union of Mineworkers which in 1987 brought its members out on strike for three weeks in what is clearly to be seen as a work stoppage of unprecedented significance in Southern African history. But there are reports that Basotho miners played a significant part in the strike, both in positions of leadership and in the rank and file.

At the same time there have been reports that Basotho men were queueing at the recruiting stations in the hope that they could take the place of miners dismissed in the strike. There have also been reports that the Russians have been assembling again - offering to act as strike breakers. We do not know how the Russians of today compare with those of thirty years ago, but it must be supposed that the Sotho element remains significant.

On the other hand, there have been suggestions that management, exasperated by the number of Basotho workers active in the NUM, is thinking of playing the ethnic card again, this time threatening to replace Basotho miners with more tractable men drawn from Zululand.

Thus, amongst the old themes of ethnicity, violence and accommodation that were played by previous generations of Basotho mineworkers, new ones can be discerned. They are being developed by workers in the struggle against the domination of mining capital and include trade union organization, the work stoppage and the strike with defined tactical objectives. But to see this form of struggle as the first indication of a general strategic sense, is to dismiss the many years of conflict which have characterized the history of the Basotho mineworker. Alhough these conflicts were often ambiguous and inadequate, they were also spirited and courageous, creating and nurturing a spirit of resistance and an awareness of the need to find more effective ways to confront the mining authorities and thereby make work more profitable and life more bearable.

Jeff Guy and Motlatsi Thabane

References

Guy, Jeff and Thabane, Motlatsi (1987) 'The Ma-rashea: A Participant's Perspective' in: B. Bozzoli (ed.) *Class Community and Conflict: South African Perspectives*, Johannesburg.

Guy, Jeff and Thabane, Motlatsi (1988) 'Technology, Ethnicity and Ideology: Basotho Miners and Shaft-Sinking on the South African Gold Mines' in: *Journal of Southern African Studies*, vol. 14, no. 2.